The British Empire

Recovering the Past

Series Editors: Edward Acton and Eric Evans

'Recovering the Past' aims to present both students and the general reader with authoritative interpretations of major historical topics. Drawing on the results of recent research by the author and others, the volumes both explain the importance of the themes they address and explore how historians have come to radically different conclusions about key issues in past politics, society and cultures. The lifeblood of history courses around controversy and reinterpretation; these accessibly written volumes help to explain why. Readers can use them for readable accounts and for the stimulus of engagement with lively debate.

Crusading and the Crusader States
Andrew Jotischky

Rome and Her Empire
David Shotter

The British Empire
Philippa Levine

The Age of the French Revolution
David Andress

The Third Reich
Dick Geary

The Rise and Fall of Communism
Stephen White

The Impact of the Industrial Revolution
Peter Gatrell

Imperial Russia
Roger Bartlett

The British Empire

Sunrise to Sunset

Philippa Levine

PEARSON
Longman

Harlow, England • London • New York • Boston • San Francisco • Toronto
Sydney • Tokyo • Singapore • Hong Kong • Seoul • Taipei • New Delhi
Cape Town • Madrid • Mexico City • Amsterdam • Munich • Paris • Milan

PEARSON EDUCATION LIMITED

Edinburgh Gate
Harlow CM20 2JE
United Kingdom
Tel: +44 (0) 1279 623623
Fax: +44 (0) 1279 431059
Website: www.pearsoned.co.uk

First edition published in Great Britain in 2007

ISBN: 978-0-582-47281-5

British Library Cataloguing in Publication Data
A CIP catalogue record for this book can be obtained from the British Library

Library of Congress Cataloging in Publication Data
Levine, Philippa.
    The British Empire / Philippa Levine. – 1st ed.
      p. cm. – (Recovering the past)
    Includes bibliographical references and index.
    ISBN-13: 978-0-582-47281-5 (alk. paper)
    ISBN-10: 0-582-47281-4 (alk. paper)
    1. Great Britain–Colonies–History. 2. Commonwealth countries–History.
  3. Imperialism–Social aspects–Great Britain. 4. Decolonization–Great
  Britain–Colonies–History. 5. Civilization, Modern–British influences.
  6. Great Britain–Foreign relations. I. Title.

  DA16.L48 2007
  909′.0971241–dc22

                                                      2006050693

10   9   8   7   6   5   4   3   2
10   09   08

Set by 35 in 10/13.5pt Sabon
Printed in Malaysia (CTP-PJB)

The Publishers' policy is to use paper manufactured from sustainable forests.

Contents

List of illustrations

List of maps

Imperial Federation map, c. 1886, by Captain J. C. Colombo (Royal Geographical Society, London, UK/The Bridgeman Art Library)

Preface

In his autobiography, first published in 1936, the Indian nation-alist leader Jawaharlal Nehru remarked rather bitterly that Indian nationalists were being chided for desiring national independence in an increasingly globalized world. 'It is curious', he pondered, 'how all roads in England – liberalism, pacifism, socialism, etc. – lead to the maintenance of the Empire.'[1]

Contrast this view, which emphasizes how central a concern empire was for the British, with that recently espoused by the historian Bernard Porter that the British were at best reluctant imperialists. As he puts it in the preface to his book *The Absent-Minded Imperialists*, 'Imperial Britain was generally a *less* imperial society than is often assumed.'[2]

Porter's findings echo those more typically held in Britain, while Nehru's are more reflective of views held by those who experienced British colonial rule, and especially those jailed, censored and even tortured for their opposition to it.

This study leans in Nehru's direction, arguing that British history is incomplete without an understanding of its considerable imperial history, and that the British acquisition of an empire was by no means accidental or incidental. Whether one looks at the eighteenth century when wars with the European powers so often grew out of colonial disputes, at the nineteenth century when schoolchildren and exhibition-goers, novel readers and stamp collectors, all learned that Britain's greatness was in large part because of its imperial mission and its imperial possessions, or at the twentieth century when the effort to curb anti-colonial nationalism throughout the Empire was a policy shared by governments otherwise committed to significantly different political paths, imperialism mattered.

It mattered to the British economy, it mattered to British definitions of national identity, and, above all, it mattered to those whose daily lives were affected by colonial rule, wherever they might live.

This study emphasizes how both Britons and colonial peoples thought about, dealt with and lived in this vast and complex system. It foregrounds the experience of empire alongside the political fallout that is so often the principal way in which imperialism is presented to us. As a result, the chapters of this book are themed in a number of different ways. For clarity the earlier chapters are geographical, each dealing with a particular site or region of imperialism and organized largely, though by no means exclusively, chronologically. Then comes a series of chapters devoted to exploring how empire was lived and experienced: who ruled and how? How were men and women treated, regarded, shaped differently by and in the Empire? How did it feel to live under colonial rule, or to impose that rule? How were these experiences different in different kinds of colonies? Following these chapters, the study returns to the political arena to detail the disintegration of the Empire as protests against it grew and as the world stage changed, especially in the years after the Second World War. Together these differently accented chapters offer a detailed view of the modern British Empire, from Ireland to India, from the West Indies to Hong Kong, from Africa to Malaysia, and beyond.

References

1   Jawaharlal Nehru, *Autobiography* (Oxford: Oxford University Press, 1985; first edition, Delhi, 1936), p. 420.

2   Bernard Porter, *The Absent-Minded Imperialists. Empire, Society, and Culture in Britain* (Oxford: Oxford University Press, 2004), p. xv.

Acknowledgements

It was only when I had completed the manuscript for this book that I realized just what a good idea it had been to take on this mammoth task. The idea was not mine but that of Heather McCallum, then the history editor at Pearson Longman, who persuaded me that this would be a book worth writing. Even after Heather left the company, she continued to be immensely supportive and enthusiastic about this project. It is to Heather that my loudest and warmest thanks are due. The series editors, Eric Evans and Edward Acton, have been wonderful colleagues throughout the writing of this book, pushing me to develop arguments, encouraging me and generally being there when I needed them. Christina Wipf-Perry, who inherited this stepchild from Heather, has seen it through the editorial process smoothly and graciously. Thanks are also due to my desk editor, Natasha Dupont, and her wonderful staff.

The library staff at the University of Southern California have made my work so very much easier than it might have been, alerting me to interesting new books and producing inter-library loan requests in record time. It is a real pleasure to acknowledge their key role in getting this book written.

As ever, Curt Aldstadt has been there for me, always supportive, always stern about the need to take time off, and skilful at luring me away from my desk for walks on the beach.

Publisher's acknowledgements

We are grateful to the following for permission to reproduce copyright material:

Figure 1, © Harris Museum and Art Gallery, Preston, Lancashire, UK/The Bridgeman Art Library; Figure 2, Private Collection/ © Michael Graham-Stewart/The Bridgeman Art Library; Figure 3, Royal Geographical Society, London, UK/The Bridgeman Art Library; Figure 4, Private Collection/ © Michael Graham-Stewart/The Bridgeman Art Library; Figure 5, Alamy/© Chris Ballentine; Figure 6 from 'The Percival Family Album', Research Library, Getty Research Institute/Los Angeles, California (96.R.84); Figure 7, The British Library; Figure 8, Bibliotheque Nationale, Paris, France/Archives Charmet/The Bridgeman Art Library; Figure 10, Punch Photo Library; Figure 11, Illustrated London News, Figure 12, Royal Commonwealth Society Photo Collection by permission of the Syndics of Cambridge University Library; Figure 13 from 'The Travel Albums from Paul Fleury's Trips to . . .', Research Library, The Getty Research Institute/Los Angeles, California (91.R.5); Figure 15, School of Oriental and African Studies/Council for World Mission/London Missionary Society; Figure 16, Illustrated London News; Figure 17, Mary Evans Picture Library; Figure 18 from 'The Plague Visitation, Bombay, 1896–97', Research Library, The Getty Research Institute/Los Angeles, California (96.R.81); Figure 20 from 'The Percival Family Album', Research Library, Getty Research Institute/Los Angeles, California (96.R.84); Figure 21, Punch Photo Library; Figure 22, National Army Museum; Figure 23, The Art Archive/British Library; Figure 24, Illustrated London News; Figure 25, Topfoto/AP.

Imperial Federation Map: Royal Geographical Society, London, UK/The Bridgeman Art Library; Maps 1 to 5, © Cambridge University Press, reproduced with permission of the authors and publisher.

In some instances we have been unable to trace the owners of copyright material, and we would appreciate any information that would enable us to do so.

CHAPTER 1

Uniting the kingdom

Three Acts of Union – from the sixteenth to the very start of the nineteenth century – cemented the legal, political and economic relationships between dominant England and the so-called Celtic fringe of Wales, Scotland and Ireland. These relationships, which by the nineteenth century saw all these regions directly ruled from the Westminster parliament, are often dubbed 'internal colonialism'. Bringing Wales, Scotland and Ireland within a broader British realm represents some of England's earliest forays into colonial rule, for though the formal statutes linking these countries take us through to the nineteenth century, English interest in and often coercion of these neighbouring regions has a very much longer history.

The first of these lands to come directly under English control was Wales, brought formally into the English fold by the 1536 Act of Union that created 27 Welsh parliamentary constituencies. For at least a hundred years prior to this, conflicts between the Welsh and the English were common and, in the borderlands between the two especially, the English imposed discriminatory regulations and practices on the Welsh as they gradually gained the upper hand. The Welsh lacked many of the rights that the English enjoyed, a pattern of inequality and prejudice that would only grow after formal annexation.

Scotland's associations with England were more complicated, and its annexation more drawn out. It was under Stuart rule in 1603 that the union of the Scottish and English crowns was formalized, with the seat of government firmly located in England. Little more than a hundred years later, in 1707, another Act of Union robbed Scotland of its own parliament: 45 seats in the Westminster House of Commons and 16 in the House of Lords were established to represent the new Scottish constituencies.

Unlike Wales, however, and largely because it had been an identifiable sovereign state before unification, Scotland maintained even after union with England its own judicial system, its own national church (Presbyterian, unlike England's Episcopal Church of England) and a separate education system. And unlike the 1536 Act that had yoked Wales to England, the 1707 Act was a product of negotiation and not brute force. Scotland was in a position to sever its ties with England and the purpose of the 1707 legislation was to prevent that. The Act thus gave the Scots considerably more latitude than the 1536 Act had allowed the Welsh. Indeed, outside the wealthier segments of society, it probably made little difference to most Scottish men and women. As we shall see, the Jacobite uprisings in the eighteenth century would change that, but before then the Union was reasonably harmonious and not wholly disruptive for Scotland.

The same could not be said for the Act of Union with Ireland, which took effect on the first day of the new century, 1 January 1801. A number of critical political factors prompted this union, largely related to Britain's vulnerability, perceived or real, to foreign invasion. Ireland's incorporation came at a time when Britain was almost constantly at war with the Catholic power of France, and sometimes with Catholic Spain, and shortly after a popular uprising in Ireland had been subdued. Ireland was, of course, a predominantly Catholic land. Wolfe Tone's 1798 Irish rebellion was a violent one, with almost 30,000 fatalities. The fact that the rebellion had been aided by the French (despite the fact that Tone was himself a Protestant) fuelled English fears, especially during the threatening years of Napoleon's rule when Britain's political and military strengths were severely tested.

With a far larger population than either Scotland or Wales, the 1800 Act granted Ireland 100 seats in the House of Commons and 32 in the House of Lords to represent its 5 million inhabitants. As with Scotland, this representation was premised on the dissolution of a separate Irish parliament, and though that all-Protestant body had long been under the English thumb, the symbolism of its abandonment was nonetheless potent in shaping the future of Irish politics.

English intrusions into Ireland date back to the twelfth century, and the Irish had experienced considerable erosion of their liberties over the years; by the sixteenth century England was actively engaged in a political, economic and religious subjugation of this neighbouring island. The dates are anything but coincidental, for the bloodshed over religion so characteristic of the Tudor years in England had deep and dangerous consequences for Catholic Ireland. By the late sixteenth century, there was some urgency to the policy of de-Catholicizing Ireland through migration and plantation, as England became definitively Anglican. A greater and greater Protestant presence was imposed from the 1560s and for the next hundred years, with a corresponding dispossession and pauperization of the Catholic Irish. When the Act of Union was passed in 1800 one promise upon which the old Irish parliament insisted before they would dissolve was that Catholics be allowed to vote and to hold public office. It was a promise that would remain unfulfilled for a further three decades. Early in 1801, it was his inability to keep that controversial promise that prompted the prime minister, William Pitt, to resign his office.

After 1801, the kingdom – now consisting of Scotland, Wales, Ireland and England – was governed solely and as one from London. The state was more deeply centralized than ever before; the term Great Britain, already in use, was now the official designation of the nation. Some historians have argued that such centralization was effective by 1640.[1] This might be so in an informal sense, but we can certainly point to 1801, the dawn of the nineteenth century, as a time when such centralizing tendencies were fully and formally in place and when internal colonialism was complete. Although Scotland retained a number of important local institutions, Britain had one parliament and a state religion secured by a Protestant succession to the monarchy.

It was fear of destabilizing this Protestant sovereignty that prompted much of Britain's internal colonialism. Ireland as a predominantly Catholic region was the principal flashpoint for these religious debates within imperial policy, but religion was politically significant in Wales and Scotland too. In Scotland, Catholicism had largely given way by 1690 to a Calvinist-inspired Presbyterianism, under the influence of John Knox. It was distinctively different in character from English Episcopalian Christianity. The influence of Presbyterians among Protestant Irish groups, mostly centred in northern Ireland, was of considerable concern to the English authorities in the eighteenth century. Presbyterianism in Scotland was acceptable, but its presence in Ireland added a complicating additional layer of religious discontent and dissent that could only add to England's problems there; the Protestant Irish strand was the origin of the Orange Movement, which quickly became deeply involved in political protests in Ireland. Meanwhile, in Wales the insistence by the Anglican Church that services be conducted solely in English secured sturdy support for non-Anglican forms of Protestantism. The successful spread especially of Methodism and of Baptism owed much to the fact that they conducted services in the local language. Likewise the translation of the

Bible into Welsh, effected during the reign of Elizabeth I, ensured that virtually every household in Wales would continue to be exposed to the Welsh language even at a time when that language was under attack. Welsh remained alive in large part because of the actions of a monarch determined to impose Anglican conformity.

Non-Anglican Protestants and Catholics throughout the kingdom were barred from public office, local or national, by the Corporation Act of 1661 and the Test Acts of 1673 and 1678. These laws were part of the legal and political mechanism designed to protect a Protestant succession to the throne and to resist reinstatement of the Catholic Stuart dynasty. They also reflected a popular and growing sentiment that parliament – although hardly a representative institution at this time – was a specifically Protestant expression of liberty, what historian Linda Colley has called the 'Protestant inheritance'.[2] This celebration of Protestantism gave voice to a profound and long-standing anti-Catholicism in England, bolstered throughout the eighteenth century by the animosity between England and its most significant imperial and commercial rival, France. Ironically, after the defeat of France in the Seven Years War in 1763, Britain's new colonial acquisitions made the Empire a far less identifiably Protestant one than it had formerly been. Catholics and non-Christians figured largely among those now subject to British imperial rule.

National stability and success depended on more, of course, than merely a continued adherence to Protestant Christianity. The needs of merchants and of bankers were vital, and the mercantilist economic principles of England in the seventeenth and eighteenth centuries meant that the state took a close interest in trade and commerce, actively regulating economic life as a way to pay the expenses of government. In the early eighteenth century, for example, rarely a year passed in which a new law designed to regulate colonial trade in some fashion, or to control customs revenue (and its enemy, piracy), did not come before parliament. England kept a tight rein on colonial trade. Colonial goods were governed by strict regulations that gave a strong advantage to the English economy. Scots merchants and traders gained access to these lucrative colonial markets as a condition of the 1707 Act of Union. This meant that they were no longer required to route goods through England and pay duties on them, but could trade directly with other colonies within the British Empire. For Ireland, the wait was longer. An Act of 1696 had ruled that goods from the American plantations could not be landed in Ireland, a law that hindered the logical trade that might otherwise have flourished between America and Ireland, given their geographical proximity. Though this restriction was eliminated in 1731, Irish trade continued throughout the eighteenth century to be primarily with England, a situation that gave England as the dominant trading partner a considerable advantage.

Wales, like the often neglected Celtic region of Cornwall on England's south-west tip, was the site of active smuggling, both across the English–Welsh border and at the ports. The loss of government revenue that efficient smuggling represented made the control of contraband and of piracy a major component in England's desire to fold these 'peripheral' areas into the polity. The prospect of economic order in border areas – meaning a crackdown on smuggling and an organized customs agency pulling in significant revenue – was a key motive for internal colonialism.

This interest in potential revenues from the Celtic periphery was seldom balanced by a corresponding commitment to investment in those regions. The Irish plantation schemes of the sixteenth and seventeenth centuries were more concerned with peopling the country with loyal Protestants than in giving economic aid to, or partnering with, the Irish. Centralization, as it would do at a later stage of empire and in more distant lands, often worked to the advantage of the dominant and not the peripheral power. In the arena of banking, for example, London became more and more powerful at the expense of provincial centres, and the establishment of the Bank of England in London in 1694 was some indication of the power lines in the fiscal world. Whereas Scottish banks remained robust until the banking reorganization of the 1840s, those in Wales and Ireland simply could not compete with their English rivals.

Economic competitiveness was crucial to political survival in this era, and here again it was English practices and activities that came to dominate, particularly from the eighteenth century onwards. The landholding practices common in Celtic cultures were often incompatible with English ideas about inheritance, wealth creation and economic efficiency. The dominance of *gavelkind*, in which land was shared by all male heirs, contrasted with the typical practice of primogeniture in England, which concentrated wealth in eldest sons. In an era when the English economy was focusing increasingly on consolidating large tracts of land for more profitable and efficient cash-crop farming, the tendency in *gavelkind* for land plots to shrink to accommodate every son was regarded as a backward-looking and inefficient system. The clan system common in the Scottish Highlands was likewise regarded as hindering economic reform, with its subletting practices based on small farms and plots. England's inability to accommodate alternative practices and lifestyles led also to

English criticisms of these other cultures as barbarous, uncivilized and unproductive, a charge that would re-emerge in relation to more distant cultures as imperialism grew, and which frequently became a justification for colonial rule or intervention.

This fear of the different and the alien was also prominent in another of the factors determining the course of internal colonialism, and that was Britain's European rivalries, most especially its enmity with France. Throughout the eighteenth century, France was England's most constant antagonist and tension between the two countries was frequently performed on the imperial stage. Between 1689 and 1815, the English and the French fought a full seven wars. Furthermore, not only did the French aid the Americans in the 1770s, but they helped the Catholic Stuart claimants in the 1715 and 1745 Jacobite uprisings in Scotland, which attempted to put a Catholic monarch back on the British throne. France and Britain fought in India, in North America and in the Caribbean. Rivalry between England and France would not die down until 1815, when the Napoleonic armies had been routed and their leader exiled. Britain also went to war with Spain and with Austria during the eighteenth century, and colonial trading rights were at the heart of these conflicts. These complex entanglements of religion, trade and expansionist rivalry directly affected the internal colonies of Scotland, Wales and Ireland. England's intent in annexing the Celtic lands had much to do with securing the borders to deter foreign invasion. Such fears were, of course, confirmed when Catholic France offered aid to the Stuart cause or in Ireland. When the 1798 rebellion in Ireland (which catalysed formal annexation in 1800) broke out, government feared that the resulting instability would allow a French invasion. This constant reading of the predatory hostility of France had powerful consequences for the Celtic fringe; the marginality of the Welsh, Scottish and Irish was commonly transmuted into a potential disloyalty to the English state, a sentiment not always, of course, inaccurate given the resentments that colonialism invariably fostered.

As a result, English control of these three regions grew, and the history of the relationship between England and the Celtic fringe is one of increasing domination and supervision. England's close control of the Celtic fringe was in part to stabilize rule at home and in part to secure the more distant outposts of empire so often under threat from rival European colonizing powers.

This control made the Celtic fringe more and more dependent, economically and politically, on England and, as a result, anxious to participate as much as possible in its complex, highly protected, trading network.

Even before formal annexation, the dependency of Wales, Scotland and Ireland was high among English priorities. The 1720 Declaratory Act passed at Westminster was, in its own words, 'for the better securing the dependency of Ireland upon the crown of Great Britain'. The Act made laws passed at Westminster binding on Ireland and also ensured that appeals cases originating in Ireland were heard in England, thereby formalizing judicial control from the centre as well. This assertion of a central authority via a Declaratory Act was, interestingly, also tried with regard to the American colonies in 1766, proclaiming parliament's right to legislate on behalf of the colonies in the wake of a quantity of unpopular and vigorously resisted legislation. Not surprisingly, neither the colonial assemblies in the Americas nor the Irish parliament welcomed such laws. The Irish Act of 1720 was repealed in 1782, and not insignificantly after the surrender of Lord Cornwallis's troops at Yorktown, a symbolically important colonial defeat for the English state, ending the American Revolution (see Chapter 3).

The Irish had made shrewd use of Britain's preoccupations in America. The American Revolution had wreaked havoc with the Irish economy, cutting off many of its markets. English merchants refused to relax any of the restrictions on Irish trade to help alleviate Ireland's crisis, and in the face of this intransigence the Irish retaliated by refusing to import British manufactured goods. More pressingly, given how many of England's troops were deployed in America, Irish volunteer militia – Protestant and Catholic – began to drill and train all over the country, a move much feared by the English government. It was in this context that the Declaratory Act was repealed and the Irish parliament reconvened in an attempt to calm discontent, especially among Irish Protestants.

The victory of the Irish was, of course, short-lived, for within 20 years the Irish parliament would once again be dissolved. Furthermore, although Wolf Tone's rebellion in 1798 called for political representation for all Irish regardless of religious creed, the Irish parliament that had clawed back its existence in 1782 was an exclusively Protestant body with little interest in representing the Catholic majority. Internal tensions like these remind us that we should not classify the Celtic lands simply as victims of colonial aggression. Although they certainly experienced such aggression, the history of internal colonialism is far more complex; the Celtic regions were often also internally divided. They were also sometimes themselves anxious to colonize. In 1695, a Scottish expedition attempted to found a colony in Spanish Central America; the Darien project was a failure, but it certainly spurred the English to annex Scotland a decade later. The

Disunity within internal colonies

English were infuriated by this independent Scottish action, fearing its effects on English colonial trade and on relations with Spain. The Scots asserted their right to exercise an independent foreign policy, but the English threat to ban exports from Scotland to England subdued the Scots' protests. Scotland was clearly the weaker power in this exchange, yet it had attempted to colonize abroad despite its own experiences with a colonizing power.

Further complicating any overly simple view is the tangible split between Lowland and Highland Scots. The troops who defeated the 1745 Jacobite rebellion included many Lowland Scots as well as English soldiers. Highlanders were often regarded by the Lowland Scots as well as by the English as savages of little education and refinement compared with the more metropolitan and urbane occupants of urbanizing Lowland Scotland. As a result, the destruction of Highland society effected after 1745 and intended to discourage further rebellion met with little opposition from influential Scottish politicians who were focused largely on the more economically developed southern regions of the country. Such divides warn us not to oversimplify, or indeed overromanticize, colonial relationships.

In Wales, it was the English migrants who saw the Welsh as savages, for the Welsh population was small (half a million in 1801) and in some respects more homogeneous than the populations of Scotland and Ireland. English fear of intermingling with the Welsh had led, even before the Union, to regulations that, for example, classified as Welsh English men who married Welsh women. This was a significant reversal of the typical status of men and women, in which the condition of the husband determined that of the wife and not vice versa. Wales, seen as backward, acquired many of the indices of modern development – universities, museums and the like – far later than the other Celtic regions, towards the end of the nineteenth century.

Aside from the need to eradicate smuggling and to quell border raids, England's main interest in Wales was in its rich mineral possessions. Until the middle of the nineteenth century Wales was known mostly for the iron-working concentrated in Glamorganshire. After that, coal production dominated. These raw materials spelled wealth and profit in the propertied echelons of society, but often ended up impoverishing the ordinary people of Wales. In many areas, there was no work other than in coal mining, and whole families worked at it, sons following their fathers into the mines, the women of the family providing domestic back-up and often also working at the coalface. Few opportunities to break this cycle were available, and this made Wales highly vulnerable to economic depression. In the twentieth century especially, unemployment in the coal-mining valleys of Wales was among the most severe in the British Isles.

Ireland offers, in some respects, the most complicated of the various histories of internal colonialism. A separate island that remained overwhelmingly Catholic, its history of involvement with an aggressively expansionist England was a long one. Historians have often regarded sixteenth-century Ireland as England's 'colonial laboratory', but the English yoke was felt far earlier. Poyning's Law, passed in 1494, forbade the Irish parliament from meeting without the consent of the English monarch, and permitted only Protestants a vote. Strict codes, collectively called the Penal Laws, restricted every aspect of the lives of Irish Catholics. Marrying into a Catholic family entailed a loss of civil rights. Harsh rules limited the type and amount of property Catholics might own, where they could work, who they could employ, where and what they might learn. They could not carry arms or practise law. While legal devices ensured that an independent Irish political structure could not develop, landholding practices there kept a large proportion of the population in penury. Land tenure in Ireland was highly unusual in that tenants and not owners were responsible for improvement and investment, yet with no security of tenure, tenants had little incentive to invest in improvements. The pattern that grew out of this system was one of widespread absentee landlords interested only in maximizing profit and unwilling to spend money on improvements, and tenants who had neither motive to improve the land nor, for the most part, the necessary finances. The plantation schemes of the sixteenth and seventeenth centuries, begun in the reign of Mary Tudor and significantly increasing in scope and size over time, only aggravated existing inequalities, for the aim of these land-colonizing schemes was to make Ireland more Protestant by granting tracts of land to the English. In this respect, the projects were in some manner successful: Irish Catholics owned 61 per cent of the land in 1641, 14 per cent in 1704 and a mere 5 per cent by the late 1770s. In almost every other respect, the plantations were a failure, catalysing sporadic and bitter unrest, to which the English response was decidedly sectarian, deliberately wrecking the symbols and relics of the Catholic faith in retaliation.

Not surprisingly, given the discontent of a disenfranchised and increasingly dispossessed population, the English maintained a large military presence in Ireland, a tactic they would later use in many other colonies. It only added insult to injury that the Irish rather than the English were expected to finance these troops.

Language

Brute force was by no means the only form of power that the English wielded, however. Throughout the Celtic lands, it was long-standing policy to discourage the use of local languages; English was the language of policy and law, of culture and, perhaps most critically, of education. We have already noted that the Church in Wales lost ground because its services were routinely conducted in English, the language of annexation and power, while its Protestant rivals worshipped frequently in Welsh. This was particularly significant, for the use of the Welsh language was far more widespread than was the use of Scottish or Irish Gaelic. Despite the ban on teaching Welsh in elementary schools, not lifted until 1907, more than half the population of Wales still spoke Welsh in the 1890s. Although smaller proportions of the Scottish and Irish populations hewed to the local language, Gaelic too was deliberately excluded from the primary school curriculum, and instruction was conducted exclusively in English. The very existence of these bans inevitably sparked a revival of languages as a source of local pride, and in the nineteenth century in particular, organizations dedicated to restoring the Celtic languages flourished. The *eisteddfod* poetry-reading competition established in Wales in the 1860s, and the 1876 Society for the Preservation of the Irish Language, are typical examples of the interest generated in the nineteenth century as both cultural and political nationalism grew stronger in the internal colonies.

Not surprisingly, it was among the wealthy and the educated in Celtic populations that the use of English was most widespread. Language became one of the principal markers of privilege, an easily measured index of assimilation and of Anglicization. It was critical, of course, for English rule to seek collaboration from within, as was the case in almost every colonial setting, and in an era in which marked inequalities of power, wealth, representation and rights were wholly unremarkable, looking to local elites for support was an obvious and a sensible strategy of colonization, and largely successful. Wealthy Scots and Irish worked hard to fashion their lands and their lifestyles to English custom and aesthetics. They built their houses according to English style, affected English dress and speech, and acted towards their tenants according to English practice. Wealthy Celts, like their English counterparts, saw the poor and the labouring classes as rough, uncivilized and often immoral. In Scotland, such divisions were also geographical, as we have seen. Lowland Scots tended to regard the more rural and isolated Highland regions as more primitive and unrefined, a throwback to earlier and ruder lifestyles, prejudices eerily reminiscent of how the English spoke of the Scots, the Welsh and the Irish. Similar discriminatory thinking would follow the huge

Irish migration across the Atlantic to America, and around the globe to Australia.

Class Lines

The division along class lines that helped secure the colonial hold was considerably strengthened by the passing of the 1832 Parliamentary Reform Act. While this overhauling of the national electoral and parliamentary system of Britain did away with some of the more egregious inequities built into the voting system, the new constituencies it created clearly put English interests ahead of those of the Celtic regions. After 1832, one in five Englishmen was entitled to vote (women had everywhere been wholly disenfranchised by the Act), compared with one in eight Scots and one in twenty Irish men. Furthermore, it was only with the Catholic Emancipation Act of 1829 that voting rights were extended to non-Protestant Christians, finally fulfilling the demand the Irish parliament had made before its dissolution in 1800.

Internal colonialism did little to alleviate the gap between the poor and the rich, instead exploiting that divide – as it would in more distant colonies – for colonial ends. What could the poor then do? In large numbers, they chose to migrate, further impoverishing depleted regions through depopulation. After the uniting of the kingdom, the Celtic population diminished relative to that of England, though even in earlier times migration was a solution, although not always an easy or a comfortable one, to the grind of poverty and hopelessness. Young Irish men and women figured prominently among indentured servants arriving in the American colonies in the seventeenth and eighteenth centuries, their labour a product of colonialism at their place of both departure and arrival. The eighteenth- and nineteenth-century British Empire was a significantly Scottish enterprise: medical practitioners, military men and civil servants in the outposts of empire – hardly among the poorest segments of society – were disproportionately Scottish. For many, the disadvantages of being Scottish in an English environment diminished, for in far-flung colonial settings the fact of being British rather than specifically English elevated one's status. In the Scottish Highlands, population control was cynically manipulated for economic ends in the nineteenth and twentieth centuries. The sinews of colonialism were thus at work inside Britain and beyond the waters surrounding it; internal colonialism, though different in some respects from the overseas enterprise, was nonetheless integral to the broader project of empire and constitutes some of its earliest episodes.

These developments and changes emanated from an expansionist and aggressive England intent on keeping intact its Protestant succession and its vigorous colonial trade. As we have seen, much of the military activity in which England engaged in the seventeenth and especially in the eighteenth century focused on keeping colonial trade and trade routes running smoothly and profitably. From about 1700, England's major trading interests shifted from Europe to the growing empire, and laws ensured that it was England's needs that took precedence in commercial arrangements. As far back as the 1650s, the infamous Navigation Acts regulated all commercial shipping: British-built ships with British crews carried goods through British ports in British territory. Commerce was conducted as a form of 'closed shop' that privileged and protected England as a matter of course, and though many restrictions were lifted over time, the protection of English trade and commerce always came first.

When George III came to the throne in 1760 he successfully pushed for more direct monarchical involvement in the running of the country. Aided by widespread anti-Catholic sentiment and the fears generated by the French Revolution, this monarchical revival culminated in the establishment of the Royal Jubilee in 1809. By the reign of Victoria, this cult of the monarch was a valuable colonial tool that imagined a harmonious unity between the disparate parts of Britain's Empire. The growth of royal visits to the colonies and the declaration of Victoria as Empress of India in 1876, along with the pomp and grandeur created for such occasions, pumped up a new populist loyalty in which the British Empire was the definitive symbol of British greatness. The emphasis on British unity so central to this rhetoric promoted a degree of amnesia about the brutalities that had accompanied internal annexation. As a result, it is all too easy to forget that the United Kingdom was a product of Britain's larger colonial enterprise, and never a 'natural' connection between the quite different groups that, as the Empire was consolidated, were brought together as Great Britain.

References

1   See, for example, Steven G. Ellis, ' "Not mere English": The British Perspective, 1400–1650', *History Today* 38 (Dec. 1998), p. 48. See also Ellis and Sarah Barber (eds), *Conquest and Union: Fashioning a British State 1485–1725* (London: Longman, 1995).

2   Linda Colley, *Britons: Forging the Nation, 1707–1837* (New Haven, Conn.: Yale University Press, 1992), p. 52.

CHAPTER 2

Slaves, merchants and trade

By the eighteenth century Britain's powerful naval superiority was as much about colonial trade, shipping goods and peoples across the globe, as it was about the warfare so typical of the period. The visible growth in Britain's global activities, interests and profitability outside Europe led to a greater awareness, and often celebration, of the phenomenon of imperialism. Empire came, in the eighteenth century, more and more to connote British-held territories rather than merely British influence overseas. In parliament, imperial concerns took up an increasing amount of time; 29 Acts on colonial trade and related items were passed between 1714 and 1739 alone. Newspapers, magazines and journals in eighteenth-century Britain devoted considerable space to discussions of Britain's imperial possessions. More goods criss-crossed the globe, as did more people. Over the course of the century, the British Empire not only grew – in size, in stature, in profitability – but it also shifted in focus. For the most part, the eighteenth century was an era characterized by Atlantic domination, with North America and, more critically for British wealth, the West Indies at the imperial centre.

It was the Atlantic slave trade, without question, that secured much of the vital wealth and political success of Europe and of the British Empire throughout the eighteenth century. Slave labour in European-held colonies was by no means a unique phenomenon. Human enslavement had a long and a varied history by the time the Atlantic slave trade became profitable, but it was western European exploitation of existing slave practices in the Mediterranean and further south in sub-Saharan Africa that created the vast and distinctive trade associated with colonialism. Along the Gold Coast of West Africa, small fishing villages were transformed during the sixteenth and seventeenth centuries into bustling centres of commerce

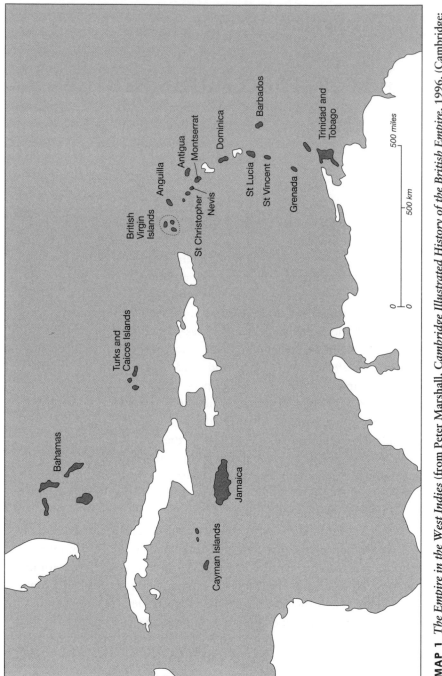

MAP 1 *The Empire in the West Indies* (from Peter Marshall, *Cambridge Illustrated History of the British Empire*, 1996, (Cambridge: Cambridge University Press, 1996), inset back cover map. © Cambridge University Press, reproduced with permission of the author and publisher).

hosting European as well as African residents. Slaves were traded alongside spices, weapons and ivory in a lively and profitable economy, and for the greater part of the eighteenth century few protested against its existence.

The imperial slave trade that supplied the Caribbean and North America was distinctive in a number of ways, however. This was a trade vast in scale, and it transported slaves much further away from their homelands than was routine in other forms of slavery. Atlantic slavery was unusual in being so racially specific; freed slaves in many societies would not have been that different from those around them. For the slaves caught up in the Atlantic trade, their skin colour made them stand out, marking them *as* slaves. New World slavery was also different in being so dominantly concerned with agricultural production. Slaves elsewhere fulfilled a far greater variety of duties and responsibilities, whereas in the Atlantic region they were put to work mainly in plantation agriculture. The goods they cultivated on the plantations that came to dominate Atlantic agriculture were also frequently plants brought to these regions through colonial exploration and travel. Both sugar and cotton were brought to the West Indies from other tropical regions, transforming the landscape, labour practices and social structure of the Caribbean dramatically. Joseph Banks, one of Britain's most celebrated naturalists, worked secretly for the Board of Trade, bringing Asian cotton varieties to the West Indies in the 1780s. Varieties of sugar native to the Pacific and the Indian Oceans helped improve sugar yields on West Indian plantations. The Atlantic slave trade, so closely associated with an era of active European imperialism, was a distinctive and unusual form of slavery.

The bulk of those whose labour would prove so profitable for Europe's sugar, tobacco and cotton production were purchased along the western African coastline, and the majority of them were taken to the Atlantic region in the years between 1740 (although the trade had begun almost two hundred years earlier) and the abolition of the slave trade in the British Empire in 1807. With an average of 60,000 slaves shipped annually for most of the eighteenth century, the effect of slavery on Africa was just as great as it was on the Caribbean, on North America, and on the imperial European powers. Slave-raiding, kidnapping and, inevitably, the extension of the tentacles of this trade to ever wider areas transformed politics in Africa as well as the life of those bound for servitude. Between the mid-fifteenth century and the late nineteenth century, some 12 million Africans were shipped in slavery to the Americas.

Their experiences could differ drastically, according to where they found themselves landed, for slaves might find themselves on a sugar colony in the West Indies, on a tobacco plantation in Virginia, growing rice in the Carolinas, or even away from the life of the plantation further north in New England, New York or Canada. A few found themselves in Britain where domestic service was the commonest form of labour allotted to African slaves. Early in the eighteenth century far more slaves were shipped to the British West Indies than to the colonies of North America, but the balance had shifted before the end of the century, with far more slaves transported to America than to the Caribbean by the dawn of the nineteenth century.

Over the course of the seventeenth and eighteenth centuries, slave labour gradually replaced the earlier and widespread use of white labour, often Irish, in British colonies. Indentured labour had been widespread in the West Indian and the American colonies before the boom in the slave trade in the eighteenth century. White colonial labour had included a good number of convicts and a group often known as 'redemptioners' who, if they failed within an agreed time to repay the captain of the ship in which they sailed, could be sold by him to pay off that debt. Convicts transported across the Atlantic consisted of both criminals (convicted largely of minor crimes such as pickpocketing, vagrancy and thieving) and political prisoners. Oliver Cromwell used transportation in the seventeenth century to rid himself of many of the Irish rebels who had opposed his plantation policies, linking colony with colony in a westward movement. Religious dissenters who persistently defied the law could also find themselves aboard a convict transport bound for the colonies along the Atlantic seaboard. These were the least free among the poor whites who worked in the Atlantic colonies. Indentured servants, by contrast, contracted with an employer for an agreed period, generally in return for a free passage to the colony where they would work. Some renewed their contracts. Some left the colonies. Some stayed on in non-indentured capacities. Their choices were often limited but they did at least enjoy the exercise of choice, unlike those brought across the Atlantic enslaved. Throughout the eighteenth century, as slave labour came to dominate, African migration massively outstripped white migration to the region. Only after abolition of the slave trade in 1807 did white migrants again start to dominate numerically.

In the earliest years of West Indian settlement, slaves and indentured servants were often indistinguishable in the work they did and in how they were treated. On occasion slaves could even successfully sue for their freedom. As the slave trade grew and the economics of colonial slave plantations hardened, however, the line between indenture and slavery, between white and black, grew more visible and much harder to cross.

The use of white labour in the plantation economy diminished radically and the importation of African slaves quickened.

Conditions aboard the slave ships were grim, with people jammed into small, unhygienic spaces and locked up below deck for large portions of the voyage. Communicable diseases ravaged these unwilling passengers: dysentery, smallpox and measles were all greatly feared. The slave ship *Arthur*, which sailed from West Africa in 1678 headed for Barbados, did not see a day go by without at least one African death. Altogether, 82 lives were lost on the two-month voyage.[1] Between 20 per cent and 40 per cent of those destined for slavery died during transport to the African coast for sale and shipping, another 3 per cent to 10 per cent died before they could be transported, and a further 15 per cent or so died aboard the slave ships at more than twice the rate of unenslaved paying shipboard passengers in this era. More than a third of those transported as slaves died before reaching their destination, and yet more died once they reached the New World, mostly from diseases to which they had never previously been exposed. The death toll was simply appalling. In 1788 the British parliament passed legislation regulating conditions aboard slaving ships to mitigate the suffering and the losses, but mortality remained high among this human cargo.

Nor was life much better when slaves arrived at their destinations. One in three slaves in the West Indies did not survive more than three years toiling in the fields of the Caribbean in the early years, although by the second half of the eighteenth century the economics of high mortality had convinced some slave owners to improve their care of their human property. Food allocations improved and the pace of work was sometimes eased by those who understood the drain on their investment that neglect could bring. It was less a humanitarian impulse than an economic incentive that prompted these changes. Nothing in the life of a slave in a British colony was easy. Slaves mostly built their own accommodation, grew their own food staples and made their own clothes from the cloth rations given to them, and all this was in addition to the long hours of field work expected of them six days a week.

Yet slaves were not without the means to control at least some of their waking hours, and they quickly learned which forms of resistance were least likely to have severe consequences and which were effective. Ira Berlin describes some of the options slaves shared with other groups of workers: 'feigning ignorance, slowing the line, minimizing the stint, breaking tools, disappearing at critical moments, and, as a last, resort, confronting their superiors directly and violently'.[2] Slaves pretended not to understand how to operate tools, or not to understand instructions. They could slyly do substandard work and, as they gained an intimate appreciation of the rhythms of agricultural production, their cooperation or lack of it could make a substantial difference to the quality and profitability of a crop.

Not surprisingly, some found escape a greater temptation than these covert forms of resistance. Those who were not caught, punished and returned to work often banded together in what came to be called Maroon communities. They lived in isolated, hard-to-reach areas to avoid capture, and they organized both raids on plantations and actual rebellions from time to time. The largest Maroon communities were in Jamaica, where there were about 1,000 escaped slaves living mainly in two groups, one windward (east) and one leeward (west) on the island. Between 1729 and 1739 the Maroon War played havoc with Jamaica's economy. A treaty between the Maroons and the authorities in 1739 granted freedom to the Maroons – in return for their agreeing to return runaway slaves to their owners. It was a curious alliance between those who had escaped and those from whom they had escaped, and it was reached over the bodies of future escapees.

By the late eighteenth century, British slave colonies had passed slave codes that laid out less the rights than the absence of rights endured by their slaves. These laws defined slaves as chattels (meaning they could be bought, sold and inherited), and made the prospect of manumission (freedom from slavery) almost impossible. They laid down punishments for slave misdeeds, and established pass laws severely restricting slave mobility. These Consolidated Slave Acts did provide an occasional concession: slaves were given one a day a fortnight (except during the harvest) other than Sundays to tend their own crops, grown on small plots given to them because the land was less amenable to profitable cultivation.

Over the course of the seventeenth century, Britain steadily increased its hold in the West Indies, consciously working to weaken Spanish power in the area and adding more and more colonies in order to rival and ultimately overtake Portuguese sugar production in Brazil. Throughout the eighteenth century Britain was dominant among slave-trading nations, transporting more slaves than any other country. The acquisition of Jamaica in 1655 proved crucial: by the dawn of the eighteenth century, the island would be Britain's most important source of sugar, though still dwarfed by the French slave sugar colony of St Domingue, destined to become modern Haiti after a major slave revolt in the early 1790s. Though sugar was not the only crop cultivated by slave labour in the British Caribbean, it was indubitably the most important. By contrast, in the American colonies there was far more diversity of production and much less emphasis on monoculture. Only 5 of Britain's 19 colonies in the Caribbean were not significant sugar producers. Tobacco, coconuts, coffee and other crops were grown too, but sugar yielded the greatest profit and required the most – as well as the most disciplined – labour. On average, sugar plantations in Jamaica by the early 1830s were worked by an average of 223 slaves compared with 128 in coffee production and 100 on livestock farms.

West Indian sugar production combined agricultural labour with modern factory practices. In order to ensure that the cane would not rot before it could be used, sugar was not only grown but partially processed in the West Indies and slave labour was found not only in the fields but in the mills, where a strict industrial schedule ensured the timely processing of the raw cane. This factory-style production was already operating in the colonies at a time when many workers in Britain were still tied to the land. Sugar was not, however, fully processed and refined in the West Indies. Strict laws governed the degree of processing that could be done prior to the cane reaching Britain. The bulk of refining was still done in Britain, but the perishable nature of the crop made the colonies sites of early industrial production. Britain's needs remained dominant, and the lives of those upon whose labour the whole operation rested were completely irrelevant to the process. The work was hard and unrelenting, although highly profitable for the plantation owners. Between 1770 and 1787, the British West Indian sugar colonies produced some 35 per cent of the sugar in the North Atlantic region, rising to about 55 per cent by the early years of the new century as slave revolts in French sugar colonies reduced production there. Since sugar was Britain's largest import from the 1750s to the 1820s, this was big business. The seemingly endless rise in British domestic sugar consumption – unmatched by any other European nation – boosted the value of this import throughout this period. The West Indian colonies in the second half of the eighteenth century were hugely import-ant to the British economy.

Slavery, unlike indentured labour, had the potential to provide the next generation of workers through reproduction. There was a clear economic incentive for ensuring that children born into a state of slavery could never exercise an option to leave the plantation. The children of slaves inherited their mother's status, and not their father's, in contrast to eighteenth-century British law in which women were minors and children derived their status in life from their fathers. Without explicit laws, children born of slave mothers might under British law have avoided enslavement if their fathers (as was so often the case) were not slaves but white men who had impregnated slave women. It was Thomas Jefferson's opinion that a slave woman who bore a child every two years was more profitable in the long run than the strongest and fastest male slave because her fertility replenished the workforce in the long term.[3] Nubile women were prized and often passed on as an inheritance in slave owners' wills as especially valuable property. Some slave owners, like Jefferson, realized the benefits of protecting slave women during their pregnancies since slave births in many places outpaced purchase of new slaves. Such was the case on Barbados, which had become a British colony in 1627 and which was a pioneer in producing the highly profitable commodity of sugar on large capital-intensive plantations using slave labour. From about the 1760s natural increase among the slave population was beginning to fulfil the island's labour requirements, but the island was not typical of the West Indian slave colonies. The conscious breeding of slaves was a practice more generally associated with American plantations where slave women were generally more fertile. The emphasis on sugar production in the West Indies, with its brutal and harsh work, adversely affected the fertility of women slaves. Male slaves were routinely assigned to the more skilled tasks associated with sugar cultivation and production, making women's labour vital to the field gangs. The heavy manual work of planting, weeding and pulling in gangs took its toll on women's health and fertility.

For some women slaves, pregnancy and early motherhood offered some respite from the hardships of slave labour. In some locations, though by no means universally, pregnant slave women enjoyed reduced workloads, a policy inspired by economic gain rather than sentiment. It was the lucky slave whose master implemented such policies. Richard Steckel's analysis of nineteenth-century plantation records in America suggests that some 54 per cent of slave pregnancies ended in stillbirth, infant mortality or early childhood mortality.[4] There is no reason to assume that the situation would have been any better at an earlier date or in British colonies. Although women might enjoy some benefits of this kind, they were vulnerable to sexual abuse since they could not spurn the sexual advances of owners or overseers without potentially severe consequences. The widespread sexual contact between white men and slave women was the reason why laws determining the status of children born to slave mothers was so important to plantation owners. Such children, without that law, might be deemed white and free.

Violence was not limited, of course, to the sexual experiences of women. Slave rebellions were common, and were invariably met with violence, although that threat did little to deter protest. Tobago saw repeated slave rioting in the 1770s as well as in the early nineteenth century. There were substantial uprisings in Antigua in 1736, in Grenada in 1795, in Trinidad in 1805, in Barbados in 1675 and 1816, in Demerara in 1823, and in Jamaica in 1760, 1776 and 1831. Slave revolts were in large part a reaction to the daily violence that defined plantation slavery. Slaves could be whipped and beaten, raped, assaulted and even killed with impunity as part of the daily routine. Their enslavement was a product of violence at every level. Coercion was central to slavery, which rested ultimately on the lash, the gun and the boot. The violence slaves experienced nevertheless went well beyond the pain of physical abuse. Slaves were men and women who had been forcibly removed from their communities and were often thrown together with strangers who spoke different languages. They were forced to go by names chosen for them by their owners, and to do any work their supervisors instructed them to do. Violence and coercion dominated their existence.

Towards the close of the eighteenth century anti-slavery sentiment began to emerge forcefully in Europe. Eighteenth-century political philosophers had mostly either ignored or found justifications for slavery, but in the 1760s the French philosopher Charles de Secondat, Baron de Montesquieu, offered a thoroughgoing critique of the practice. The influential Scottish economist Adam Smith also registered an unease with slavery, which he saw as incompatible with human advancement. For Smith free will, which slaves so palpably lacked, was the motor that would drive improvement, and free labour was most especially central to his vision of the interplay of morals, economics and governance. If Smith's rationale for opposing slavery was connected to the economic system he thought would improve the world, many anti-slavery activists were motivated by religious sentiment, and a variety of evangelical Christian and other Protestant groups played a significant role in the movement. A religious motivation did not necessarily, or indeed particularly frequently, imply that abolitionists saw slaves as their equals. A common argument wielded by the anti-slavery movement, not dissimilar to Smith's concern about unfreedom, was that slavery degraded and brutalized those who suffered under its yoke. Typical of this sentiment was the dramatic speech William Wilberforce delivered in the House of Commons in 1789 in which he claimed that 'all improvement in Africa has been defeated by her intercourse with Britain'. The slave trade had 'enslaved their [Africans'] minds, blackened their character, and sunk them so low in the scale of animal beings that some think the apes are of a higher class'.[5] Many abolitionists

FIGURE 1 *Anti-slavery medallion, 1787* (Harris Museum and Art Gallery, Preston, Lancashire, UK/The Bridgeman Art Library)

saw their role as creating an environment in which Africans could be raised to civilization, a state they believed fully lacking in their life of enslavement and realizable through the redemption of Christianity. Note how the chained slave in the medallion is in an attitude of prayer and supplication.

The anti-slavery movement in Britain grew rapidly in the late eighteenth century. By the 1770s the Quakers had broken off all association with slaveholders and slave traders, requiring their members to divest themselves of any slave-related business interests. The Mansfield decision, handed down by the courts in 1772, ruled that James Somersett, a former slave now in Britain, could not be forcibly returned to enslavement in the North American colonies because on British soil the former slave was free. The case was important for it destroyed any claims to the legitimacy of slavery within Britain. A few years later, in 1787, activists founded the Society for the Abolition of the Slave Trade, circulating a petition against slavery that year that produced about 60,000 signatures. The first Bill for abolishing the slave trade reached parliament in 1791, although it failed to pass. Women became actively involved in anti-slavery protests, raising funds, writing letters of protest, and becoming increasingly politically aware. For a substantial group of women, anti-slavery activism would open their eyes to the inequalities under which women in Britain lived, prompting them to fight for women's rights as well. Yet despite this diverse and significant activity, economics as much as moral sentiment may have helped the anti-slavery case, as the push for a free trade system grew stronger in early nineteenth-century politics.[6] Moreover, Britain was not the pioneer of abolition. Denmark had become the first country to abolish the slave trade in 1803, and rumours that America planned to do so were circulating widely at the time Britain embraced abolition. (Denmark's abolition passed into law in 1792, but became effective only in 1803.)

The effect of anti-slavery agitation was, not surprisingly, piecemeal and scattered. Whereas Upper Canada ended the importation of slaves in 1793, Britain did not halt the slave trade until 1807 and slave emancipation finally passed successfully through the British parliament in 1833. Many were horrified by the terms of the 1833 emancipation proclamation, which the government justified as necessary to save the planters from economic ruin. Although slavery was abolished as of August 1834, slaves were required for a period of seven years to devote three-quarters of their work hours to their former owners in return for food and clothing. This compensation to the slaveholders was in addition to a generous cash payout that totalled about £20 million. The seven-year apprenticeship

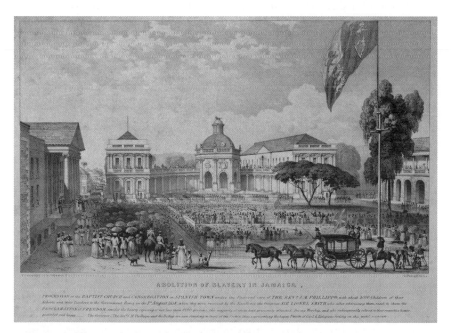

FIGURE 2 *Thomas Picken,* The Abolition of Slavery in Jamaica, *1838* (Private Collection/© Michael Graham-Stewart/The Bridgeman Art Library)

scheme ended early in 1838, but by then it had already led many former slaves to move to uncultivated areas to avoid such onerous post-slavery service. By the end of the 1830s, some 800,000 slaves had won their freedom in the British colonies of the West Indies and on the sugar-producing island of Mauritius in the Indian Ocean.

The abolition of slavery in the 1830s had come very swiftly upon the heels of one of the largest slave rebellions in British territory. It was in 1831 that the 'Baptist War' convulsed large sections of Jamaica. Crops and property were destroyed, and the frustration and anger of slaves was made dramatically visible. Although this uprising alone cannot explain emancipation, it certainly helped precipitate a shift from an even more gradualist plan than that implemented in 1833.

Elsewhere in the British Empire, and especially in East Africa, slavery was not abandoned even after emancipation. The principle of separation between slave trading and slaveholding that had shaped the passage of reforms in Britain continued to influence laws elsewhere. In the last quarter of the nineteenth century slave trading was prohibited in many parts of British Africa, mostly using a strategy known as 'legal-status' abolition. Rather like the Mansfield decision of 1772, this tactic permitted slavery no legal standing. This meant that courts of law could not enforce possession of a slave. The same tactic had been applied in British India in 1843, yet in large parts of the Empire, and particularly in parts of Africa, slaveholding was not formally outlawed until the twentieth century.

The number of freed and escaped slaves in the Empire was expanding long before the 1830s. When the American Revolution ended in the early 1780s many former slaves found their way to Canada and Britain, mostly in conditions of poverty. Faced with this unexpected wave of poor migrants, Sierra Leone was founded as an experimental free black colony in 1787. The earliest colonization scheme failed and the experiment struggled for some years, but the colony nonetheless survived. It became a Crown Colony in 1808, although it never fulfilled the dream of its promoters that it would become a self-sustaining agricultural plantation economy worked by free labour. It was, however, as much a colonial product of slavery as the sugar so avidly consumed by the British in their tea and their cakes.

While reformers were worrying over whether Sierra Leone could demonstrate African capacity for free labour, British trade even after 1807 continued to profit significantly from slave-produced commodities, and British manufacturers were active in producing goods that were linked intimately to slavery, such as shackles and irons. The abolition of the slave trade did not presuppose any diminution in the export of slave-grown sugar, just as the emancipation law of 1833 had no effect on the sale of slave-grown cotton from America to Britain. Long after Britain eschewed slavery legally, its economy and trade profited substantially from slave production.

Since slave-grown sugar was the most valuable British import of the eighteenth century, the West Indies in many ways dominated the late eighteenth-century British Empire, and after emancipation the Caribbean diminished rapidly in importance within the Empire. The story was quite different in the era of slavery, when planters not only grew rich from their enterprises but exercised considerable political power in Britain and in the colonies. Indeed, the plantation colonies enjoyed considerably more power than most of Britain's other colonies in the eighteenth century. The Atlantic colonies themselves were self-governing, with legislative assemblies and a property-based franchise. Barbados led the way, its first assembly being convened in 1639. Their significance for the health of the British economy also allowed the West Indian planters to extract considerable concessions from the imperial parliament, which increased their wealth and restricted non-British competition. Besides, more than a few members of parliament had significant sugar interests.

One source of irritation that would have significant consequences was the capacity of the West Indian lobby to extract concessions from the imperial government that were opposed by their neighbours in the North American colonies. The Molasses Act of 1733, for example, imposed wickedly high duties on foreign (meaning non-British) sugar imports to the American colonies as well as outlawing the importation of French sugar and molasses into Ireland. America went on buying sugar from the French and from other producers when it was cheaper than British sugar, but resentment over the preference shown to the West Indian interest at their expense burned deep.

In an era before free trade came to dominate economic philosophy and in which the principles of mercantilism ruled, such protectionist desires were widespread and indeed often secured by naval and military action. Historians of the eighteenth century often describe Britain as a 'fiscal–military' state where close ties between economic policy and diplomacy determined political action.[7] Both economics and diplomacy were intimately connected to the growing profitability of empire that helped keep government financially afloat.

A number of laws governed who could trade with whom and who could transport British goods across the ocean, and in these various laws we see the principles of mercantilism clearly enshrined. The trade in humans followed these same economic principles. The British slave trade had begun as a monopoly venture, the privilege granted first and unsuccessfully in 1663 to the Company of Royal Adventurers, and nine years later to a newcomer, the Royal African Company. In essence, chartered companies – whatever the goods they traded in – paid the Crown in exchange for being granted a trade monopoly. In 1698 the Royal African Company lost its monopoly and the trade in bodies became one of the very first experiments in free trade undertaken by Britons when the slave trade was opened to private traders.

But though there were, by the middle of the eighteenth century, some 150 British slaving ships actively trading, slaving was not wholly without restraint. In 1713, in the Treaty of Utrecht marking the end of the War of the Spanish Succession, in which Britain also acquired Gibraltar and Acadia (modern Nova Scotia, roughly speaking), Spain granted England the sole right (called the *asiento*) for 30 years to supply slaves to the Spanish Empire. The government gave those rights to the South Sea Company, stipulating that they in turn buy their slaves from the Royal African Company (which gave up slaving altogether in 1731, weakened by the competition). British planters, fiercely protective of monopolies that increased their wealth, were deeply opposed, arguing that Spain would get the best slaves and that British planters would have to make do with Spain's rejects.

Mercantilism, then, had very little in the way of a humane face. It was an economic system in which the colonies were expected to supply to the metropolis raw goods in exchange for manufactured goods, and in which each party enjoyed a monopoly position in the market of the other, although the colonies always remained subordinate to British needs. This would be one of the principal sources of tension between Britain and its North American colonies in the second half of the eighteenth century, as the next chapter will discuss. This monopolistic exchange of goods was always and ultimately backed by force; in the case of Britain, by the immense power of its navy.

From the 1650s, the Navigation Acts regulated colonial trade by ensuring that colonial goods were carried only on British and British colonial ships and by effectively directing all export and re-export through Britain. To sweeten the pill, the colonies in return had a monopoly on the home market. The colonies were thus encouraged, and in some senses coerced, into concentrating on producing goods unobtainable but in demand within Britain and to buying manufactured goods solely from

Britain. After 1696 colonial trade was supervised by a new Board of Trade and Plantations, generally referred to simply as the Board of Trade. The Board increased central supervision of private trading, mainly to realize the state's portion of this extraordinary wealth, mostly derived from the collection of customs and excise duties. Likewise, slaves bound for British colonies were, in the eighteenth century, carried almost exclusively on British slave ships.

Commerce in the eighteenth century was a busy and vigorous enterprise, and social theorists of the period often argued that the elaborate commercial life that so typified the European powers represented the very pinnacle of civilization. It was not uncommon in the eighteenth century to regard a lack of interest in commerce and business as a defining characteristic of 'primitive' peoples. For an era of colonial expansion premised primarily on trade, it was a perfect justification for colonial conquest and for the appropriation of uncultivated land. Economists, philosophers and politicians generally agreed that less civilized peoples, unappreciative of consumerism, of manufacture and of trade, would benefit from the influences of civilized trading nations. Whereas in other periods, differences in religion or skin colour might be the focal point of difference between colonist and colonized, in the eighteenth century it was often commerce that defined civilization and marked difference. The tendency to encourage a trade in which commodities came *to* Britain and manufactured goods *left* Britain only reinforced this view. The relatively low level of consumption in the colonies was sometimes taken as evidence of the barbarous state of 'native' peoples, a convenient explanation for the distinct lack of interest in British goods traders often encountered in Africa and Asia, and for the poverty that so very often accompanied colonial influence for indigenous peoples. It would, of course, also prove a convenient justification for transatlantic slavery.

Mercantilism had originated in a desire to acquire ever greater quantities of silver, then considered the most valuable of all substances. In the mercantilist view the purpose of trade was to increase the store of silver, so wealth-generating trade such as that between Britain and the Caribbean, or Britain and the American colonies, was regarded as the right kind of trade. The lack of interest that non-European peoples displayed for European goods was further complicated by the one interest they did show, which was in silver. Silver, the mercantilists complained, was the only item for which Asian traders demonstrated any enthusiasm, but buying with silver obviously diminished rather than increased stock. In a mercantilist economy, then, a carefully controlled slave trade that disallowed certain kinds of exchanges and that kept trade within a British world was an expression of right, while the Asian lack of interest in British and British colonial goods was evidence of a distance from civilized commerce.

If trade in people as well as goods was one of the most salient characteristics of British imperialism in this period, the other dominant theme was imperial rivalry. The eighteenth century in particular was punctuated by outbursts of naval and military violence between rival European powers, with France, Spain and Britain dominating as the aggressors. The buoyancy of the slave economies of the West Indies allowed politicians to raise revenues for fighting, and it is no accident that the stream of wars that erupted between the main contenders for European expansion was staged not in Europe, but largely in colonial territory. The European colonial competitors fought one another in the Caribbean, in India, in North America, colonial possessions rapidly changing hands with no consideration for the opinions or needs of the indigenous peoples living there.

It was increasingly against the French that the British pitted themselves, more especially as the power and significance of the older Spanish Empire – especially in the Caribbean – waned. Between 1680 and 1815, there were seven Anglo-French wars, the most decisive perhaps being the Seven Years War, which ended in 1763. Britain acquired considerable new lands, but at a cost. The war was a huge drain on Britain's finances and on many of its colonies (not least because of trade blockades), and the cost of administering the newly acquired territories was also high. Moreover, the war left Britain vulnerable in one of its most important colonial regions, America. Both British Americans and Britain's European rivals would, not much more than a decade later, exploit that weakness in the American War of Independence, as we shall shortly see.

The British Empire nonetheless grew significantly as a result of the territories acquired in the 1763 Treaty of Paris that ended the Seven Years War. In the Caribbean, Britain gained Grenada, Dominica, St Vincent and Tobago. In North America, Quebec, Prince Edward Island and both East and West Florida all became British. Britain's interests in South Asia were also expanding considerably at this time. Not surprisingly, many historians see the Peace of Paris as a watershed: where before this the British Empire was predominantly organized around and acquired for trade, after 1763 the scope, size and heterogeneity of British imperial holdings increased the political, as opposed to the exclusively economic, realm. The rationale for empire shifted at least some degree away from the purely economic.

Yet curiously this growth in the size and diversity of the British Empire coincided with another and very different kind of growth, that of resentment and tension from within. In North America, two major forms of dissatisfaction with British rule were brewing: American colonists in the older territories were chafing at the economic and political restrictions that bound them and, in the previously French territories now controlled by Britain, French-speaking (Francophone) Catholics resented the anti-Catholic elements of the British political system that limited their participation.

Catholic irritation was not, however, confined to colonies such as Quebec. Much closer to the centre of imperial power, Ireland was also in turmoil, as Chapter 1 has shown. The 1798 rebellion may have sealed Ireland's fate for more than a century, but it also underscored the vulnerabilities Britain faced within its Empire. Even closer to home than Ireland, the growing anti-slavery lobby threatened the continued use of slave labour at much the same time that a new generation of economic theorists – spearheaded by Adam Smith – attacked the restrictive practices of mercantilism and preached to considerable effect the doctrine of free trade. Although hindsight gives us the benefit of knowing that none of these potential and actual crises would bring down the Empire, and that the practice of colonialism would prove flexible enough to incorporate the major ideological changes ushered in by the free trade and anti-slavery lobbyists, those living through these changes must have wondered not if, but when, the Empire would collapse. For many, of course, the events that unfolded in America in the 1770s must have seemed to spell such doom.

References

1   Jennifer L. Morgan, *Laboring Women. Reproduction and Gender in New World Slavery* (Philadelphia: University of Pennsylvania Press, 2004), p. 53.

2   Ira Berlin, *Many Thousand Gone. The First Two Centuries of Slavery in North America* (Cambridge, Mass.: The Belknap Press of Harvard University Press, 1998), p. 11.

3   Edwin M. Betts (ed.), *Thomas Jefferson's Farm Book: With Commentary and Relevant Extracts from Other Writings* (Charlottesville: University Press of Virginia, 1976), p. 46.

4   Richard Steckel, 'A Dreadful Childhood: The Excess Mortality of American Slaves', in Kenneth Kiple (ed.), *African Exchange: Towards a Biological History of Black People* (Durham, NC: Duke University Press, 1998), p. 220.

5 Wilberforce's parliamentary speech of May 1789, quoted in Barbara Harlow with Mia Carter, *Archives of Empire, Vol. II: The Scramble for Africa* (Durham, NC: Duke University Press, 2003), p. 97.

6 The most celebrated and controversial example of this argument is that of Eric Williams in his landmark study, *Capitalism and Slavery* (Chapel Hill: University of North Carolina Press, 1944).

7 Philip Harling and Peter Mandler, 'From "Fiscal–military" State to Laissez-faire State, 1760–1850', *Journal of British Studies* 32 (1993), pp. 44–70.

CHAPTER 3

Settling the 'New World'

The Atlantic colonies that would, in time, become America were developing at roughly the same time as those of the Caribbean, and indeed the histories of these two sets of colonies were closely linked until the end of the eighteenth century. Some early settlement attempts in the 1580s, in what is now Virginia and, much further north, in Newfoundland, were succeeded in the seventeenth century by settlements that proved more durable. The colony of Virginia was founded in 1607, named after Queen Elizabeth (the so-called 'Virgin Queen'). Over the course of the seventeenth century more and more settlers left Britain, some seeking work, some seeking land, and some to gain religious freedom in the new American colonies. These new American colonies were founded, and in the early days peopled, in large part by white settlers choosing to migrate. This has led to some characterizations of the colonization of America as a phenomenon achieved by migration rather than conquest, one in which colonial peoples enjoyed a good deal of political freedom. That view is accurate only if we choose to ignore three important groups: the convict and indentured labour so important to early American prosperity; the native American peoples whose subjection and marginalization by settler society was necessary for the new population to enjoy the freedoms and successes they sought; and the growing body of slaves carried to the region and forced to work there.

Early settlers frequently thought of themselves as British, and of the native indigenes they encountered in the colonies, as well as slaves brought forcibly from Africa, as foreign. The effects of colonization on America's indigenous peoples were colossal, affecting their health, their wealth, their social structures, their customs and traditions, and their habitat. Most notorious was the impact of previously unknown diseases brought to the continent by Europeans. With no prior exposure to diseases such as smallpox, measles, influenza, tuberculosis and diphtheria, Native Americans were highly vulnerable, having no immunity. When epidemic disease spread through a Native American settlement, it could easily fell almost every member; in the early days of settlement, epidemics were the most common killer. New forms of land use and the enclosure of land for settlement considerably altered the local ecology over time, often depleting resources such as the wild game that local peoples had traditionally relied upon for food. Changes in land use led also to a gradual shift from subsistence agriculture among Native American tribes to a dependence on trade and commerce. It was a change that made tribes more reliant on settlers, as well as changing radically the seasonal settlement and movement that many tribes had traditionally followed. Fur trading, especially, became a critical source of Native American revenue, but the large-scale trapping of animals affected the environment, often in destructive ways. The introduction of European-style firearms was also destabilizing; the power of guns made them a valuable commodity, and Native American groups competed with one another for possession of them. Such competition led to an increase in inter-tribal conflict, itself made deadlier by the growing use of guns. Still, inter-tribal warfare was less significant in the destruction of an older Native American way of life than were the wars of European settlers. These affected Native Americans even though they were concerned with issues far removed from indigenous life. The rivalry between Britain and its imperial competitors in Europe, and the hunger for large tracts of land, put considerable strain on Native Americans drawn in to these conflicts, weakening their ability to survive in the face of settler America.

Those who did survive, however, not only adapted to the changes around them, but quickly learned the ways of European-style diplomacy. By the eighteenth century, especially as refugees from weakened tribes joined together, their communities became increasingly diverse. Native Americans learned to play the various European rivals off against one another for their own advantage, and there was also a good degree of cross-cultural exchange. The modern American Thanksgiving table owes much to what settlers learned from the locals: turkey, corn on the cob, maple syrup and pumpkins were all foodstuffs that settlers learned how to prepare from Native Americans. Nonetheless, and despite this tough determination to survive in a hostile world, by the time of the American Revolution American Indians along the Atlantic seaboard were largely dependent economically on the European settlers, and this meant they had little political muscle.

The significant support that Native Americans gave to the British during the Revolutionary War was not repaid, and many at the time thought the failure of the peace settlement of 1783 (discussed below) even to make mention of their future was a shabby return for Native American loyalty. Yet the British cultivated Native Americans after white America won its independence from the Empire, although they consistently refused to help them during the wars that erupted between the new American republic and the native population in the 1780s and 1790s. Their support for the British during the war did not endear American Indian populations to their new masters, and the treaties America increasingly enacted with numerous tribes were seldom generous to the indigenous peoples.

If Amerindian populations were dwindling in the seventeenth and eighteenth centuries in the wake of contact, the settler population was growing fast. Around 20,000 migrants arrived in the New World between 1620 and 1640, in 1730 the population was around 629,000, and by 1783 almost $1\frac{1}{2}$ million white Europeans had settled there. By 1800, the population totalled more than 5 million. The earliest migrants were predominantly young, male and single, a typical pattern in settler colonies. In the later period, as the colonies became established, families began to migrate. By the 1630s some 500 miles of coastline along the north-eastern seaboard of North America was British, and by 1759 there were 13 colonies, mostly thriving. The largest populations by the mid-eighteenth century were to be found in the tobacco-growing colonies of Virginia and Maryland, whose combined population totalled some 372,000 by 1750. The New England colonies had the next largest concentration of population.

What made the American colonies so attractive? The story most often told is, of course, that of the 1629 voyage aboard the *Mayflower* that signals freedom of conscience and of religion, and certainly the Puritans do figure significantly in the early history of the American colonies. The bulk of white settlers who came to the Americas were non-Anglican Protestants, and in the eighteenth and nineteenth centuries the colonies became known as places where small religious sects could flourish. One important feature of American life was that, overall, there was no majority religion, which partially explains the strong strand of religious toleration that made America so distinctive. Only two of the 13 colonies – Massachusetts and Connecticut – ever had formal state churches, a radically different situation from Britain where the power of the Anglican Church prevented Christian non-Anglicans as well as Catholics and Jews from enjoying full political participation.

Religion, however, was only a part of the complex of reasons why settler colonialism was so very successful in America. In the growing commercial environment that by the eighteenth century was so clearly definitive of Britain, these colonies offered goods unavailable in Britain as well as becoming an increasingly valuable depot for supplying the nearby slave colonies of the West Indies to their south. By the late eighteenth century, North Atlantic markets were of crucial importance for a host of goods: sugar, tobacco, coffee, cotton, cocoa and rum. In the more northerly colonies, timber with which to build and fit ships was equally important and the fur trade, too, was highly profitable. By the middle of the eighteenth century, settler capitalism was well established, and many of the restrictions theoretically imposed by Britain's mercantilist policies were routinely ignored by American merchants and traders with little fear of retaliation.

Land was perhaps the most important factor in colonial advancement, as well as a source of considerable strife between settlers drawn by its availability and cheapness and Native Americans increasingly required to abide by property laws utterly alien to their culture. Much of the struggle between the newcomers and the indigenous population reflected a fundamental difference in attitudes and relationship to the land. Both settlers and Native Americans complained constantly about the other's trespass. This persistent tension led to frontier violence and raids, the killing and stealing of livestock, the burning of crops and of compounds; none of this was sanctioned by colonial governments, but it was a fact of life on the frontier. There was no single form of land acquisition in colonial America; different colonies had different methods of parcelling out land. In some colonies, particularly in the north, land was largely allotted to groups and communities, while further south it was more likely to be sold to individuals. In the south, a system known as headright offered free land to those who would pay their own passage there. But land was, by British standards, cheap and plentiful and migrants came not just from England (the larger number in pre-Revolutionary America) but from Germany and Switzerland, Scandinavia, Holland and Ireland. The larger proportion of the earliest Irish migrants were not Catholic, but Ulstermen who would come to be known in America as Scotch-Irish. They were Scottish Protestants who had left Scotland for northern Ireland, and came to America in large part because they felt adrift in predominantly Catholic Ireland. Between the end of the Seven Years War in 1763 and the start of the War of Independence in 1775, some 55,000 Protestant Irish, 40,000 Scots, 30,000 English and 12,000 Germans arrived in the 13 colonies, as did around 84,500 African slaves.

Although land was a significant attraction, at least half of all migrants who landed in America in the seventeenth and eighteenth centuries came not to purchase land but as indentured labourers, tied for a fixed term to an employer who paid their passage and guaranteed them food and lodging for the duration of their contract. Although American history is full of grand tales of the poor made good – the 'rags to riches' stories of the popular press – few who started out in America as indentured servants ever saw fabulous wealth. Most stayed poor, and would continue to work outside indenture for wages rather than eventually acquiring land. This suited a society that was increasingly commercially oriented, for the cheapness of land made labourers sometimes hard to find, since so many could afford to buy modest plots of land. Although such a situation sounds as if it would be favourable to workers since they were in short supply, that was not so: indenture and the mercantilist imposition of maximum wages in many of the colonies served to keep firm the distinction between those who owned property and those who worked for wages. As the next chapter will show, this critical relationship between landownership and labour would re-emerge in colonial Australia.

Eighteenth-century America can, however, be characterized as a largely middle-class place, in that there was a large population of landholders, a small wage-earning working class and no significant aristocracy. The preponderance among this landholding class of non-Anglican Protestants, wedded to a stern work ethic and fervently believing in the importance of the individual, would help shape the new republic in myriad ways.

Settler colonies enjoyed a degree of political freedom that was only ever extended to those colonies where a white migrant population came to dominate. The system of 'representative government' we see in the American Atlantic colonies operated via elected assemblies. As in Britain, the franchise was based on property ownership and limited to adult men. Women and landless men were excluded, along with Native Americans; the British usually chose not even to regard the latter as British subjects. Whereas issues such as defence and taxation – which would both prove contentious in the 1770s – remained in the hands of the imperial government in London, the local assemblies in the colonies had the power to pass laws specific to the locale. In the early years of colonization, and until the mid-eighteenth century, the British government was mostly uninterested in the operation of internal colonial politics unless they interfered with revenue. It was trade that they wished to control, and it was only when trade and politics began to clash that British politicians paid attention to matters of governance in the American colonies.

In part this lack of interest is typical of the eighteenth-century Empire, overwhelmingly concerned with commerce and revenue. But in the case of the American colonies in the earlier years of the eighteenth century, as in the preceding century, it was also because they were regarded as ultimately less profitable than the West Indian colonies. Their main role was to supply the West Indies with foodstuffs, livestock, timber and cloth so that the slave colonies could focus their attention on the products for which they were renowned and on which the returns were so attractive. In return, the West Indies supplied the American colonies with sugar, rum and molasses in a classic example of how the British wanted colonial trade to work: Britain and its colonies linked in a complex network of production and supply, and excluding goods from outside the British world. The steady growth of the settler population in North America boosted this system, making the American colonies increasingly important, but also growingly restive about the limitations imposed from Britain on their trade. By the middle of the eighteenth century they had moved from relatively lacklustre economic units to become critical markets for both export and re-export, alongside their growing role as suppliers both to the West Indies and to Britain.

It was, however, impossible to insulate commerce from the political ferment of an era in which Britain was so often sparring with its European competitors in these very regions. Much of the Anglo-French conflict in the Atlantic and the Caribbean was commercial rivalry, especially with regard to sugar. And it was here that trouble really began to brew between the American colonists and the British government, most especially in and after the Seven Years War, which ended in 1763. The lure of wealth often proved greater than the pull of patriotism, and during that war, New England colonists had resolutely refused to cease their trade with Britain's enemies, sometimes provisioning the very ships that were fighting against Britain. This disregard of wartime loyalties for business reasons may represent an extreme example, but the flouting or ignoring of such sanctions, laws and duties was far from uncommon in the Atlantic economy. For most of the eighteenth century, and despite laws in 1763 and 1764 designed to prevent it, North American traders purchased French as well as English sugar. The impossibility of enforcement in the North American sugar trade became something of a legend in rebel circles; as the economic historian Eric Williams put it, 'lawlessness was erected into a cardinal virtue of American economic practice.'[1] Trouble was brewing between Britain and its American colonists, and that unrest drew as much on the role of the West Indies in the Empire as it did on local dissatisfactions within the 13 colonies. After the Seven Years War, right at the moment of swelling restlessness in the American colonies, they became even more important as part of the defence and protection of the neighbouring sugar colonies. Though Britain had gained Caribbean territory as a result of the war, the fighting had been costly and the French still dominated sugar production. Britain's territorial acquisitions and victory had to be carefully balanced against the financial strains they inevitably spawned.

But the war also had another cost, one that would become increasingly apparent in the 1770s. It fuelled the resentments already being expressed by American colonists regarding the restrictions by which they felt themselves hampered, restrictions that the burden of war had made more apparent. There is no doubt that the Seven Years War affected the American colonies adversely, even given the deals New England merchants were striking with the enemy French. The war reverberated in America after 1763 in two ways. It spilled over into colonial frustration with taxation by the British. Not wholly unfairly, many colonists argued that they had contributed both soldiers and money to the war effort, and that further taxation was a burden, and though this did not flare into a major issue it burned steadily and rancorously in the background. More pressingly, there was deep resentment not only of the presence of increased troops garrisoned in the colonies, but of being taxed for their maintenance. The British sought a greater military presence in the region to deter their European rivals and to have troops closer to hand in case of trouble in the West Indies. The Americans did not fully trust British motives, and felt that the troops were a symbol of imperial and authoritarian rule. British insensitivity and obduracy in the following years intensified such suspicions as well as fuelling the dissatisfaction of the Americans, hastening increasing rebellion. The extensive disregard of the many economic restrictions that we have already noted is a good index of American discontent with mercantilism.

But alongside the suspicion engendered by the presence of British troops and a resentment of what they regarded as economic inequalities, the colonists also chafed at political restrictions. The elective assemblies were frequently stonewalled by colonial governors loyal to the English and appointed by the Crown. Rebel colonists felt that their interests – political and economic – were consistently overridden by and subservient to those of far-away Britain. The actions of the imperial parliament in the late 1760s and early 1770s did little to appease them. Shortly after the war, in 1764, the Plantation Act (sometimes called the Sugar Act) raised American hackles by calling for the return of sugar duties. Although the rate of duty was lowered, this was the same duty that had angered Americans in 1733 (in the Molasses Act discussed in Chapter 2), and which they had largely ignored. The difference, however, was that this time around there were signs that the duty would actually be enforced. A year later the infamous Stamp Act, levying duties on business and legal transactions, ramped up the level of American anger. Twelve of the thirteen colonies protested against the Act, and although the British quickly repealed it, their subsequent actions were guaranteed to inflame existing discord. In 1766, a Declaratory Act similar to that relating to Ireland in 1720 (discussed in Chapter 1) asserted parliament's right to impose upon the colonies any taxes it chose. Despite this strong talk, however, by 1768 virtually all duties had been repealed in the face of vigorous resistance. The only duty retained was on tea, and it would prove fateful. Ironically, tea was not an important revenue-raising commodity in the Atlantic colonies, and the duty had been retained mostly as a symbol of the principles of the Declaratory Act, of Britain's right as an imperial authority to control taxation. But though tea was of little fiscal importance in this region of the world, it was a major trading commodity elsewhere. Its intrusion into American colonial politics in the 1770s underscores the links between different parts of a growing, and growingly diverse, British Empire in the later years of the eighteenth century.

Across the globe in South Asia, tea was among the most important assets of the fast-growing East India Company, which, while Britain was waging war in and near British Caribbean territories, was increasing its territorial and political clout in India. At the heart of the Company's Indian holdings was the province of Bengal in eastern India, and Bengal in the late 1760s was in the grip of a vicious famine that was annihilating both the local population and the East India Company's assets. More concerned with the Company's loss of profits than the hunger of the local population, Britain decided that the Company would benefit from selling its tea exports in America directly rather than through American importers. In reality, the Tea Act of 1773 was really not an American revenue measure at all, but rather a scheme to reduce duties by selling directly to the consumer in the hope that an expanded market across the Atlantic would help the East India Company overcome its serious fiscal problems in the East. The East India Company was much disliked by the American colonists, for whom it was a symbol of the monopolistic mechanisms of trade that so irked them. The result of the Tea Act, which favoured the East India Company over America, was the famous Boston Tea Party of December 1773 in which disgruntled colonists stormed three ships carrying cargoes of tea, and docked in the Boston harbour, throwing the tea overboard in protest. This colourful episode has popularly been seen as the fuse that lit the Revolutionary War, but in fact many Americans were appalled by what they regarded as the extremism of the rebel action.

It was the British response, however, that proved the more troubling. Not only did the British retaliate by closing the ports, putting the livelihood of many unassociated with the action in jeopardy, but parliament withdrew colonial civil and political rights. Early in 1774 they imposed the punitive Coercive Acts and the constitution-changing Massachusetts Government Act. The Massachusetts law substituted a nominated assembly for the elected one, articulating Britain's political supremacy over the colonies. These actions alone would have been inflammatory given the tense state of the colonies, but another law passed at the same time aroused further American suspicion and displeasure. In the 1763 treaty ending the Seven Years War, the British had acquired tracts of French-speaking Canada that they combined into the colony of Quebec. The Quebec Act of 1774 laid down the political system that would govern the new colony, and it was one that the Americans did not like at all. Not only did it guarantee religious toleration for Catholics, the majority population there, but it established a nominated rather than an elected assembly in which Catholics outnumbered Protestants. Already dubious about Britain's motives, Protestant Americans worried that such political arrangements would migrate south. The American Mutiny (Quartering) Act of 1765, which enlarged the power of colonial governors with respect to the quartering of troops, did nothing to quell American notions that their political liberties were potentially under threat from the imperial centre. The British clearly had little interest in substantive appeasement, and this slew of aggressive decisions suggests both a certain misplaced confidence in their power and rather poor judgement.

It was in this tense and difficult atmosphere that the two Continental Congresses of 1774 and 1776 convened, the latter producing America's Declaration of Independence. There were plenty of skirmishes between British troops and American rebels in the 1770s before war was formally declared in 1775. The British would have preferred a war waged solely on land, and though that would seem to contradict the clear dominance Britain enjoyed in naval terms, there were good strategic reasons for this that serve as another valuable reminder of the interconnection of imperial sites and concerns. The British knew that using their navy would attract the attention of the French, given the proximity of the West Indian colonies over which Britain and France had so recently and so bitterly fought. The error in judgement the British made was that it would be naval activity that would motivate French interest. In the event, land war did nothing to deter the French from seeking an advantage over their imperial rivals. In early 1778, a Franco-American alliance gave the American rebels increased military muscle, and expanded the war from a purely local if serious conflict to one also directly and deeply affecting other colonial sites, principally the West Indies.

To the disappointment of the American rebels, the West Indians did not rally to the cause of independence, remaining loyal to the British. Their loyalty may well have been strategic; as chains of small islands, they were highly vulnerable and had over the years experienced many wars. Since three-quarters or more of the population was under slavery, the question of political freedom was far more restricted than in the American colonies. Planters already enjoyed a good deal of influence in Britain and were generally supportive of mercantilist trade, as we saw in Chapter 2. Dominica, St Vincent and Grenada fell to the French during the Revolutionary War, but were later restored to Britain. Other colonies experienced considerable disruption both to their trade and to obtaining supplies; it was, of course, most often and most forcefully the slave population who paid the price of this hardship.

By late 1781, it was becoming apparent that the British could not win this war. Spain had joined the forces pitted against Britain in the summer of 1779, laying siege to the British colony of Gibraltar on their southern tip, a long way from America but symbolic of imperial connections. The surrender to the Americans of Charles Cornwallis at Yorktown in October of that year signalled defeat; Lord North, as a result, lost control of the British parliament. In February 1782 a motion asserting the impracticability of war passed in the House of Commons, and within the month North had resigned as prime minister. By November, the basic outline of a peace agreement was in place, and in September 1783 the Treaty of Versailles finally ended all hostilities, and returned to Britain most of the colonies seized by Spain and France during the conflict, as well as returning those French colonies Britain had captured. In that year, Britain also agreed to a policy of free trade with the new United States. By 1800 trade with the USA was running at £40 million a year. Hostility was buried as commerce reasserted its hold; there was a rapid rise in British imports from its former colonies and the loss of the American colonies barely affected British prosperity.

The loss of America clearly did not lead to the demise of the British Empire, or to any significant loss of British imperial power. Britain rapidly acquired new territories elsewhere in the world and would, over the course of the nineteenth century, go on to increase its imperial holdings substantially. Why, then, is the American War considered important? In some ways, it was precisely because it shifted the focus of British imperial interest in new directions that would be sustained into the mid-twentieth century. There are, however, other reasons too. Britain's defeat in the American Revolutionary War was one of only very few defeats that the country sustained over the course of the eighteenth century and, given the considerable fighting in which Britain engaged in that time, this alone is remarkable. Moreover, while in the earlier wars of the eighteenth century Britain had been fighting against other nations and national interests, this war was between Britons, and pitted Britain against a British and Protestant adversary (albeit one enjoying substantial aid from Britain's Catholic rivals). The loss of America and the growing interest in the colonies of Asia made Britain's Empire far less Anglophone, far less Protestant, far less white and less self-governing. And with the French and the Spanish supporting the American colonies against Britain, the war also isolated Britain within Europe.

The outcome of the war affected not just the direction of future growth within the British Empire, but also the fortunes of the West Indies. The decline of the sugar islands was not sudden, but over the course of the next 20 years or so, their wealth and power diminished. Competition with the powerful French sugar industry, a declining share of American trade and, in 1807, the abolition of the slave trade spelled the end of West Indian predominance within the British Empire. The shift in imperial interest in a largely easterly direction also unquestionably hurt the fortunes of the sugar islands.

Not all of Britain's Atlantic holdings were lost in 1783, of course. American colonists who remained loyal to the English Crown often fled north to the Canadian colonies, and these became an important site for various experiments in colonial governance. It would be in British Canada that the new code of 'responsible self-government' would first be instituted. Canada posed some awkward problems for the colonial state, however, since so many of its settler inhabitants were French and Catholic, France having gained a considerable foothold in the north Atlantic by the eighteenth century. Catholicism for the British was still, at the time of American independence, tied symbolically to disloyalty; it was not even a hundred years since the English state had secured a Protestant succession to the throne and passed laws that prevented non-Anglicans of all persuasions from holding public office. The insistence in the new American constitution on separating Church and State was a reaction to Britain's restrictive and unequal religious divisions.

In the Canadian context, the loyalty of Catholics living under British rule proved very important, and the constitutional arrangements we see in late eighteenth- and early nineteenth-century Canada reflect the attempt of imperial politicians to deflect French separatism in the region. Using the experience of America as a guide, Britain granted a limited form of representative government to the Canadian colonies in 1791, with a franchise based on freehold property and with governors who enjoyed a power of veto. By encouraging British emigration to Canada and awarding land grants to loyalists who left America, the government also quietly hoped to increase the British proportion of this mixed population. Lower Canada (Quebec), however, remained predominantly French and by the 1830s rebellion threatened to dissolve the fragile truce between British and French colonists in British Canada. As will be discussed in Chapter 6, the need to find a system that would quell this tension would result in a solution that would be transported to white settler colonies throughout the Empire during the nineteenth century. Although the system of representative self-government did little to deflect the tensions between British Canada and French Canada, it would prove to be the system that sustained white settler colonialism for the remainder of the nineteenth century and into the twentieth. Canada would prove an important resource within the Empire. From a population of some half a million in 1815, Canada had almost 19 million people in 1911, and was responsible for 16.5 per cent of British trade. Often neglected in histories of the British Empire, Canada was a significant arena for political experiment as the Empire matured in the nineteenth century.

Reference

1   Eric E. Williams, *Capitalism and Slavery* (Chapel Hill: University of North Carolina Press, 1994), p. 119.

CHAPTER 4

After America

At the end of the eighteenth century, although it had lost a good deal of its North American possessions, Britain was a major colonial power, with territorial possessions spread far and wide, in which there were a multitude of languages, customs and religions. After a century of recurrent warfare – mostly with the French and the Spanish – the British had established their supremacy among European expansionist powers. In part, this was due to Britain's considerable maritime power, developed because, as a small island, Britain needed to protect its shores.

With the loss of the American colonies and the decline in the importance of the West Indian colonies, British imperial interests began to swing from the Atlantic world towards the Pacific and Asia, which had been steadily developing as colonial sites of interest since at least the 1750s. The new forms of white settlement that would emerge in the Pacific at the end of the eighteenth and into the nineteenth century were politically very different from those of the 13 American colonies. By the 1860s these new colonies of settlement, Australia and New Zealand, had followed the Canadian colonies in being granted 'responsible self-government', and they would remain central to the growing idea of a British Commonwealth.

Exploration in the Pacific preceded actual settlement, and the 1760s and 1770s were particularly active decades of maritime exploration. The motives for the many voyages to the Pacific region in these years were varied. There was, of course, the constant search for resources and wealth that had long prompted entrepreneurs and explorers to set sail for distant lands. There was also a keen interest in finding good ports and harbours where ships could dock, rest and resupply on long sea voyages. Beyond this, we might note a revitalized attention to science in the eighteenth century, linked to imperial exploration's revealing of new flora and fauna, as well as of different cultures. The work of explorer–scientists in this era influenced poetry and art as much as it shaped the course of empire; the romantic view of the South Seas and the Pacific became part and parcel of late eighteenth-century English culture. Late eighteenth-century expeditions rarely sailed without a retinue of scientists; the most famous of the British sailor–explorers of this period, Captain James Cook, hosted a large group of scientists on his Pacific adventures, many of whom would be active in subsequently promoting the commercial development of the Pacific and other regions of colonization. We have already noted in Chapter 2 the work of Joseph Banks in bringing cotton to the West Indies.

Cook's first voyage left English shores in August 1768, landing at Tahiti some nine months later. Samuel Wallis had already staked a British claim to Tahiti in 1767, but Cook sailed more extensively in the area, landing at several spots on the east Australian coast during the first of his three voyages, and claiming the Australian continent in the name of Britain. Other European colonizers were close behind, spurred by the increased British interest in the region. The Spanish and the French mounted Pacific expeditions in the 1770s, and what would become Australia was commonly known as New Holland at this time, reflecting the active Dutch presence in the region. There was also a growing American interest in the Pacific, dominated by the trading ships of New England.

The British made no attempts to settle these Pacific islands, although the impact of contact with Europeans would still have a devastating impact on the local population; Tahiti's population diminished from around 40,000 in 1770 to a tiny 9,000 in the 1830s. It would be 1788, and the creation of the first penal colony in the Pacific, before permanent colonialism would emerge in this region. But why did Britain choose to send convicts on such a long, expensive and perilous voyage? Throughout the seventeenth and early eighteenth centuries, *Terra Australis* (or New Holland) had generally been regarded as a fabulous and mythic spot rather than a land that would realize profit for European commerce. The Pacific voyaging and exploration that gained ground in the later eighteenth century significantly altered that opinion, even though it was only the eastern Australian coastline that was known. At the same time, Britain had lost its main penal colony after the American War of Independence, but not its desire to transport convicts. The waters around Britain were littered with convict ships, known as hulks, where convicts were locked up at night, spending their days working in the ports and harbours where these unsanitary ships were moored. Though few of the convict hulks were seaworthy, this style of imprisonment reveals the depth and centrality of

Britain's maritime personality. Sailing convicts to a distant land seemed a routine activity, and if that land might offer naval and commercial advantages as well, then the state would win on numerous counts, offloading unwanted people and, through their labour, gaining potential profits, goods and bases for future commerce and military security.

After the American Revolution, the government quickly turned its attention to establishing an alternative penal colony, for the Americas had absorbed around 1,000 transportees annually. Africa was considered and rejected, and in 1786 Botany Bay on the east coast of New Holland was adopted. Certainly the site offered a place from which escape would be unattractive and difficult, and whose distance from home might be seen as a disincentive to would-be criminals. There was a hope, too, that the harbour would provide a naval base for further expansion in the region, and that whaling, also lost after American independence, might be profitably resumed in these waters. Norfolk Island, an isolated island some 1,400 kilometres east of Botany Bay, also offered the prospect of both a timber and a flax industry, commodities vital to the navy, and since European imperial rivals were also scouting the area, establishing a working, occupied colony would strengthen Britain's own claims in the region.

This was, of course, a hugely ambitious project, not only because of the distance and uncertainty regarding the land but because it was to be a colony built in effect by convicts, by Britain's discards. This posed interesting questions regarding how the colony would be administered. Clearly, it could not operate as the American colonies had done, since prisoners by definition were not free, and aside from them the only other settlers were the marines who accompanied them and who acted as their guards after the voyage was over. The new colony, as a result, was a curious hybrid, a military colony run by naval officers, but with a civil legal system since this was the system under which the convicts had been sentenced. The hope was to transform criminals into productive colonists who would ready the land for profitable settlement.

The First Fleet, consisting of eleven ships carrying around 1,050 people (of whom some 750 were convicts) as well as animals, farm implements and food supplies intended to last two years, left Portsmouth in May 1787. The Fleet reached Botany Bay in mid-January of the following year but quickly realized that it was by no means an ideal landing spot. Sailing north, they docked instead 12 kilometres away at Port Jackson on 26 January 1788, a date still celebrated annually as Australia Day.

The new migrants had arrived at the hottest time of year and soon found that raising crops was a difficult business and that the unfamiliar timbers of the region did not yield easily to their axes. Life was hard and sparse for these first settlers; only twelve acres of land had been successfully cultivated after six months in the new colony, the livestock, unused to the harsh conditions of an Australian summer, were dying, and food and medical supplies had to be strictly rationed. A party sent east to Norfolk Island was similarly impoverished as neither the pine trees nor the flax there proved usable. In 1803, Van Diemen's Land (renamed Tasmania in 1856), an island off the south-east corner of Australia, was also settled. Sealing was already an established industry here before formal colonization began but it, too, was far from an easy living.

Despite these unpromising beginnings, the settlements slowly but surely gained a foothold, even if in the first decade or two shortages and crises occurred regularly. The Napoleonic Wars between 1793 and 1815 brought both hardship and, at the same time, increased British attention to the region. Fighting against the French, whose interest in the Pacific had not waned, Britain's presence on the east coast of New Holland was an important strategic and military one. Yet the war also brought about a decline in transportee numbers since ships were diverted to wartime use, and passage across the waters became less safe. Still, the colony's future was, by 1815, assured. By 1800, there were some 5,000 white colonists on the eastern mainland and another 1,000 on Norfolk Island, and although it was already becoming popular in England to regard the convict's lot as a happy one resulting in substantial landownership, convicts were daily reminded that theirs was a punitive condition. In the earliest years, convicts were assigned either to public works or to an individual master, and were allowed time to work for themselves and earn an income alongside the work they performed as part of their sentence. Women convicts, far fewer in number, worked mostly in domestic service or on production lines in the female factories, whereas the work for men covered all areas, since the colony was quite literally being built by them. Floggings were plentiful for those who challenged the system, and convicts were expected to return to work the day after a lashing, whatever their physical condition. By 1800, many of the private employers reliant on convict labour were themselves former convicts who had served out their sentences or who had received an early pardon. Two-thirds of the colonists were free by that date, though few had the means to return to England and many chose in any case to stay on in what was now called New South Wales.

In the mid-nineteenth century, convict conditions, if anything, became harsher. Convicts could no longer work for themselves: the free time in which to do so had been taken away. Many fewer were pardoned early, and the fractious were far likelier to be sent to one of the isolated settlements now developing up and down the coast and on Van Diemen's Land to the south. The land grants that had made the English public so sceptical of transportation as a punishment disappeared, creating a landless workforce of former convicts to people the industries of the new colonies.

When the Napoleonic Wars ended, transportation once more quickened. By 1820 there were 32,000 colonists in New South Wales and Van Diemen's Land, and by 1850 the white population had grown to 400,000. In addition to a constant flow of migrants, both voluntary and convict, the dramatic growth in population was also a result of natural increase. The settler population was mostly a youthful one, and the growth in the number of children in the colony was striking. Children constituted some 3 per cent of the initial settlers (some born on the voyage, a few accompanying their parents). By the end of 1799, they accounted for almost 17 per cent of the population.

The youth of the settlers was only one reason for this rapid increase in population. Though women colonists were small in number, colonial policies all aimed to domesticate them and to foster the principles of Christian family life at the centre of colonial culture. The early land grants given to convict men (but not to women) on the expiration of their sentences were augmented if the man was married, and boosted even further if he had children. Women's reproductive potential was, in a sense, part and parcel of the social landscape envisaged by the architects of the new settlement. Women represented approximately one-sixth of all transportees, and were invariably of childbearing age; they were a conscious instrument of colonial policy and, by the early 1800s, the larger number of them were either formally married or cohabiting with men.

Their lives were certainly no easier than that of men. Women were severely economically disadvantaged, since they were not entitled to land grants in their own right and were restricted in the employment open to them, despite the fact that many of them had labour skills from their prior life in Britain. Unlike men who could, should they choose, work their passage home as shipboard labourers, women seldom had the means or opportunity to return to Britain. In the first days of settlement, women's rations were two-thirds those awarded to men. It would be the early twentieth century before there were roughly equal numbers of men and women in the population. Interestingly, however, the Australian colonies would be among the first governments to grant women the right to vote. South Australia led the way, granting women voting rights in local government elections in 1861 and in parliamentary elections in 1894.

Women were not the only group of convicts singled out for differential treatment. Political prisoners, many of them Irish, were routinely separated from one another, for fear they would organize rebellions (as some indeed did). Another interesting group is the thousand or so Africans, former slaves, who had been taken to Britain and were subsequently convicted of crimes and sentenced to transportation.

Transportation came to an end in 1867. New South Wales had abandoned transportation in 1840, resuming the practice briefly in 1847. Van Diemen's Land discarded the practice in 1853. The Swan River Colony (now Western Australia) began transporting convicts only in 1850, and it was here that the last transport deposited its human cargo in 1867. In the years between 1788 and 1867, somewhere between 150,000 and 160,000 convicts arrived in Australia; about 60 per cent were English, 34 per cent Irish and 5 per cent Scots.

All of this activity was unfolding against the backdrop of a substantial indigenous population whose principal experience of colonialism was the loss of their hunting grounds, their livelihood and their place in the world. Regarded as primitive by the settlers because they wore scant clothing, did not engage in settled agriculture or build in western ways, the Aboriginal population suffered considerably at the hands of the continent's new residents, despite spirited attempts both to resist and to live amicably alongside them. The extension of western-style agriculture severely limited Aboriginal movement and access to foodstuffs, as that most distinctive of western ideas, private property, was fenced off or actively policed. As in colonial America, diseases brought from the west wreaked havoc on populations exposed to them for the first time. The size of the aboriginal population plummeted from roughly 300,000 at the moment of initial white settlement to some 80,000 in the 1880s, leading many white Australians as well as anthropologists and scientists, to classify them – wrongly – as a dying race.

In the very earliest days of settlement, officials exercised some caution in their relations with Aboriginal Australians, although Aboriginal men were kidnapped and held in the white settlements in the hope that they would act as translators of indigenous custom and culture. Needless to say, such tactics were much resented, and men thus confined almost always escaped as soon as they could. By the 1790s, punitive raids against resistant Aboriginal groups were sanctioned, and the killings began to mount. Yet far more Aboriginals died because of disease or malnutrition than from the guns of settlers. It was exposure to unfamiliar diseases and the loss of traditional forms of food-gathering that ultimately had the most devastating effect on Australia's earlier inhabitants.

Outside the cities, on farms and sheep and cattle stations, Aboriginal labour was crucial to success, for settlers relied upon indigenous know-

FIGURE 3 *'Thomas Baines, Mr Phibbs and Bowman engaging the blacks who attempted to burn us out . . . Depot Creek, Victoria'. Accounts of struggles with Aboriginal Australians frequently emphasized Aboriginal violence.* (Royal Geographical Society, London, UK/The Bridgeman Art Library)

ledge of a harsh land where water was sparse and dangerous storms could blow up in minutes. Trackers assisted surveyors, settlers and others to navigate and pass through the hinterlands, yet despite their importance in helping settlers, Aboriginal workers were often poorly treated. Unlike white workers, they were frequently paid in rations rather than in money, a practice long since abandoned in western labour markets where waged work was a central symbol of the modern workplace. Local peoples, as in many other colonies, were regarded as pre- or un-modern, and as unlikely and often unable to adapt to the modern western conditions that colonialism brought with it as it swept round the globe. As in the case of Australian labour practices, this led to massive inequalities between settlers and indigenous peoples all over the Empire. Though the Australian colonies were, by the late nineteenth century, a shining example of new and progressive labour conditions and practices, such benefits were restricted to white Australians.

The most notorious relations between white settlers and Aboriginal Australians were those in Van Diemen's Land in the early nineteenth century. In 1830, relations between settlers and Aboriginals were tense. The killing of some settlers prompted the colony's governor, George

Arthur, to declare a state of martial law. A 'Black Line' – literally a human chain stretched across the island and comprising some 2,000 armed soldiers as well as civilians – was designed to force the Aboriginal population southward, and then to round them up and contain them on allotted lands. The plan was an abject failure. In its wake, Arthur commissioned a tradesman, George Robinson, to bring in the island's Aboriginals. Using less confrontational methods Robinson's success probably sealed the fate of the black population, for this apparent exercise in protection isolated the entire population on inhospitable Flinders Island, where their numbers declined precipitously. By the 1880s there were no full-blooded Aboriginals still alive in Van Diemen's Land.

The idea of Aboriginal protection became a popular one from the 1830s, at about the same time that slavery was abolished within the Empire. It found a more sympathetic audience in Britain than in the colonies themselves. In that decade, the imperial parliament in London investigated the effect of colonialism on native peoples, and in London concerned humanitarians, mostly evangelicals, founded the British and Foreign Aborigines' Protection Society. In time, the Australian colonies would introduce Aboriginal Protection Acts, the first of which was in the colony of Victoria (in south-east Australia) in 1869. Despite their name, the Acts were more concerned with control than protection, routinely prescribing where Aboriginals might live, who they could marry, what work they could do, and addressing many other aspects of their daily life. This was paternalist legislation founded on a belief that Aborigines were incapable of making responsible decisions; such laws also effectively drew distinct boundaries between white and Aboriginal spaces, invariably to the disadvantage of the latter.

Land, and the use of land, was at the heart of much of the conflict between the Aboriginal and the settler inhabitants of the new colony from its inception. As far as the British were concerned, the Aboriginal populations did nothing productive with the land on which they lived: there was no settled agriculture, no market in agricultural produce, no farming of the land. It was a view that failed to understand the rich alternative ways in which Aboriginal peoples sustained themselves through the land. After all, when white settlers first arrived the Aboriginal peoples were healthy and numerous, living well for the most part off land that looked to the British uncultivated. It was this colonial perspective that led to the development of the legal concept of *terra nullius*, in which the British reasoned that land not put to productive use was available for settlement. This view justified the seizing of huge areas of the continent, pushing indigenous peoples increasingly to the margins of this newly farmed, cultivated and built-upon soil.

Land was a key component in the shaping of the new colony's culture and politics. The ability of settler colonialism to survive was staked on the promise of what the land might productively yield and, as the various Australian colonies grew economically, older British ideas about property ownership re-emerged. As we have seen, the very earliest years of settlement relied not just on convict labour but on a hope and a belief that giving men, even former convicts, land would be an incentive for them to work hard and produce wealth. The slow but steady success of that gamble in a sense also effected its undoing; as in Britain, a line was increasingly drawn in settler Australia between the propertied and the unpropertied as well as between white and Aboriginal. By the mid-nineteenth century, land was made available for purchase rather than being given away free, although there were those known as squatters who had illegally but successfully assumed control of vast tracts of land, principally for the grazing of animals. Their position would be much debated in government, although it remained largely unresolved, at least at the legal level. Still, by mid-century, and most especially in the cities, white Australian society was clearly divided among those who owned property and those who sold their labour to property owners. Wholly different from Britain, however, a universal male franchise was typical for the lower chamber of government, the assembly, after responsible self-government was conferred on the colonies of New South Wales, Victoria and South Australia in 1855, of Tasmania in 1856 and of Queensland in 1859.

What did this term 'responsible self-government' mean? Imported from the British Canadian colonies, it was a device that distinguished settler colonies from the larger portion of the Empire where far fewer Britons lived, and where they did so generally on a temporary basis only. It drew on the forms of governance that had been in place across the Atlantic in earlier years. Unlike colonies where there were few white settlers and that were increasingly considered insufficiently capable of governing their own affairs, the Australian and other white settler colonies were regarded as outposts of British society and civilization. Responsible self-government created colonial mini-versions of the British parliament, a two-house government in which the assembly approximated the House of Commons as an elected house, while the council consisted of those appointed by the colonial governor. Since there was no formal aristocracy to inherit seats in the new colonies as there would have been in the British House of Lords, this upper house had appointed members. Prior to responsible self-government, the governor wielded considerable power. He made legal decisions, ruled on economic and fiscal matters, on the granting of land, on marriage contracts and on many other facets of colonial life.

Throughout the first hundred and more years of settler colony history, however, many key powers remained with the imperial parliament at Westminster. Governors were appointed by the Colonial Office in London, rather than in Australia, just as they had been in the Atlantic colonies. Laws passed in the colonies could be overturned by the imperial parliament who also retained control of fiscal, monetary and tax issues, and of defence. Furthermore, of course, when responsible self-government was granted, not only was the decision to do so taken in London but it followed that the governing structures of the colonies would closely resemble those at the centre of the Empire. Responsible self-government thus depended upon the colony's acceptance of political structures created in an English idiom.

The creation of a series of 'miniature Britains' in the 1850s rested on the transformation of the Australian colonies from penal settlements to free settlements. Free settlers had been coming to the Australian colonies in significant numbers since 1793. From the 1830s, sponsored colonization began to alter the social structure of Australia as free settlers rapidly outpaced the prisoner population. By the late 1840s, free migrants – many of them poor – outnumbered those whose passage to the colonies had been via the criminal courts.

Before the 1840s especially, there were also a good few British indentured servants in the Australian colonies, but indenture proved unpopular and unsuccessful. Employers complained that the indentured were lazier than the convicts, while those under contract chafed at the disparity between their low wages and what free labourers could command in a still sparsely populated country. They energetically sought early release from their contracts and seldom renewed them on expiry. Indenture among whites in Australia simply faded away over time although, as we shall shortly see, this did not mark the end of indenture in the Australian colonies.

State-assisted migration from Britain began in 1831, with free passages and cheap land on offer to those willing to start new lives across the globe. Agents for the scheme were paid per head for those they signed up, and the numbers of voluntary migrants rose dramatically. In the 1820s, before these schemes were introduced, some 8,000 free settlers arrived in the Australian colonies, but numbers, not surprisingly, jumped dramatically with the introduction of state-assisted schemes. In the 1830s, around 30,000 made the journey, rising to about 80,000 in the 1840s. The free and assisted passages that made emigration an option for poorer Britons were financed by a shift within Australia from land grants to land sales. The new settlers were largely people of modest means, many of them from the rural regions of southern England where wages were low and social relations between employers and workers still very rigid. Over time, and especially once famine hit Ireland, a significant proportion of migrants would come from poverty-stricken Ireland. There was also a concerted, though not always successful, push to encourage single women to migrate as a means of solving the distinctive imbalance between male and female populations.

With so many migrants arriving, settlements spread further and further and new colonies beyond New South Wales were created. By the late 1850s there were six colonies, by no means identical in population, politics or governance, but a sure sign that what, from 1814 or so, was called Australia would endure. The Swan River Colony was first established in 1829, and that of South Australia in 1836. The founding of new colonies was prompted not only by the tide of emigration from Britain but by a variety of local political interests as well. As had been the case with Van Diemen's Land in 1802–3, the Swan River Colony was initiated in large part to deter the French from attempting any settlements, this time in the south-west. Planned initially as a settlement solely of voluntary migrants, although including those under indenture, the struggles of the early residents led to the late introduction of transportation in 1850. Despite the Swan River Colony's desire to be convict-free, it would be, as we have seen, the last of the colonies to abolish transportation.

South Australia, by contrast, proved successful in limiting its population to free settlers. Here the principles of 'systematic colonization' laid out by Edward Gibbon Wakefield were implemented, as they would be, too, in parts of New Zealand. Wakefield proposed to create communities that were aligned to the laws of economics as they were popularly understood in the nineteenth century. Arguing that selling land too cheaply upset the critical balance between land, labour and capital, Wakefield looked to create both a landowning class and a landless labouring class, replicating the traditional contours of British society. He saw this social structure as guaranteeing a labour supply, in this case composed of free settlers rather than convicts forced to work. If everyone could afford land, argued Wakefield, then labour costs would rise prohibitively since there would be no inducement to seek waged work. It was a classically nineteenth-century statement of the relationship between the social order and the economy. After some initial struggles – typical of settler history in these lands – South Australia thrived. It remained a free settler colony and, unusually, one in which the ratio of men to women was more balanced than in the other Australian colonies.

Vital to the expansion of Australian settlement was exploration. Matthew Flinders, a naval officer, had sailed around Australia at the very start of the nineteenth century, proving that it was indeed a continent. Inland, explorers heading west from Port Jackson crossed the Blue Mountains in 1813, enabling settlement towards the interior of the country. In the 1820s many new penal stations were established up and down the east coast. Major expeditions to northern and central Australia in the 1840s also opened up the interior, although the settler population clung mostly to the coastal areas, as the population still does today. As a result, and despite the emphasis on land acquisition and the development of large-scale pastoral agriculture, Australia developed as a highly urbanized culture, the vast majority of its population (although not always its wealth) clustered in cities by the middle of the nineteenth century. In 1850, 40 per cent of the population already lived in urban environments, a proportion that would grow substantially over time.

The characteristically urban profile of the Australian colonies should not blind us, nonetheless, to the central importance of pastoral agriculture to the economy. Wool and, later, dairy and beef cattle dominated the economy, although in the very earliest years whaling and sealing had been key industries. The penetration inland and the creation of large sheep and cattle stations so destructive to Aboriginal lifestyles made wool a staple of the Australian economy by 1850. Coal mining was on the rise by the early 1800s and gold became significant in the 1850s. Copper and silver also proved economically important.

As convict labour diminished a dual labour system grew up, quite distinctive when compared with many of Britain's other colonies. As we have seen, changes in land policy led to the creation of a large white working class, many engaged in much the same kind of work as might have been on offer in Britain. But in the tropical northerly reaches of the continent, as settlement expanded, fears of climatic unsuitability had a striking effect on the labour market. There was some use of Aboriginal workers but many white Australians regarded them as unstable, and many Aboriginals in any case had little interest in the kind of work offered by white employers. Instead, there was a growing use in the north, and at a time when its use was waning elsewhere in Australia, of indentured labourers, some of whom were from India and China, but who mostly came from nearby Melanesia. Pacific Islanders worked in plantation-style agriculture, especially in the growing sugar industry of Queensland. The use of non-white indentured labour in Australian colonies lasted into the early twentieth century, long after white indenture had disappeared. It was more commonly in use in places where there was no white labour force to be employed, and it was crucial to the cultivation of the northerly tropical regions of Australia. The networks that allowed workers from different parts of the Empire and beyond to take work in other lands is a fascinating, and often quite brutal, example of transnational colonial connections at work, as we shall see again in Chapter 8.

Some 1,600 kilometres south-east of Australia, and across the Tasman Sea, lay what would become in the 1840s the new British colony of New Zealand, also a white settler land although in many respects markedly different from Australia. First claimed for Britain by Cook in 1769/70, and initially a dependency of New South Wales, New Zealand had a less harsh climate and a more tractable soil than Australia's east coast, and it had timber suitable for shipbuilding. There was considerable commercial activity there even before formal colonization. Both the Americans and the French operated whaling stations, and wealthy Australian speculators were busy buying up tracts of land. In 1839, Edward Gibbon Wakefield's New Zealand Company undertook the organizing of a permanent settlement on the North Island. All of this activity was the work of private entrepreneurs and would have been unthinkable without the acquiescence of New Zealand's indigenous Maori peoples. The government's lack of interest in pursuing more formal colonization had more than a little to do with the perception of Maori society as well organized and militarily proficient, and not all that easy to subdue.

Life would change for the Maori and for the early settlers when, in 1840, New Zealand became a Protectorate (and a dependency of New South Wales), with the signing of the Treaty of Waitangi. Prompted in part by a suspicion of increased French activity in the region, the treaty was to a large extent engineered by missionaries and reformers who argued that the intense economic speculation in New Zealand was producing anarchic conditions harmful most especially to the Maori. The Protestant missionaries were also anxious to curb their French Catholic rivals, already quite active on New Zealand's South Island.

The treaty was a curious one for, in principle, it recognized Maori ownership of land, a very different context for colonization from that experienced by the Aboriginal Australians. The treaty offered protection and British subjecthood to the Maori in exchange for an exclusive British right to purchase lands the Maori might wish to sell. In practice, Maori reluctance to sell was often overlooked, and the effect of the treaty was the acquisition of a very substantial quantity of land by colonizers at extremely low prices. The shift of land ownership not surprisingly precipitated increasing friction between Maori and Pakeha (as the white settlers were known by them) over governance. By the mid-1840s what have become known as the New Zealand Wars had begun, first in the north and then spreading. The ultimate, though not easily achieved, defeat of the Maori had the inevitable consequence of dispossessing and marginalizing New Zealand's indigenous peoples as white settler colonialism spread. By 1861, two-thirds of New Zealand land had been sold, with the inevitable result that there was a rise in the white settler population and a corresponding decline in the Maori population. In the 1840s alone Pakeha numbers in New Zealand rose from 2,000 to about 10,000, whereas the Maori population was, over the course of the nineteenth century, halved from around 200,000 to 100,000. Still, when white women were awarded the vote in 1893 (the earliest granting of a national franchise to women in any British territory), the Maori were also enfranchised, just one month later. This, and the four Maori seats in parliament that had been guaranteed since the 1860s, did little to restore the previous prosperity or dominance of New Zealand's indigenous people, although it nonetheless offers a very different version of settler colonialism than that to be seen in neighbouring Australia. As was always the case, however, settler colonialism relied on the subjugation of claims by prior residents. New Zealand's economic situation remained precarious throughout these years of war, although the Australian gold rush of the 1850s eased things by providing a local market for New Zealand produce. New Zealand acquired a federal constitution and a general assembly in 1852, and the two islands (north and south) were united as one state in 1876, a quarter of a century before Australia's federation.

The white settler model was not the only form of colonialism operating in the region as British attention turned east from the late eighteenth century. In south-east Asia and the Malay archipelago, the British were by no means the dominant imperial power. The Dutch had a long history in the region, and a Spanish and French presence was considerable. In the sixteenth century, the East Indies – the chain of islands comprising Java, Sumatra, the Bandas and the Moluccas – were assumed to be the most profitable, and India (the subject of our next chapter) was often regarded as a stop en route to reach these sources of wealth. But the Spice Islands proved tough for the British, both because of the actions of local elites and rulers and because of the success there of their European rivals. In 1700 the British had only one settlement in the area, at Bencoolen on Sumatra's west coast.

Typically, the British took advantage of wartime conditions to wrest control of some of these places from their European competitors. During the Napoleonic Wars Britain captured many of the Dutch possessions in this region. But the balance of power and of economic profitability had shifted considerably, and the British no longer coveted the Spice Islands for their commodities, but rather for protecting India from territorial encirclement by the French, since the Dutch, at this time, were under the influence of Napoleon. By 1811, Britain had captured all the major Dutch colonies, among them Java and the Trincomalee harbour at Ceylon. Though most were restored to the Dutch after Napoleon's defeat when a new kingdom of the Netherlands was established, Britain was careful to maintain a strategic and commercial foothold in the region. The Dutch were welcome to return as long as a place for British trade and passage was guaranteed. In 1819, adding to the British possessions on the Malay peninsula around the Straits of Malacca, Sir Thomas Stamford Raffles acquired for the East India Company an island that in 1826 would become part of the new colony of the Straits Settlements. In its early years Penang was the principal settlement at the Straits, but over time Singapore would come to dominate the colony, economically and politically. In these early years, since the colony was an East India Company possession, it was administered via India and by the company. The Straits became a Crown Colony in 1867, and it was only then that more complete British intervention in the area fully occurred. Even before then the colony was both a highly profitable acquisition and a valuable location from which to conduct diplomatic relations with both Siam (modern Thailand) and the Malay states.

The period between the loss of the Americas and the end of the Napoleonic Wars was thus a busy period of colonization for the British, and the Napoleonic Wars in particular saw an active period of acquisition on the part of the British. The motives were partly strategic and partly economic, limiting the power of rivals and simultaneously maximizing profitability. The introduction in 1815 of the 'Crown Colony' reflects this period of activity and also a change in thinking about the process of colonization and the future of the British Empire. The new device of the Crown Colony, which placed a colonial territory under the direct authority of the British Crown, allowed the use of British laws and institutions (such as courts and police forces) without the need for any local ratification. The imperial parliament in London had full control in such colonies and local legislative bodies could be required to assent to London's decisions. Not all colonies were Crown Colonies, of course. India, for example, never had that status and nor did many colonies designated as Protectorates. Technically, the Protectorate remained under the sovereignty of a local ruler under British protection and gave the inhabitants no right to British citizenship. In practice, Britain acquired a good deal of control, and most of its Protectorates moved to Crown Colony status at some stage. Most white settler colonies were granted responsible self-government by mid-century, radically altering their political relationship with the centre. Essential to this expansion was the principle that colonies should be self-financing entities.

The one settler colony without responsible self-government by the 1850s was the Cape Colony in coastal southern Africa, and since the settlers there were largely in this period not British and struggles between them, the Africans and the British were common, this is not surprising. The British had first occupied the Cape in 1795, mostly to prevent the French from doing so. It was only after occupation that its value as a port en route to India really became clear. The area catapulted back and forth between Dutch and British claims in the early 1800s, until at the end of the Napoleonic Wars the territory was finally and formally ceded to the British as Cape Colony. The Dutch settler farmers – the Boers – who had been there for a hundred years or so, thus became British subjects, a change that in the 1830s would cause considerable disruption in the area. Enraged by the British abolition of slavery in 1833, and the abolition of indenture among the indigenous Khoisan people in 1828, some 15,000 Boers (known also as Afrikaners) attempted to found their own land across the Orange River. This northerly 1835 exodus, known as the 'Great Trek', forced Britain's hand: were the Boers to be permitted secession or should Britain bear the expense of administering another colony? Southern Africa was not yet a really valuable economic location, for the discovery of gold and diamonds was still decades away. Nor was plantation-style agriculture yet fully established. The British thus took their time in deciding on how to react to this Boer challenge, and it was almost a decade before, in 1843, they chose to move, annexing what the Afrikaners now called Natalia. The Dutch settlers scattered over the region, winning a pocket of independent land from the British in 1852. Tensions would

FIGURE 4 *Cartoon by George Cruikshank, 1819: '"All among the Hottentots capering ashore"!! or the blessings of emigration to the Cape of Good Hope (ie) To be half roasted by the sun and devoured by the natives!! recommend. To the serious consideration of all thos[e] who are about to emigrate'* (Private Collection/© Michael Graham-Stewart/The Bridgeman Art Library)

mount between the Boers and the British throughout the century, tensions that often had a far more deleterious effect on local African populations than on the Europeans themselves.

Beyond the southern tip, Africa was of limited interest to the British before the late nineteenth century. There was little colonization of the continent before the 1890s, other than at Sierra Leone and the Gambia. Both of these were related to Britain's new policies on slaving: Sierra Leone (as Chapter 2 detailed) was created as a site for the return of freed Africans while The Gambia housed Britain's anti-slaving squadron.

There was expansion in this period, however, in other regions. The tiny and isolated Falkland Islands in the South Atlantic (called by the Spaniards the Malvinas) aroused European interest in the late eighteenth century because of their proximity to the route between the Atlantic and the Pacific Oceans. Not surprisingly, therefore, they also became the subject of European rivalry between the French, the Spanish and the British. The first white settlers there were French: two years later, in 1766, a small British contingent settled to the west. Together the French and the Spanish tried to drive out the British in 1770, but though the British remained unsubdued, it was not a territory for which they were willing to fight. They withdrew their settlement in the late 1770s, though continuing to claim ownership. The Spaniards, who had taken control of the French settlements in 1767, withdrew in 1811 and little attention was paid to these remote islands until, in the early 1830s, newly independent Argentina claimed possession on the curious grounds that the Falklands had once been, like Argentina, part of the Spanish Empire. Britain promptly despatched a naval expedition to the South Atlantic and declared the Falkland Islands a Crown Colony in 1832.

Although friction with France dominated much of Britain's colonial doings in the early nineteenth as well as the eighteenth centuries, the British and the Spanish also clashed, as in the Falklands and in many of the complicated wars discussed in the previous two chapters. One other long-term bone of colonial contention between the two countries was Gibraltar, on the southernmost tip of Spain This promontory on the Iberian peninsula, just a few kilometres from the North African coast, was first claimed by the British in 1704. By the 1713 Treaty of Utrecht, resident Gibraltarians continued to enjoy rights that, had the territory been wholly British, would have been denied them as Catholics. Gibraltar proved useful for British naval forays in the Mediterranean where, as a result of the Napoleonic Wars, they added Malta and the Ionian Islands to their colonial spoils, extending the Empire quite significantly into European territory.

Such captures as these demonstrate just how much of Britain's imperial strength derived from naval prowess. The colonial acquisitions and consolidations we have tracked gave Britain an immense advantage, in effect a global chain of harbours, a powerful and dominant navy, and an empire that, by 1815, was the largest in the modern world. From a concentration for most of the eighteenth century on the Atlantic, and centred on the West Indies and America, the Empire had not only expanded considerably in the Pacific but had secured an impressive network of ports and harbours that gave Britain that imperial pre-eminence that would so colour its modern history.

CHAPTER 5

Britain in India

In the colonial scheme of things, Britain's imperial interests in India were among its most important as early as the seventeenth century. It would, of course, be the middle of the nineteenth century before the British government laid formal claim to ruling large parts of India, but that did not mean that British India was not central to Britain's Empire at a far earlier date.

India was not a single country or entity, but rather a collection of states ruled in different ways, and frequently with markedly different languages and customs. There was no single Indian language or religion. Small and large areas were governed by local dynasties, and by the eighteenth century much of northern and central India was ruled by the powerful Moguls. British imperial influence in the subcontinent came on the heels of this empire. The last wave of Muslim Moguls had arrived in India from central Asia in the sixteenth century, cleverly forging alliances with powerful Hindu elites in India and rapidly establishing significant control. Mogul power and wealth was considerable and early British traders were obliged to pay homage to the Mogul rulers. In the seventeenth century European merchants typically traded in Asia by permission of local rulers whose power and military might were at least the equal of the Europeans.

The dominating British enterprise in India was the East India Company (EIC), launched in London in 1600 by a powerful financial elite. The EIC was a chartered company, enjoying a monopoly over British trade with the east. The chartered company was an economic and political device of mutual benefit to a company and its backers and to the government of the country in which the company was established. The position of such corporations changed over time, and by the eighteenth century, in return for a share of the profits (and sometimes also favourable loans), the government granted the companies tremendous political and military as well as economic freedom in a given area. The EIC enjoyed not only a trade monopoly but the government's agreement that it might directly negotiate with local rulers, and might engage in warfare to defend company privileges (though it was forbidden to initiate hostilities). It also enjoyed the right to control British citizens within company territory. As a joint-stock enterprise, the EIC was well suited to expensive long-distance trade, for its size meant it could raise more money and spread the risk involved over a larger group of investors, a strategy unavailable to small traders. These monopolistic policies, part of the mercantile system, were typical of the way in which global business was conducted before the free trade era of the nineteenth century. Clearly, such policies married economics and governance in important ways, since much more than control over commerce was granted to those doing business around the globe.

India was of growing importance among Britain's colonies even beyond its commercial capacity. The EIC's hold on India was tightening at much the same time that the American colonies broke away from Britain. The loss of America was as much a psychological as an economic blow. The failure of British trade in the East Indies (Indonesia and the Spice Islands) and the barriers to trade in China before the 1840s made India a particularly important site of British interest, their principal foothold in Asia. Success in India acted as a counterbalance to Britain's inability to rein in the American revolt. India became more and more important not only for its products but increasingly as a symbol of Britain's overseas power after the loss of America. India would occupy British attention until the middle of the twentieth century, strongly influencing other colonial decisions and acting as a training ground for scores of colonial officials.

The need to protect India from the encroachment of rival powers often shaped colonial policy in the nineteenth century, just as in the eighteenth century protection of the sugar colonies had been paramount. Fear of neighbouring Burma led to the first of the Anglo-Burmese wars in the mid-1820s, prompted by Burmese expansion into Indian territories. Friction with the Burmese kingdom of Ava would lead eventually in 1886 to Britain's annexation of parts of Burma, taken under the wing of Indian administration. Rivalry with European powers also prompted land-grabbing. As we have already noted, Britain seized the island of Mauritius in the Indian Ocean from the French, and Java from the Dutch, in 1810. Close to India, in Ceylon the British poached on territories formerly under the control of Portuguese and Dutch interests, annexing the island in 1796. To the east the British commandeered interests (including Singapore on

the Malay peninsula) that, in their earliest colonial days, were administered, like Ceylon, through the East India Company. The Malay colonies
were used early on by the company, in an echo of Australian transportation,
as a dumping ground for Indian convicts used as forced labour. There
were also a whole series of strategically placed sites en route to India and
seized by the British during the French war, including the Seychelles
(1794), the Cape of Good Hope (1795) and Malta (1800; annexed 1814).
The Andaman Islands in the Indian Ocean were first colonized as a convict colony in 1789, but the settlement lasted only until 1796. It would be
populated again as a convict colony for British India in 1858.

To the east, China was closely connected to British interests in India,
for a significant fraction of the East India Company's profits derived from
the sale in China of opium grown in India. The efforts of the Chinese
leadership to stem the flow of Indian opium would lead in 1839 and again
in 1856 to war and to Britain's acquisition in 1841 of the island of Hong
Kong, just off the southern coast of mainland China. In 1839 Britain also
took possession of Aden, its proximity to the Red Sea and the Arabian
Sea making it a vital coaling station for ships en route to India. It was
governed from Bombay for almost a hundred years.

With these new, and sometimes temporarily held, colonial possessions,
Britain formed a circle of protection around India, near and far, and in
essence the East India Company became a transnational corporation with
tentacles all over the world, holding together both its fiscal and its political interests. These close ties – political, military, geographical, economic
– exemplify the interconnection of imperial interest and expansion, each
colony influencing and shaping other British possessions. A mass of
factors was always involved in the acquisition and the maintaining of
colonies; it was never a single factor that decided which areas of the world
would come under British rule. And as the Empire grew in size, these more
global considerations became more and more important. India – and,
before 1857, the EIC – was frequently central to these considerations.

Yet in the late 1680s the company's future in India had been uncertain.
The sum of £15,000 in compensation for defensive military actions paid
to the Emperor Aurangzeb helped ensure that the EIC did not lose its
trading rights, but what this failed military aggression clearly demonstrates is that the company, even before the dawn of the eighteenth century,
no longer felt constrained to engage only in peaceful trade. That important shift in policy would have far-reaching consequences. By 1700 the
company had established the three presidencies of Bombay (to the west),
Madras (in the south) and Bengal (to the east). Though they were small in

area, the company had also, by this time, leased more than 20 trading posts from the Moguls. In return for these, the rulers of India expected aid in stemming piracy and, perhaps most importantly, in organizing the collecting of land revenues. The East India Company's role in collecting taxes from property (especially in Bengal) was increasingly important. Its part in the administration of the system brought huge wealth both to the company and to individual officials. Over time, and despite its origins as a trading entity, the EIC's focus shifted from trade to taxation.

Company trade was regulated by a *firman* from the emperor, which granted the company trading rights in designated areas in return for either rent or an annual fee. In its early years, company jurisdiction was only over very small areas of India, a situation that would change with astonishing rapidity after the 1750s. The Mogul Empire was changing direction, moving from a heavily centralized power to a more regional and decentralized entity. Europeans read this change as indicating the empire's decline, and these changes did render the Moguls vulnerable to attack and invasion, as well as to the intrigues of other Indian rulers (of whom there were many) anxious to enjoy a share of India's lucrative trade. The company, too, had been transformed early in the eighteenth century. After far-reaching criticism of its methods and practices, it had re-formed in 1709 as the United Company of Merchants Trading to the East Indies. It was a change by which the company became, in many respects, a national institution, and a highly profitable one. Between 1709 and 1748 there were only two occasions on which the company was unable to pay dividends to its shareholders. At the start of the eighteenth century, the EIC's trade was focused heavily on India, from where some 90 per cent of its major cargoes originated. Textiles were among the most profitable of its goods. In Sumatra the company also traded in pepper and in China in tea, silk and chinaware.

It was when the East India Company defeated Mogul forces in 1757 that the expansion of British India really began in earnest. The company had explicitly violated its agreement with the Moguls by fortifying Calcutta (the centre of British Bengali operations) against the French. They also engaged in a host of illegal and dubious commercial practices in the region. Angered, the nawab of Bengal, Siraj-ud-Daula, reacted by capturing Calcutta in June 1756. His imprisonment of Europeans in what became notorious as the 'Black Hole' of Calcutta – and the death of some of the prisoners – ignited British anger. The quick and decisive defeat of the nawab's forces by company troops led by Colonel Robert Clive at the Battle of Plassey resulted in a change in leadership. The new nawab,

Mir Jafar, was very much under the British thumb, at least early in his rule. Bengal, and especially Calcutta, became the central power base of the company over the course of the century. The growing importance of Bengal in trading also helped enhance its supremacy.

From the 1760s, as more territory and power accrued, the presidencies took on responsibilities traditionally the province of governments rather than commercial companies. With their courts of law and their armies, the three presidencies effectively ruled larger and larger tracts of the subcontinent, deploying their armies against intractable rulers as much as against the French whose interest in the region had not waned and who hoped to weaken the British through supporting local rebellions. The decisive defeat of the French interest came in the early 1760s, when victory in a series of skirmishes in south-east India consolidated Britain's position. The company took advantage of the ousting of the French from India and the failing power of the increasingly fragmented Mogul Empire. British patronage of regional rulers speeded the disintegration of the older Mogul

FIGURE 5 *Brighton Pavilion: built in 1784 and purchased in the early nineteenth century by the Prince Regent. John Nash oversaw the rebuilding of the palace between 1815 and 1821 in a mixture of classical and Indian styles, often labelled 'Hindoo-Gothic'* (Alamy/Chris Ballentine)

power structure while stabilizing and entrenching a British foothold. Coupled with Britain's willingness to colonize, if sometimes only temporarily, in regions helpful to Indian expansion, such as Mauritius and Java, these tactics secured the company's extraordinary transformation. Moreover, the fact that it still continued to pay fat dividends to its British shareholders gave the company considerable weight in Britain.

Yet there was both serious internal dissension and concern in government circles about the conduct of individual officials and about the company's arrogation of power. EIC officials came to be seen as greedy, unscrupulous and self-seeking, and those who ostensibly controlled direction and policy from London felt increasingly in the late eighteenth century as if they could not control their own employees. Novelists poked fun at the 'nabobs' and they were often resented and despised in Britain, seen as a corrupt and spoiled nouveau riche. The most famous of the nabobs was Robert Clive who won battles, commercial concessions and territory for the company. Always a controversial figure, Clive did much in the 1760s to steer the company towards its new role in India, though at times he was more popular with the public than with his employers. His most celebrated accomplishment apart from the victory at Plassey in 1757 was engineering the *diwani* (revenue control) of Bengal in 1765. By this agreement (also known as the Treaty of Allahabad), the company won the sole right to collect revenues on behalf of the emperor, now Shah Alam, in Bengal and in neighbouring Bihar and Orissa. In return the emperor was to be paid the enormous sum of 2.6 million rupees a year. At the same time, Clive enriched his own coffers considerably, returning to Britain immeasurably wealthier.

This intensification of the company's financial role not only altered its own profile but had a lasting impact on patterns of landownership in eastern India. The 'Permanent Settlement' engineered by Lord Cornwallis in 1793 created a new landowning class of local wealthy Indians who had functioned previously as tax collectors. Tax assessments on land remained unchanged over time, offering an incentive for a new and profitable form of property-holding by purchase. The effect was to alter the basis of property ownership substantially, investing individuals with rights of ownership previously shared among all those with an interest in the cultivation of land. Whereas the system significantly enriched the affluent tax-collecting *zamindari* or *talukadar* and, of course, the company, ordinary farmers and agricultural labourers were forced to pay substantial land taxes. Since these remained unchanged whatever the yield of the harvest, they paid heavily under the new system for their traditional livelihood. It was – for the wealthy, at least – a profitable system that put India at the centre of British imperial interests.

For all the wealth this created, and despite Clive's considerable political skills, the company ran aground in the late 1760s. Political intrigue, charges of corruption, expensive military campaigns and a market crash that seriously threatened EIC stock pushed the British government into action. It was abundantly clear by the 1770s that the government needed to regulate the affairs of the company if Britain's national interests in India were to remain viable. India was too profitable and prestigious a possession by then to risk losing, and in 1773 the prime minister, Lord North, changed the course of British colonialism in India. His Regulating Act, though cautious and exploratory, established the government's authority over the company's activities in India. The Act created the position of governor general to oversee all three presidencies. The court of directors made the nomination, but could appoint to the position only with government approval. A new supreme court at Calcutta in Bengal, which replaced Delhi as the centre of power in India, had judges appointed from London. The system created considerable resentment in the presidencies, angered by their loss of autonomy, as well as among the company's directors in London who resented the government's interference.

This tension between officials on the ground and government in London would become an enduring hallmark of British imperialism. It had, in some senses, already been apparent in the American context, for it was opposition to what American colonists regarded as undue control from London that catalysed rebellion. The principle of government intervention was the chief cause of friction. Warren Hastings, the first governor general in India from 1774 to 1785, endured almost constant disharmony in relations between London and the colonial government. Despite long experience in the company's service in India he faced opposition on a number of fronts and, with his uncompromising views on what forms imperial Indian governance should take, he was always a controversial figure. India in these years received a tremendous amount of attention in the London press, and debates about the moral status both of British and company involvement were vigorous.

It was in part because of some of the stalemates Hastings had faced in his years in office that Pitt's government reconsidered the 1773 Act under which Hastings was appointed. That Act was replaced by a more comprehensive law after eleven years, and after the fall of the British government at the end of 1783 over its policy on India. By then, the American rebels had changed the face of British imperialism, making India even more important and more attractive a possession, and tilting the axis of British imperial expansion towards Asia; and of course, unlike the 13 colonies, there was no settler tradition or elective government in India to challenge the new structures. In many respects, the India Act of 1784 extended and expanded upon the earlier Act, strengthening both the power of the governor general and of the profitable Bengal presidency over Madras and Bombay. The governor general acquired the power of veto over his council and over the decisions of the two other presidencies. His appointment remained officially in company hands, but since the government had the power of recall the procedure became one of careful negotiation between government and the EIC; after Hastings, those appointed to the position were routinely outsiders to the company. The governorship became a politically motivated appointment. The Act also created a Board of Control based in Britain. The company did not lose its trade monopoly, its role in revenue collection, or its right to appoint and dismiss its own officials, but the board now gained jurisdiction over the company's civil, military and revenue affairs in India. The law gave Britain's politicians new power to control the political and diplomatic roles of the company. Although the total shift from control by a chartered corporation to direct government rule did not take place until 1858, a heightened degree of government supervision and interest was already changing how large parts of India were ruled and by whom.

For all the expansion of power, however, the East India Company found its prominent new role in British India a costly one, and its growing control of India was accompanied by an anxiety over balancing the books and realizing the necessary profits. The heavy cost of the machinery of government as well as of maintaining standing armies, as the company did in all three presidencies, cut into profits considerably, thus prompting the government, always concerned with the profitability of trade, to intervene in company affairs. Governor General Cornwallis had begun the task of professionalizing the company's growing administrative staff, creating competitive pay scales and a merit-centred ethos long before the British civil service adopted such practices. It was a policy prompted in large measure by the perpetual outcry in Britain over the corrupt practices of company servants. After 1805, company civil servants were sent to the EIC's own college in Britain, Haileybury, where they underwent a two-year preparatory training before being posted to India. Along with Calcutta's College of Fort William (founded in 1802) where new recruits received language training, Haileybury gave the Indian civil service a unique level of preparation among government servants.

Each presidency also supported its own army, composed largely of Indian soldiers (sepoys) commanded by a white officer class. In the second half of the eighteenth century their numbers swelled strikingly. There were some 18,000 troops in the three presidencies in 1763; 40 years later there were over 150,000. In Bengal alone, the 1756 contingent of 3,000 soldiers rose in a mere decade to 26,000. The soldiers were needed to keep order at a time of increasing restiveness among local rulers and to ward off threats, especially from the French, in the late 1790s. Yet the expansion of territory effected by this soldiery was also the source of their financing; without the revenue brought in by what the military achieved, there could be no expansion in their number. The military component of the company was a self-propelling entity necessary for rule but also itself creating the need for the relentless expansion of territory and therefore revenue so characteristic of the later eighteenth century. The high expense of the military continued into the new century, directly influencing the course of economic policy.

In the years after 1858 the composition of the army in India would change radically, but in the years of company rule the presidency armies were overwhelmingly Indian. Poor men were recruited into the armies by the promise of regular pay and food and a pension. At a time when the British army was regarded contemptuously as a haven for those who needed to hide, the armies of the company were well-trained and well-disciplined forces. Indians employed in the civil administration, equally, were well educated, though in the 1830s there was considerable debate over the wisdom of encouraging an English-style education among Indian elites. Much of urban India (in cities such as Lucknow and Calcutta) possessed an active elite culture in the early nineteenth century with a lively literary and theatrical scene and a well-established musical and dance tradition. British interests lay with whether or not an English education would secure the long-term loyalty of this essential class of administrators. They were essential not only because, like all colonial ventures, success relied in part on a degree of collaboration and collusion, but also because there were insufficient numbers of Britons to keep the enterprise afloat. Without the work of Indians – whether in clerical and administrative positions, in farm labour or building construction, or in the armed forces – British India simply could not have functioned.

The number of Britons residing in India remained small until after direct rule was imposed in 1858; in the 1830s, the British component of the population was 45,000 out of a total population of 150 million. Even after 1858, the numbers were never vast, though there were significant changes in who came to India over the course of the nineteenth century. In the earliest years of British influence, aside from the occasional adventurer, the majority of Britons in India were company officials working either in trade or in the military. As the company became a political body, traders gave way to emissaries and administrators. The numbers still remained small, and this population was almost exclusively male, for there were no job opportunities for British women; the company rarely permitted officials to bring their wives with them to India, and the military allowed marriage for only a small percentage of the rank and file. The trickle of British women going to India grew in the nineteenth century, as first missionaries and then other women began to settle. However, the majority of women in India throughout the British period were the wives of officials, civil and military. As a result, areas of British settlement and residence in Indian towns and cities were slowly transformed into family-oriented areas resembling more and more the environment left behind in Britain.

The indigenous population, meanwhile, became increasingly mobile. Changes in land use and in patterns of landownership under both Mogul and British rule disrupted traditional occupations, and shortages and famines – never unknown in the region – became more frequent and more severe. The Bengal famine of 1770, caused by a mix of high taxation and a drought, killed a third of the local population. Many sought new job opportunities catering to British needs as traditional employments diminished. From the 1830s many Indians signed on as indentured labourers, either on the tea plantations in Assam in eastern India and nearby Ceylon or on the rice plantations in British Burma, or in more distant lands. The abolition of slavery in 1833 created a need for a new workforce in traditional areas of slave agriculture. The early abandonment of apprenticeship schemes for former slaves in 1838 quickened the pace of recruitment. India's large rural population seemed an obvious source for plantation labour and recruiters targeted areas where work was scarce. The pre-colonial existence of debt bondage in India – where debts were paid off through labour, not necessarily that of the debtor, and often in fact of a younger family member – perhaps made the prospect of indenture less alarming, and certainly the severe depression of the late 1820s to 1850s spurred the supply of such workers.

A very different set of political influences, meanwhile, were at work in Britain. The influence of the free trade movement, hostile to the protectionism and monopoly that had so characterized the eighteenth-century mercantile system, was increasingly strong in Britain, and when the EIC's

charter came up for renewal by parliament in 1813, the free trade lobby
was ready. The company lost most of its monopoly in India, retaining it
only on opium and salt. Since together these items represented 25 per cent
of the company's income, and since trade played less and less prominent
a part in the company's operations, the loss was in some ways symbolic,
more a reflection of political than economic concerns. Though the company
experienced some diminution in its commercial ventures, its power in the
three presidencies was more and more comprehensive, and its military
was untouched by the changes to the charter. The charter renewal did
introduce, however, a small contingent (40,000 maximum) of royal forces
to India, supplementing the growing size of the EIC armies. Twenty years
later, in the 1833 charter renewal, the victory of the free traders was
complete: the company lost its last remaining monopoly in China, and
India was opened fully to private traders.

The activities of the EIC over the course of the first half of the nineteenth
century make it hard to remember that this was a trading and commercial
organization. Philip Lawson describes the company after 1813 as 'a
department of state'.[1] From the 1820s on, and acting exactly like a government, Indian administrations tackled a host of social improvement issues
in India, moving away from the earlier principles of 'orientalism' that had
avoided overt influence on local cultures. This new direction in policy was
typified by Thomas Babington Macaulay, a member of the Bengal Supreme
Council, and by William Bentinck, governor general from 1828 to 1835.
Macaulay, in a famous tract known as his 'minute on education' (1835)
argued that English should be the language of state in India, and that
westernization would improve the condition of India and guarantee the
loyalties of India's educated classes. Bentinck, meanwhile, presided over a
series of social reforms in the 1830s that attacked what were regarded as
barbarous local customs.

In the same year that Bentinck was appointed governor general,
Calcutta-based activist and prolific author Ram Mohan Roy founded a
reform organization, the Brahmo Samaj, that would be of tremendous
influence in eastern India. A Hindu-based organization dedicated to
extirpating idol worship and the caste system, the Brahmo Samaj was also
active in social reform. Many of the same issues on the organization's
agenda also caught Bentinck's attention, prominent among them the
ancient practice of widow sacrifice (suttee), in which a widow threw
herself upon her husband's burning funeral pyre, dying in recognition of
his centrality to her existence. An EIC regulation of 1813 had declared
suttee legal as long as it was a voluntary act. Roy, arguing that the practice

was not necessary to religious observance, published in both Bengali and English a tract condemning the practice in 1818. Journalistic and literary accounts of women's hideous screams of agony captured the British imagination, while for Roy and his followers the practice was a brutal corruption of Hindu tenets. In 1829 Bentinck outlawed it, though this did little to extirpate the practice. In remote areas few would have known of the change in the law, and in any case the incidence of suttee seems to have been regionally specific and confined to the higher castes. Some historians have argued that the law was counterproductive, advertising the practice more widely, and also making it seem an act subversive of British rule.

The ban on suttee was only one of a number of reforms undertaken in the years of EIC governance and aimed at Indian women. In 1856, a Widow Remarriage Act permitted Hindu widows to remarry, but forced them to forfeit rights in their deceased husband's estate. This was also an issue that Indian reformers, led by Ishwar Chandra Vidyasagar, had campaigned about for decades. But the form the law took robbed low-caste women of economic opportunities, since the prohibition on remarriage had generally been practised only among the higher castes. Ordinary women had always remarried, but under the new law could no longer inherit from their husbands when they did so.

Widow remarriage and suttee reform alike failed to take into account the differences between practice in elite and in poor families. In assuming that high-caste Brahmin orthodoxy was widespread, reforms of this sort often made the lives of lower-caste and poorer women more difficult. As Barbara Ramusack has noted, neither British nor Indian reformers saw any need for the counsel of Indian women in formulating their actions.[2] All these laws presumed the lesser status of women in Indian culture and society and emphasized a highly elitist interpretation of Hinduism based solely on Brahmin texts. This thinking became the basis for much of the colonial accommodation to local custom in the nineteenth century, a policy that reinvested the Hindu caste system with power and gave the men of the priestly Brahmin caste a disproportionate influence in discussions of what constituted proper Hinduism and proper Indian behaviour. It was a colonial tendency that would recur in other parts of the Empire with equally detrimental and divisive results. It reflected, too, a conscious power shift on the part of the British, favouring Hindu over Muslim.

Measures of reform almost always involved a critique of what were seen as typically Indian behaviours or ideas, and implemented conduct and values favoured by British elite culture. With each successive diminution in company power at the time of charter renewal, the metropolitan voices of reform – spearheaded by free traders and evangelicals – became more influential. Bolstered by Indian activism in many of the same areas of concern, early nineteenth-century governments intervened ever more closely in Indian religion, culture and social life. The effect was often to emphasize the more conservative strands of local society. The Hindu caste system, now enforced through the courts, became, if anything, more pervasive and more stultifying, and Britain's interest in maintaining Indian princes as local rulers helped to keep tradition securely in place. British economic policy discouraged competition with the metropole, making large parts of India more rural and agrarian just as Europe was industrializing.

These reforms point to the declining role of the EIC and the rising government interest in India – many of these reforms would probably not have been initiated by the EIC alone. The company's long-standing policy on religion had been one of toleration and non-intervention. Christian missionaries were long forbidden to work in India, and it was only in 1813 that the evangelical lobby was able to overcome the EIC's mistrust of missionary activity. Even then their victory was only partial. Missionaries required licences in areas under company control and were watched carefully. It would be another 20 years before missionaries gained complete freedom of mobility and organization in India.

For all the interest in the alleged social ills of the country, there was one critical arena that remained untouched, and that was the opium trade between India (the source of production) and China (the point of sale). The dulling and addictive effects of opiates were already known in Britain, and in the popular imagination opium was associated with the 'Chinaman'. Throughout the nineteenth century, a city's Chinatown (whether in Britain, Australia, Hong Kong or Canada) was invariably depicted as a place teeming with haze-filled opium dens where insensate addicts dozed and dreamed. Yet the trade – unwelcome to the Chinese authorities – was hugely lucrative for the EIC and for the Chinese middlemen to whom they sold the drug. The Chinese government's hostility to the importation of opium to China did not deter Indian production, although it did force the company to find ways around Chinese anti-opium laws. In effect, the company endorsed a huge and sophisticated smuggling ring. In terms of income, it was worth the risk. Without opium there would be a trade deficit on the Chinese trading route. China had little interest in the other goods available from British traders; its own pottery and textiles were far superior, and it had tea in abundance. If the Chinese did not buy the company's opium there was little else to sell them, and tea bought from China had to be paid for in cash since the Chinese were uninterested in the other goods on offer. The only way to address the deficits that this large outlay of cash entailed was from the sale of opium.

Although illegal in China, the opium trade was enormously profitable and constantly growing, with the result that opium became one of the most important products managed and traded by the East India Company. Large numbers of workers in India relied on the income from growing poppies, and the company offered incentives to farmers involved in its production. The company thus invested considerable time and effort in developing this trade. Before the large-scale cultivation of opium poppies in India, Turkey had been the world's principal source of opium. The disintegration of the Ottoman Empire during the nineteenth century made the development of Indian cultivation a viable business proposition, so much so that in 1830 the British government gave permission for more extensive opium cultivation in India. The effect, not surprisingly, was to reduce cultivation of other agricultural products in the race for the easy profits associated with the opium poppy.

The company's monopoly on opium had been the work of Warren Hastings, first governor general of India. Over time, the monopoly tightened; by 1793, poppy growers in India could sell only to the EIC. Despite its central role in the movement of opium from India to China, the company worked hard to disguise its position in the trade. It sold the opium at auction in Calcutta, from where it was shipped by private firms rather than in company vessels to China and distributed by smugglers. The proceeds from the sales, however, were always paid to the EIC's own China office.

A clash between China's Manchu leaders and British traders over the illegal importation into China of huge quantities of the drug was inevitable. China was concerned both about high levels of opium addiction among its populace and about the drain on the country's stocks of silver, which were being diverted to pay for opium. The first of the two Opium Wars broke out when Chinese customs officials impounded opium shipments arriving at Canton (now Guangzhou). Britain, already irritated by a Chinese offensive to curb the trade, deployed a naval detachment to shell important Chinese ports and trading sites in protest, and was successful not only in forcing trade concessions from the Chinese, but also in acquiring the new colony of Hong Kong. This three-year war, from 1839 to 1842, occurred at much the same time as social reformers were declaring the moral bankruptcy of Indian society. Yet other than the evangelical lobby, surprisingly few British voices were raised in protest over the selling of opium until late in the nineteenth century. The war was depicted in the British press and in parliament as a principled dispute over free trade rather than about drug peddling. Both government and the EIC focused attention on China's refusal to allow foreign merchants commercial access to the country. The continued monopoly the company enjoyed in trading opium was conveniently forgotten, as was the fact that its sale violated Chinese law. In practice, the war – conducted not by the company but by the British government – was a convenient way to force open the China trade that had for so long eluded the British. In his 1845 novel *Sybil*, future Conservative prime minister Benjamin Disraeli satirized the most famous of the opium merchants, William Jardine, as the fictional 'McDruggy fresh from Canton, with a million in opium in each pocket, denouncing corruption and bellowing free trade'.[3]

The 1842 Treaty of Nanking made no mention of opium despite the fact that it had been the catalyst for the 1839 war. By 1849, the trade through Hong Kong was worth about £6 million a year. Opium continued to be a valued commodity throughout the nineteenth century, and was the second largest source of revenue for India after land taxes. Sales and trading were as brisk in the 1890s as they had been early in the century. The trade also remained the province of highly respectable business ventures. After the loss of the EIC monopoly in 1833, other companies could profit from the trade and some of the most prominent of Hong Kong's commercial entities owed their success to their entry into the opium trade. After the Second Opium War (1856–60), the trade was effectively legalized by the establishment of formal tariffs for the importing of opium.

Opium's huge profitability has always been more important to those who trade in it than have been the consequences of addiction to it. What makes the colonial opium trade so interesting is that it was controlled not by underground and illegal organizations but by some of the largest and most successful businesses of the period, and with the direct knowledge of successive British governments. Moreover, in the case of the EIC, it was a business enterprise involved simultaneously, via its political wing, in the implementation of law and order in British India. In effect, then, the nineteenth century opium trade was more than connived at by government: it was actively encouraged. Furthermore, that encouragement did not deter officials from claiming moral, religious and civilizational superiority over both those who grew the product and those to whom they trafficked it. Few outside the highly moralistic circles of evangelism saw the contradictions at work in an arena where politics, economics, religion and culture so fully coalesced. Ironically, the Treaty of Tientsin in 1858, which put opium trading on a legal footing, also saw the opening of China to Christian missionaries for the first time! The age of reform and of high morals was also quite palpably an age of rapacity.

The first half of the nineteenth century was a time of considerable expansion in British India. Annexation and a series of military skirmishes all required considerable military force, and the military in India was the largest in Asia, with 16 European regiments and 170 sepoy regiments. In the first quarter of the nineteenth century the Indian army was involved in a series of colonial wars that augmented Britain's territory in the region substantially. Britain annexed the Carnatic in 1801, Sind in 1843, the Punjab in 1849 and Oudh in 1856.

The EIC was increasingly acting like a government, imposing British values and British definitions, while incorporating more and more territory. From the mid-1840s, under the leadership of Lord Dalhousie, the tentacles of westernization spread further and further. Dalhousie eased the way for the construction of railways, steam-shipping and irrigation schemes. He laid plans for Indian universities and introduced changes in the military, and in 1854 set up a postal service. He altered the systems of land tenure that held back cultivation. He also ushered in the deeply unpopular 'doctrine of lapse', which broadened British opportunities for expansion by requiring that Indian states without a male heir were forfeited to the British. However, in the process of these many reforms, he angered many entrenched interests.

Local dissatisfaction with this system of dual government found many outlets. The company had won the right in 1813 to introduce a non-fixed tax system (*ryotwari*) in newly acquired territories. Peasant cultivators in these areas found themselves heavily taxed to compensate for the situation in Bengal where, under the Permanent Settlement, taxes could not be raised. Intervention in a few social issues by no means signalled an intent to overhaul and certainly not to modernize India. Local rebellions and resistance to company rule were not uncommon, and there was a general feeling that the British imposed alien values on local peoples. In the company armies there was resentment at British insensitivity: for example, a new army regulation in 1856 required service wherever posted, potentially jeopardizing the caste standing of Hindu sepoys, since crossing the 'black waters' (meaning going overseas) involved a loss of caste for high-caste Hindus. Yet during the latter half of the nineteenth century, the army required such service of Indian soldiers in large numbers. They were deployed in many colonial hot spots: in Ethiopia in 1867, in Egypt in

1882, in Burma in 1885, and in many parts of Africa in the 1890s and beyond, including in the Boer War.

The army was often a restive institution, and it was a military rebellion that prompted the end of dual government in India. The fuse that lit the 1857 rebellion among Indian soldiers was about religious taboo. Though it was only a catalyst for a range of differences between the sepoys and their command, the rumour that the cartridges of the new-issue Enfield rifles were greased with animal fat found fertile ground. The very breadth of the rumour – that the fat was both beef and pork, and thus anathema to Hindu and Muslim alike – itself suggests a profound degree of unhappiness, as does the long history of prior if less widespread mutinies among Indian soldiers. Earlier mutinies – at Barrackpur in 1824, in the Northwest Frontier Provinces in 1844 and in the Punjab in 1849, to name just a few – had been stopped before they could spread. In 1857, however, tensions between the British and their Indian subjects (and not just in the army) had mounted considerably and resentment at the EIC's often high-handed methods of governance was common. Moreover, soldiers understood only too well that Dalhousie's army reforms imperilled their long-standing privileges. What began as a military mutiny in the Bengal Army spread beyond the soldiery to include agrarian protest and much more, though it remained focused in the north. The 1857 revolt was far more than merely a soldiers' protest. It expressed in many ways the burgeoning gulf between British authority and Indian subject. This revolt covered a whole range of frustrations – over extortionate tax demands, extensive overt racism, insensitivity to local culture and religion, and incessant territorial expansion.

The rebellion, which began in May 1857 at Meerut, spread rapidly and caught the British by surprise. It was more than a year before the uprising was fully contained, and in the meantime the destruction of life and property was abundant. Violence was met with violence. The British exacted brutal punishment for the revolt, in a reaction to some of the more violent episodes of the rebellion. Many Britons were murdered, and it was the slaying of British women and children that most angered the British, both in India and in Britain. Accounts of the rebellion often focused on this, an emphasis that made the Indians seem cowardly, cruel and unchivalrous. Such a focus also allowed British opinion to minimize other elements of the rebellion. Civilian and in some areas even landlord support for the mutiny was, in many regions, quite strong and often explicit in demanding the reinstatement of pre-British ruling dynasties, most particularly the Moguls and the western Indian Marathas, only recently subdued by the

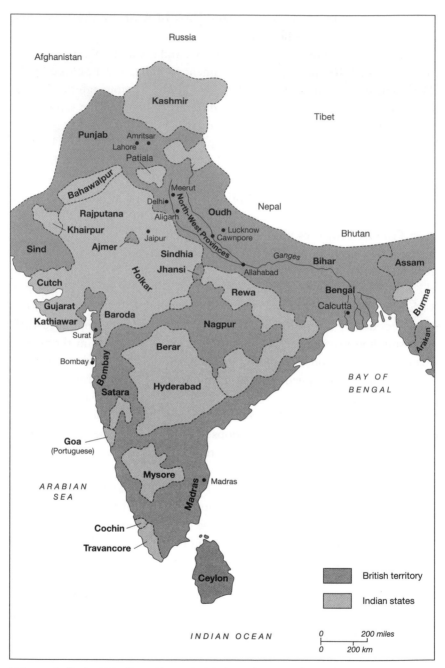

Russia

Afghanistan

Kashmir

Tibet

Punjab

Amritsar

Lahore

Patiala

Bahawalpur

Meerut

Delhi

North-West Provinces

Rajputana

Aligarh

Oudh

Nepal

Khairpur

Ajmer

Jaipur

Lucknow

Cawnpore

Bhutan

Sind

Sindhia

Jhansi

Holkar

Ganges

Allahabad

Bihar

Assam

Cutch

Rewa

Bengal

Burma

Gujarat

Baroda

Calcutta

Kathiawar

Surat

Nagpur

Arakan

Bombay

Berar

Bombay

Satara

Hyderabad

BAY OF
BENGAL

Goa
(Portuguese)

Mysore

Madras

Madras

ARABIAN
SEA

Cochin

Travancore

Ceylon

British territory

Indian states

INDIAN OCEAN

| 0 | 200 miles |
| 0 | 200 km |

MAP 2 *India in 1857* (from Simon Smith, *British Imperialism 1750–1970*, (Cambridge: Cambridge University Press, 1988), p. 52. © Cambridge University Press, reproduced with permission of the author and publisher.)

FIGURE 6 *Mutiny tents, Indian soldiers, 1857* (Getty Research Institute/ Los Angleles, California (96.R.84))

British. The political elements of rebellion were played down while violence against unarmed British citizens was accentuated.

In any event, not only were the British anything but gracious in victory but the result of the mutiny was to oust the EIC and to impose direct British rule in its place, through the Government of India Act, passed in August 1858. The EIC was dissolved and a new Indian civil service established, with appointment by competitive examination. Officials reported directly to the British government via a newly created department in London, the India Office. India, unlike any other colony, now had its own separate government department. The governor general, also called the viceroy to demonstrate that he was the formal representative of the Crown, reported directly to the Secretary of State for India. The separate presidency governments were retained and were still subordinate to the governor general.

The dissolution of the EIC did not, of course, bring all of India under British control. Several hundred independent territories dotted the subcontinent, and in these the principle of paramountcy governed relations after 1858. Queen Victoria's proclamation of 1858 guaranteed the princes in these independent states their territory in exchange for a pledge of loyalty to the British Crown. The British retained the right, however, to intervene where a ruler colluded with an enemy of the Crown or in cases of 'gross misrule'. In reality, as had been the case under EIC governance, many of these princely states were independent in name only, and were subjugated to British interests and needs. As the nationalist movement took hold in parts of India from the 1880s onwards, many saw these hereditary princely states as anachronistic remnants of an earlier era deliberately kept alive by the British for their own political ends. It would be 1971 before India would fully abolish the principle of rule by inheritance in these states. By then, the full complement of the problems associated with it were apparent. The continued impasse over Kashmir so well known today can be traced in part to this policy; it was one of a handful of princely states unwilling in 1947 to accede to one or other of the newly created nations of India and Pakistan. Today both of these countries lay claim to Kashmir.

In practice, in many parts of India as much stayed the same after 1858 as changed. Officials often stayed on in the same positions. Lord Canning remained in office as governor general, despite the debacle of 1857. Instead of being employed by the company, officials and soldiers now became Crown employees. The new Council of India, advisory to the Secretary of State and replacing the old Board of Control, was at least partially in the hands of company men for some time. Their experience and knowledge was invaluable, but their loyalties were sometimes to an older tradition of rule.

For the Indian population, the most obvious difference may well have been the increase in the number of British soldiers they saw in their lands. Shaken by what was read as the disloyalty of Indian soldiers to the military establishment, the new system, still reliant on military muscle, doubled the number of British soldiers in India. After the Mutiny, there were never less than 60,000 British soldiers stationed in India. Cantonments grew to accommodate their numbers and the military lobby demanded ever fatter budgets. Sepoy numbers, though reduced, continued to outstrip those of white soldiers, but the palpably larger presence of British soldiers was seen as a deterrent to further trouble. Changes to local recruiting practice were made, with preference being given to illiterate and ill-educated men who were seen as likelier to accept an unquestioning oath of loyalty and from the so-called martial races, often conveniently defined as those who had remained loyal in 1857.

The first few years of direct rule saw a great deal of activity codifying and establishing new policy and rule. In 1860 an Indian Penal Code, and in 1861 a Code of Criminal Procedure, laid down the legal principles that would henceforth govern Britain's Indian subjects. In 1861 the Indian High Courts Act created high courts at Madras, Calcutta and Bombay, which exercised civil and criminal appellate jurisdiction similar to that in Britain. In 1871 the British inaugurated a decennial census in India, and seven years later a survey, instruments similar to those operating in Britain and designed to make the control of the population easier.

In the late nineteenth century India witnessed the flourishing of a nationalist movement as middle-class urban populations most especially grew frustrated with their lack of a political voice. India remained a major market for British trade, its chief export market in the early twentieth century. India, meanwhile, remained predominantly agricultural, aided by the rapid growth of railway lines to and from the major ports. And there was a huge prestige factor, for now Britain could boast the largest single territory under European rule in the world. The year 1858 represented for Britain a commitment, not only to long-term rule in India, but also to a broader, deeper vision of the British Empire than had hitherto been possible; although that year might not be a watershed in Indian history, it was a major one for the history of the British Empire.

References

1   Philip Lawson, *The East India Company. A History* (London: Longman, 1993), p. 144.

2   Barbara N. Ramusack, 'Women in South and South East Asia', in Ramusack and Sharon Sievers (eds), *Women in Asia: Restoring Women to History* (Bloomington: Indiana University Press, 1999), p. 42.

3   Benjamin Disraeli (1845), *Sybil, or: The Two Nations* (Harmondsworth, Middlesex: Penguin, 1954), p. 55.

CHAPTER 6

Global growth

Over the course of the nineteenth century, Britain added 10 million square miles and 400 million people to its colonial holdings. It would, by the end of the century, still be the largest of the European empires, scattered across the globe in a bewildering variety of political and administrative forms. The diversity of the Empire was not only geographical and cultural, but also administrative. There was no one formula for rule or for takeover and, much like the Empire of the eighteenth century, there was perpetual debate about both the moral standing of colonialism and about particular colonies.

However, although there was no singular and characteristic policy dominating the seemingly unstoppable growth of the Empire, that does not necessarily mean that British colonialism was somehow an accidental or even a reluctant series of random acquisitions. Such a view, most famously voiced by the late nineteenth-century historian Sir John Seeley, has enjoyed considerable popularity among historians. Seeley's elegant quip – that Britain's Empire was acquired in a 'fit of absence of mind'[1] – has influenced many interpreters of nineteenth-century British imperialism.[2] Others, not pushing the point quite so far, see the British political establishment as dominated, especially after the 1850s, by reluctant imperialists, unwillingly annexing territory or unenthusiastically nudging local rulers into accepting British influence.[3] Yet given the vast areas brought under British control during the course of the century and under leadership from a variety of political positions, the image of a reluctant or accidental imperialism is not awfully persuasive. Huge areas of Africa became British; only in North Africa, dominated by the French, was British influence negligible. Dozens of small islands in the Pacific were appropriated as well as large portions of the Malay archipelago in south-east Asia. India came under direct rule for the first time in its colonial history with Britain. Much of Burma, to India's east, was brought under the Indian administration. Australia and New Zealand developed rapidly, and huge tracts of westerly land were added to Britain's Canadian possessions. Hong Kong, first acquired in 1841, expanded its boundaries over the course of the century. In many of these places the British fought wars to hold on to the territories they had acquired, as well as negotiating treaties that favoured British influence in areas where outright control was not considered feasible. Though parliament after parliament worried over the potential costs of empire, this vast, constantly growing proliferation of territory and over so long a period can hardly have been an accident.

The highly influential work of Ronald Robinson and John Gallagher, who coined the much-used phrase 'the imperialism of free trade' in the 1950s, saw Britain's acts of nineteenth-century colonization as formal only when absolutely necessary.[4] Their emphasis lay on a reading of British imperialism shaped as much by informal imperialism (in China, in the Middle East and in South America, for example) as by formal annexation. It was a reading of colonialism that stressed its economic elements above all else, and that saw Britain as undertaking formal colonization only as a last resort.

Robinson and Gallagher's assessment reminds us usefully that the British Empire was a complex entity with tentacles that reached beyond formal legal and political borders. Still, the implication that the British were reluctant to make colonization a reality minimizes the huge territorial gains of the nineteenth century. Certainly the British Empire was neither a simple, nor a simply defined, beast, but its heterogeneous structure should not lead us to minimize its effects and power throughout its history.

As the territory under British stewardship accrued, events in distant places forced the British into unanticipated action to protect acquisitions and to stem unrest. Unforeseen problems certainly meant that both politicians in Britain and colonists in the field sometimes had to extemporize, and this on-the-spot decision-making could be described as accidental in that it was not specifically planned. Even in such cases, the stratagems of expediency were often weighed against the consequences for related possessions and the Empire as a whole. Britain may not have wanted to expend money on its colonies, but it was hardly a wallflower among the European imperial powers. Colonial acquisition during the course of the nineteenth century was neither accidental nor reluctant, but a fundamental part of an aggressive expansionist policy designed to bolster Britain's leading world role in politics and trade. Empire was about making money, it

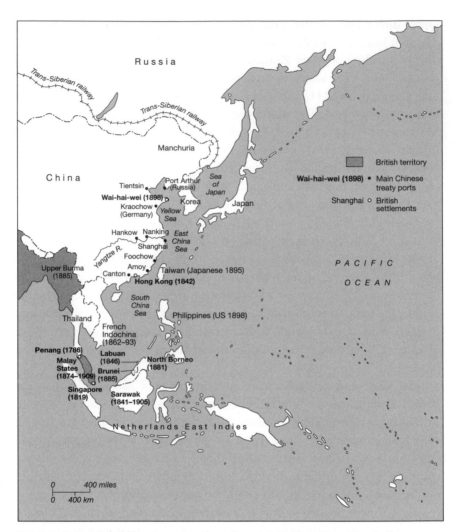

MAP 3 *Britain's holdings in east and south-east Asia* (from Peter Marshall, *Cambridge Illustrated History of the British Empire*, 1996, (Cambridge: Cambridge University Press, 1996), p. 55. © Cambridge University Press, reproduced with permission of the author and publisher.)

was about visible forms of power, and it was about the high moral ground. The civilizing mission was also the money-making mission, and both were trumpeted as elements of Britain's heritage and history.

The intense period of colonial rivalry in Africa in the last 15 years or so of the nineteenth century has encouraged historians to see these years as Britain's most expansionist. These certainly were significant gains, but the entire century is marked by expansion. The shift to direct rule in India in 1858, the occupation of Egypt in 1882 and the chartering of a trio of commercial companies in Africa in the 1880s characterize the later period, yet the first half of the century was also a time of great activity and of expansion. As we have seen, British India spread in a number of directions, Hong Kong and Singapore were in British hands by the mid-nineteenth century, and the growth of British influence and territory in southern Africa was considerable. The nineteenth century also saw considerable reorganization in the Empire. In 1768 parliament had created the new post of Secretary of State for the American or Colonial Department, a position abandoned at the time of American independence. In 1801, a similar position was revived, Secretary of State for the War and Colonial Departments, the title highlighting the often aggressive means by which colonial territory became British. This office acquired a permanent home in 1854 when the Colonial Office and the War Office became two separate entities.

These bureaucratic changes suggest that government was by no means uninterested in the supervision of the growing Empire even early in the century. We might fruitfully, then, see the entire nineteenth century as one of imperial gain and aggrandisement, perhaps with different motivations at different moments, but with a forward momentum throughout the entire century. As Christopher Bayly puts it, the partition of Africa at the end of century was 'a mere footnote' when compared with acquisitions earlier in the century.[5] The nineteenth century generally was a time of sweeping conquest, land reorganization and vast growth.

The nineteenth-century Empire was a diverse and scattered assortment of territories, some hugely valuable in commercial or strategic terms, others of little more than psychological value. No single policy connected them, no studied philosophy of governance reigned over them all. No one motive had driven this diverse agglomeration of possessions. The forms of rule were as different as the languages spoken, the food eaten, and the customs observed in the motley collection of lands that in the nineteenth century succumbed to British power or influence. There were settler colonies where, in the mid-nineteenth century, significant strides towards self-government were made. There were territories conquered by troops or handed over to British rule by local rulers. There were places where British agents and residents offered advice but could not, at least formally, make local rulers knuckle under the British thumb. There were treaty ports in Asia (at places such as Nagasaki and Okinawa) where the British had significant economic power and no mean amount of political sway as well. There were also those places where no formal trappings of British rule existed, but that came within Britain's 'sphere of influence', a favourite phrase of the day.

One of the most important principles of colonialism to emerge during the nineteenth century was 'responsible self-government'. The Upper Canada assembly had promoted the principle of a united legislature in Canada from 1822, and the theme was taken up in the 1839 report of Lord Durham on how best to manage the Canadian colonies. Durham envisaged a united Canada exercising control over its internal affairs, with the imperial parliament in London maintaining control over constitutional questions, foreign policy and trade. Canada was a vital element in the Atlantic Empire, and self-government was a way to secure its continued loyalty, especially given the tensions there between French and British Canadians. Within a decade, this principle of self-government began to take shape not just in Canada but across the white settler colonies. Those colonies deemed sufficiently politically mature were granted authority to pass laws on their own behalf in a two-thirds elective (one-third appointed) political system modelled on that of Britain. The imperial government in Britain maintained authority in key areas such as defence and foreign policy, although as a cost-cutting measure Britain abandoned its military presence in all these colonies in 1870. As we saw in Chapter 4, this experiment in government occurred mostly in the 1850s in colonies of white settlement, underlining the racial distinctions commonly applied in colonial governance. Only those areas where white European settlers had stayed to build new lives were seen as fit for this experiment in self-determination; non-white populations were invariably classed as too backward to be entrusted with such powers.

The creation of elected assemblies occurred mostly in the 1840s and 1850s with the various colonies of what would, in 1867, become the Dominion of Canada as the first to benefit. By 1854 Nova Scotia, the Province of Canada, Prince Edward Island and New Brunswick all enjoyed responsible self-government. As Chapter 4 has shown, the bulk of the Australian colonies followed suit in the 1850s. Only Western Australia, the last of the penal settlements, would have to wait until the 1890s. New Zealand acquired responsible self-government in 1856. Until 1872, the Cape Colony had the lesser status of representative self-government, in which the British-appointed governor general retained a much higher degree of control. In both responsible and representative self-government, the non-elected governor retained the right to veto laws passed by the elected representatives, but his control over a representative government was far greater. The hurried passage through parliament of the Colonial Laws Validity Act in 1865 gave Westminster the right to invalidate any laws passed by colonial assemblies that ran counter to British statute law. This brake on white settler rights would remain a bone of contention among the white settler colonies until the law was dissolved in 1931.

Responsible self-government was attractive to British politicians because it was a cheap form of rule. Colonies paid for their own administration and their own troops, and it was no coincidence that Australian self-government followed the discovery of gold, and in Cape Colony followed the diamonds unearthed in quantity there. Although no such distinctive riches prompted the changes in the Canadian provinces, there the prospect of losing the remaining British North American lands to the United States would have been both humiliating and commercially costly. Money was central to these decisions for, beyond the cost of maintaining a colony, there were also crucial trade relationships. White settler colonies, particularly early on, needed British markets and Britain needed imports from these areas. Responsible self-government allowed Britain to maintain favourable trading relationships on the cheap, while bolstering the fledgling economies of the settler lands.

The new elective system was at first sometimes unstable, with governments often falling before their term of office formally expired. Yet there was no question of these colonies being returned to dependent status. The only incidence of that came some 30 years after the end of slavery when the white elites of the West Indian sugar colonies (except Barbados) opted out of responsible self-government to avoid facing a majority black electorate. The workings of race in determining how a colony would be administered were always and everywhere crucial. Writing in 1906, W. H. Mercer unapologetically distinguished between colonies 'occupied for the purposes of taking the products of the country with the aid of coloured labour', and colonies 'which are meant to be settlements of men of white race'.[6]

While settler colonies moved in the direction of independence, many other areas were, in the course of the century, brought under direct British rule. Some were captured during war, such as Hong Kong, Mauritius and the Seychelles. Some, as was Fiji, were ceded to the British by local rulers. The Fijian Islands are unusual in that they really are an example of a reluctant British imperialism. Plagued by local rivalry the Christian ruler, Thakombau, had been trying for some time to cede the islands to a western power. The British accepted his offer in 1874, largely to prevent Fiji's acquisition by another European power. In other instances, simple annexation sufficed, as in Ashanti and North Borneo. Singapore was acquired by purchase. These new territories were largely tropical or semi-tropical, with little or no European population prior to colonization. Although many of these were Crown Colonies, in Africa Protectorates were more common. Protectorates did not have governors; instead, the top-ranking colonial official was a commissioner.

Though these were the principal forms of colonial rule in the nineteenth century, they do not exhaust its diversity. India, after all, though its form of governance resembled that of a Crown Colony, had its own London administration at the India Office, and India itself administered a number of colonial territories: Burma, Aden from 1838, Purim from 1857, Socorro from 1886 and the Andaman Islands (1858), as well as parts of the Malay archipelago into the 1830s.

Closer to home, but far removed from the principles of responsible self-government, was Ireland. The 1800 Act of Union, as we have seen, had resulted in a small number of Irish MPs being elected to Westminster. The complicated divisions between rich and poor, Protestant and Catholic, landowning and peasant classes in Ireland were in no manner solved by the Act of Union. Indeed, Ireland would be, throughout the nineteenth century, a problem that would bring down governments. Long before the severe famine of the mid-1840s forced mass emigration from Ireland and caused incalculable misery and suffering, Irish nationalists and those championing the cause of the dispossessed peasantry there reminded British politicians that not all imperial questions were located at a distance. Throughout the century, Irish activists would threaten to destabilize metropolitan politics in their quest for self-determination.

This lack of colonial uniformity reflects some interesting characteristics of the British imperial order. There is no question that in every case finding the least expensive method of colonization was a priority, though seldom one that prompted Britain to get out of the business of expansion. Relatedly, since sending a military detachment to subdue people was a costly business and not a guaranteed success, there was also always a question about what rule was appropriate and in which contexts. A consideration of these factors helped to determine what kind of colonial presence would be imposed.

There were also significant areas, as Robinson and Gallagher argued, with no formal British presence but where Britain still exercised substantial influence. For the most part, this was the case in areas not considered realistic candidates for any form of direct rule but where strategic or commercial considerations made the area important to British interests. In central and south America, for example, Britain had very few formal possessions – only British Honduras and British Guiana – but considerable economic influence, especially in Argentina and Brazil. British trade dominated these countries and their debt burden made them heavily dependent on British investors, allowing a significant British foothold in the region without any need for formal colonial governance. In part, the reluctance to colonize formally was a fiscal one, since conquest was invariably an expensive business. The Latin American case, however, was more complicated. Britain mostly worked to acquire free trade treaties (but which gave preference to Britain) in places such as Brazil and Argentina after they became independent early in the nineteenth century. The policy was successful in so far as Britain was, throughout the century, the main European nation trading in the region. The British seldom chose to colonize places where there was already a European presence or a European style of rule. Alongside the long history of Spanish and Portuguese colonial rule, the increasing presence and interest of the United States in the region further complicated the picture.

A trade treaty with Siam (now Thailand) signed in 1855, and which effectively ushered in a free trade policy in the south-east Asian kingdom, became the model for Britain's informal imperialism. Though it was strategic reasons that made the states along the Persian Gulf important to the British in this period (rather than oil, which would become important later), here too treaties in the nineteenth century made many small countries effective satellites in the British colonial system. The sheikdoms of Bahrain (1861 and 1892), Kuwait (1899) and the sultanate of Muscat and Oman (1891) all came within the sphere of British influence during the course of the nineteenth century.

One of the most politically complicated of the possessions acquired in the nineteenth century was Egypt, on the tip of north-east Africa and across from the Arabian states of the Persian Gulf. Britain's involvement there pre-dated the military occupation of 1882 and was closely tied to the fate of the Ottoman Empire and to shipping routes to India. Egypt was nominally a part of the Ottoman Empire, though the sultan was too weak by the mid-nineteenth century to have any genuine control there. For most of the century, British colonial interests dictated a pro-Ottoman policy despite public and political misgivings about many aspects of culture and rule in the Ottoman lands. The Ottoman holdings stretched from North Africa to the Black Sea, encompassing a diverse multi-ethnic array of peoples within a Muslim state, and straddling eastern and western cultures. In the nineteenth century, the Ottoman Empire was struggling to maintain its integrity. A strong internal military elite resisted the changes demanded of the empire by its western allies. Minorities were increasingly demanding, and in 1829 Greece wrested its independence from the Empire. Syria almost followed suit in 1831. Growing Austrian and Russian interest in the Ottoman Balkan possessions weakened another flank of their empire, while Russia in 1854 actually invaded Ottoman territory, setting off the Crimean War.

Britain stood by the Ottoman Empire for most of the century, seeing it as a critical barrier to French and Russian interest in the all-important routes to India. It was this concern that prompted Britain to send aid when Syria threatened to break away, and again during the Crimean War. One of the major overland trade routes to India was through the Syrian desert, a route the British were anxious to protect. British support, however, came at a price. In 1838 the British forced a free trade treaty (Balta Liman) on the Ottoman sultan that had detrimental effects on the local economy while benefiting the British, a situation further undermining the sultan's hold. As the Ottoman Empire, centred on Turkey, weakened, British interest waned. The reluctance to seize Ottoman lands, strong early in the century, dwindled in the face of British need. In 1878, needing a supply line to the eastern Mediterranean, Britain seized and colonized the Ottoman island of Cyprus, and at the end of the century, when the British entered into a power-sharing condominium in the Sudan with Egypt, Ottoman claims were simply ignored.

It was on Egypt, however, that British interests in the Ottoman region came to focus. Over the years a large European trading population had moved there, controlling the considerable export and import trade of the region. The Europeans prospered under the Ottoman legal system of 'Capitulations', which allowed them freedom from local jurisdiction. Cotton had become an especially important export when, during the American Civil War, Britain's supplies of raw cotton had been compromised, seriously affecting the prosperity of the important British textile industry. With the building of the Suez Canal, begun in 1855 and opened in 1869, Egypt became even more important to the British. The canal, located in Egypt, gradually eliminated the longer overland routes to India. When the British intervened in Egyptian affairs, the bulk of the shipping passing through the canal was British, and in 1875 Prime Minister Benjamin Disraeli had engineered the purchase by Britain of a 44 per cent stake in the canal's ownership. Europe's interest in the canal was widespread: Giuseppe Verdi's opera, *Aida*, was commissioned for the opening of the canal, though it was not in the end performed until 1871 when the new Cairo Opera House opened.

In the face of economic chaos in Egypt, the British and the French assumed dual control of the Egyptian economy to manage the country's considerable debt and to protect the financial interests of investors from their own countries. Their intervention was disrupted in 1882 by a nationalist uprising spurred by resentment of this foreign interference. The French were less and less interested in managing Egyptian affairs, so the British unilaterally embarked in May 1882 on a naval bombardment of the port of Alexandria. Instead of quelling the unrest, this show of force sparked riots. A manoeuvre intended to display British force and persuade the Egyptians to accept informal British influence backfired, and the nationalist refusal to surrender forced Britain into military action. By September 1882 Egypt was under military occupation and became a part of the British Empire. Lord Cromer arrived in 1882 as the first consul general, and Egypt would remain under British influence until the 1950s.

The colonization of Egypt came at the start of a very busy period of British expansion in Africa. Often known as the 'scramble for Africa', the period from about 1885 until the end of the century was one in which colonial growth was predominantly, though never exclusively, centred on Africa. Africa had been an important site for colonial trade in the eighteenth century, though there were few British territories there. From the sixteenth century onwards there were trading stations along the west African coast, and in the nineteenth century some were placed under crown rule: Sierra Leone (whose port of Freetown was an important freshwater stop on many international shipping and trade routes) in 1808, The Gambia in 1816 and the Gold Coast in 1821.

Africa's colonial importance before the nineteenth century lay not in territorial possession but in its provision of a critical export: human slaves. In this respect Africa was at the heart of the Atlantic slave trade and crucial to many of Britain's other colonies as well as to the slave states of America. With the ban on slaving imposed by the British in 1807 relations shifted, and in the early nineteenth century Britain's presence on the west African coast took the form of naval anti-slave squadrons detailed to prevent slaving vessels from their work. It was as a base for anti-slaving squadrons that The Gambia became important in the 1820s. These squadrons were often ineffective, and their task was an arduous one for many involved in the trade saw no reason to abide by British injunctions to cease business. In the 1830s, when the institution of slavery was fully abolished in the British Empire, west African slave traders – who were not British subjects – received no compensation for their losses, unlike the West Indian planters who were British subjects. The loss of income must have been severe and not easily replaced. Trading interests in the westerly region of Africa slowly shifted to an interest in palm oil, which, before the mass export of petroleum oil, was of crucial importance in the lubrication of machinery as well as a major component in soap-making. Slavery was part of the rationale for the occupation of Lagos in 1861. It was an aggressive move designed to open up trade, to display British force to local rulers, to break up continued slaving and to prevent further French incursion in the area.

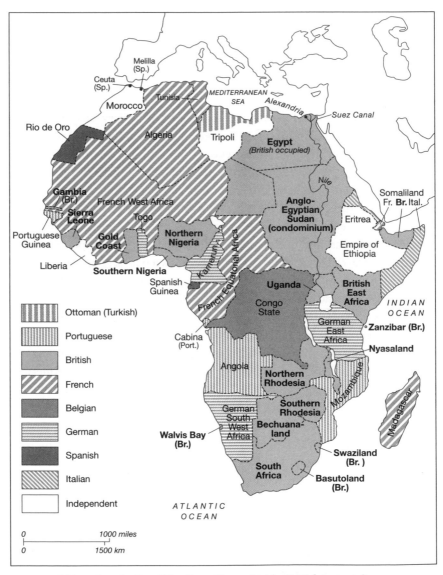

MAP 4 *Africa after the Boer War* (from Simon Smith, *British Imperialism 1750–1970*, (Cambridge: Cambridge University Press, 1988), p. 76. © Cambridge University Press, reproduced with permission of the author and publisher.)

These changes to an African profile dominated by something other than human slavery reoriented the colonial geography of interest in Africa to other parts of the continent and away from the Atlantic routes. The mid-century years saw a tremendous amount of African exploration by British adventurers: David Livingstone traversed the continent in 1853, John Hanning Speke reached Uganda in 1857. Southern Africa, meanwhile, attracted British interest early in the nineteenth century. The Cape area on the southern tip of the continent was a perfect stopping point for ships sailing between India and Britain, which made securing the Cape for British interests a priority. Annexation of land in the region began in earnest in the early 1840s. British Kaffraria was established in 1847 as a home for the Xhosa people, and incorporated into Cape Colony in 1866. The incentives in southern Africa were considerably intensified by the discovery of gold and diamonds. Diamonds were first found in the region in 1867; the discovery of gold in the Transvaal followed a few years later. Griqualand West was annexed in 1871 to ensure that the recently discovered diamond deposits there were British property. The prospect of the wealth that these precious finds would bring made southern Africa a newly important focus of British interest.

Yet even in this region of Africa, the typical method of colonization the British favoured was commercial, a strategy that in some ways returned them to an earlier era of colonization. For it was the chartered company that, in Africa especially, was responsible for much late nineteenth-century colonization. The state moved in with formal or semi-formal administrative arrangements only late in the proceedings, if at all. From the late 1880s, three new chartered companies – the Royal Niger Company in West Africa (1886), the British East Africa Company (1888) and the British South Africa Company (1889) – paved the way for imperial expansion in Africa, a method much cheaper for government than formal direct rule. The British North Borneo Company, a far smaller operation, had been established a little earlier, in 1881.

It was in some respects a curious practice for, other than a few major products, Africa offered a relatively scant array of exportable items. Ivory was as important as gold or diamonds in this period, and 85 per cent of the world's ivory came from Africa. In West Africa, the growth of the palm oil industry was important. But overall, Africa was a less economically profitable environment than many of the other areas coveted by the British. It attracted less British investment, except the gold and diamond industries of the south, than other areas of the empire, and throughout the colonial era remained considerably less developed than other regions.

In part, this was also because colonizers had to deal with both indigenous African powers, themselves interested in expansion and by no means always deferential to the British, and also with the spread of Islam in the region, a phenomenon that tended to produce resistance to European colonization. In the Sudan and Somaliland, in particular, Islamic rebellion reminded the British that their rivals were not solely among other European powers. The Mahdist jihad of the 1880s in the Sudan produced one of the great mythic tales of British expansion, the death of General Gordon at Khartoum in 1885. The Ethiopians were an expansionist force to be reckoned with in this region but elsewhere, too, the British found resistance and competition – from the Baganda in East Africa and the Ndebele in South Africa, for example. The attempts to avoid clashes with these powers was one reason why the policy of indirect rule, so eloquently enunciated by Frederick Lugard, was the chosen method for late nineteenth and early twentieth-century African colonialism.[7] Accommodation with local rulers and an insistence on retaining customary practice meant less likelihood of unrest, a built-in tendency to conservatism, and less need for a large, locally based British bureaucracy.

In this way, during the last 15 years or so of the nineteenth century, the British feverishly acquired territory all over Africa. The Niger Districts Protectorate was established in 1885, and the following year the chartering of the Royal Niger Company. In 1890, Britain concluded agreements with Germany and France to resolve disputes about ownership of African lands in Zanzibar, Tanganyika and the Niger region. The year 1891 was a busy one for colonization and diplomacy: there were treaties with the Italians, the Dutch and the Portuguese delineating territory in and near Africa, the Central African Protectorate was created, and Northern Zambesia was allocated to the British South Africa Company. The rest of the decade was one of intense growth and diplomacy in the region, and by the end of the 1890s tropical Africa had been divided fully between the major European powers, with scant regard for indigenous claims.

Resistance to the growth of British annexation and rule was by no means confined to powerful groups in Africa. Throughout the nineteenth century, and perhaps particularly in the mid-century years, the British presence was challenged in many areas. In a number of colonial regions instability or resistance was serious enough to provoke, as in India in 1857, a dramatic change in the colonial presence. The 1857 Mutiny, discussed in the previous chapter, may be the best known of the uprisings of the period, but it was by no means the only moment at which colonized peoples signalled their dissatisfaction with European dominance. Some ten years before, a rebellion in nearby Ceylon had been quelled by British troops. In the same year as the Indian rebellion there was a Chinese uprising in Sarawak, with another close on its heels in 1859. In Hong Kong, a Chinese plan to poison the local white residents by lacing their bread with arsenic caused a great deal of sickness. Riots destabilized much of the Malay archipelago in the 1850s and 1860s. The emergence of the Straits Settlements as a Crown Colony in 1867 was driven in part by the need to control serious unrest and violence in the area. The threat to British trade was likewise a factor in the 1874 treaty of Pangkor whereby protected Malay states agreed to allow British residencies. The Perak War of 1875 was prompted by the assassination of the British Resident there, and in a reaction to the assassination and subsequent riots Britain's quelling of the rebels allowed greater colonial influence in the region. The residencies plan focused on restoring order to the region by reducing dynastic conflict between local rulers, and between different ethnic Chinese groups. British suspicion that other European powers might have designs on the region also played a significant role. That the British were themselves involved in rivalries with other European powers also interested in the region was, despite its importance, seldom acknowledged as a similarly destabilizing factor.

Colonial wars abounded. Defeat in Afghanistan came in the same year for the British (1879) as defeat at the hands of the Zulus at Isandhlwana and major disputes with the Irish Land League. Across the Pacific, the Maori wars engulfed the new colony of New Zealand in the 1860s. A serious rebellion at Morant Bay in Jamaica in 1865 made headlines in Britain. Governor Eyre was vilified by some and acclaimed by others for his swift and brutal response to this uprising among former slaves. The press in Britain reported insurrections of this sort avidly, and in many cases, such as the Jamaica uprising, the events became something of a cause célèbre. Chapter 8 will consider the response of colonized peoples more closely, but here I want to suggest that the interest of the press in reporting colonial agitation hardly suggests a nation indifferent to colonialism, or shying away from expanding the boundaries of its formal rule. Though the theme of reluctance has been so frequently favoured by interpreters of nineteenth-century colonialism, the speed and scope of growth, the public interest in colonial conquest evinced by storybooks and exhibitions and by the formation of pro-imperial bodies such as the British Empire League and the Imperial Federation League, and the constant attentiveness of the press to colonial affairs, hint rather at a nation whose very identity was bound up with possessing, ruling and keeping hold of an empire of epic proportion.

The question remains as to what motivated Britain's massive augmentation in the nineteenth century of the Empire. Many factors played into the palpable growth of the British colonial world in this period. In some cases there were economic or strategic reasons for Britain's interest. Technology significantly altered the possibilities for rule and this, too, played a part. The re-emergence of serious rivalry with other European powers (a major eighteenth-century theme) as the latter caught up with Britain's industrial pre-eminence increasingly influenced the colonial power structure. In addition, of course, as an island, Britain had attended carefully and for a long time to its naval defences, a strategy that had given it unparalleled command of the world's oceans. Moreover, as the Empire grew, the need to defend existing territory often resulted in expansion to increase buffer zones or to provide ships with convenient safe harbours on long voyages. Britain's commitment to remaining in India, cemented in 1858 with direct rule, resulted in colonial growth elsewhere in the world. There were the coaling stations and ports for ships bound for India, there was the Suez Canal, and there was expansion on the ground in south Asia too, in response to what was then perceived as a Russian threat to what is now Pakistan. The borders of British India pushed further north in the nineteenth century, along with incursions into Afghanistan, in the name of defending India. The fear of Russia as a rival expansionist power had been growing since the defeat of Napoleon in 1815. Britain's support of the Ottoman Empire, as we have seen, was maintained in part because Russian interest in Ottoman territories threatened shipping routes to India. Britain's role in the Crimean War and in the Russo-Turkish war some 20 years later was premised on protecting India and routes to it. The build-up of the Russian military presence in central Asia in the 1860s and 1870s intensified fears in India, though the Russians never in fact got even as close as Afghanistan.

Towards the end of the century, rivalry between Britain and other European powers also began once more to intensify. Many of the gains on the African continent and in the Pacific were motivated by a perceived need to counter or to keep up with what other European colonists were doing. Belgium, Germany and France, in particular, vied for African lands, often quietly fomenting local discontent to weaken the territories of rival powers. Elsewhere, the substantial Dutch and French interests in south-east Asia influenced British decisions in the region, as did the growing imperial aspirations of Germany under Chancellor Bismarck. Germany in the years after its unification began actively colonizing not only in Africa but in south-east Asia and in the Pacific. It was fear of German predominance that led the British to support American colonization of the Philippines in 1898 and to annex – via Queensland – a large segment of New Guinea in 1884. The Berlin conference of 1884–5 underlined the colonial prominence of newly unified Germany. This meeting of the European colonial powers, the USA and Turkey to establish the principles of European colonial conquest in Africa was initiated by Bismarck and held on his territory. Fourteen nations met for 15 weeks, and ended by endorsing, without reference to indigenous desires or needs, free access for European powers to the African interior. The claim to territory had to be proven by what the conference chillingly called 'effective occupation'. Though the conference agreed in broad terms on the need to respect the welfare of local peoples, any claims they had to sovereignty were passed over, and they were represented instead as peoples in need of various forms of European protection. An extraordinary dismissal of the rights of colonized peoples, the conference also staked Germany's claim as a major European colonial power. The emergence of new rivals as well as the reassertion of old competition marked a new economic phase in both Europe and the colonies. Britain was no longer the dominant economy on the world stage, and indeed by the 1860s it was apparent that such predominance would not easily be regained. However, what Britain already had was a substantial and credible empire, and this, in the second half of the nineteenth century, was the basis of the country's continued claims to political authority.

Thus, although many of the new territories claimed by Britain in the later nineteenth century may have offered little practical benefit by way of valuable goods for export, the size and intensity of British imperialism gradually came to overtake economic supremacy in Britain's quest for continued political predominance. Certainly many of the colonies could and did provide Britain with valuable trade (and it was not always a mutually beneficial relationship, by any means). Australia, New Zealand, India, Southern Africa, Singapore, Hong Kong, and the sugar colonies of Fiji and Mauritius all created wealth for expatriate Britons and for the British nation, but many of the territories acquired later were never particularly profitable. Tropical colonies provided three major export groups: agricultural raw materials including rubber, palm oil, and cotton; foodstuffs (cocoa, coffee, tea and sugar were the principal ones) and minerals (petroleum oil, tin, copper, diamonds and gold). But in many of the newer colonies, production was slow or limited, distribution was difficult, and yields were unimpressive. Nonetheless, taken as whole, their presence on the British map added to the influence of the Empire, its prestige as the largest and most widespread among the European empires of the era.

Britain was, by the mid-1870s, enmeshed in a serious if unevenly distributed economic depression. Prohibitive tariffs imposed by other European nations (Germany from 1879, France from 1881, Italy from 1887, and the USA after 1890) undermined the principle of free trade, and it was becoming increasingly clear that Britain would never again dominate world trade and industry as it earlier had. Investment and interest shifted slowly towards the colonies, which provided less restrictive export and import markets. In theory, the colonies operated in a free trade environment, but in practice most were dominated by Britain as supplier and as buyer, and when free settler colonies began to seek trade agreements with other nations, as Canada did in the late nineteenth century, the British authorities were alarmed. The effect of British predominance in colonial economies was not always beneficial, however, for the system tended to focus production on a narrow range of commodities needed by the British and developed in response to British markets. This lack of diversity inevitably made colonial economies vulnerable to market shifts, a susceptibility exacerbated by the distinct lack of industry in most colonies, making them dependent on the UK for industrial products and machinery. It was not until Joseph Chamberlain headed the Colonial Office in 1895 that colonial development became an important item on the political agenda. Most of Chamberlain's schemes for development proved unfeasible, but his term of office made the issue more prominent with later administrations.

The new technologies of the period contributed considerably to the expansion of empire. It became quicker and easier to traverse the world as shipbuilding techniques improved along with innovations such as the Suez Canal. The advent of the telegraph in the 1860s made communications immediate in hitherto impossible ways. The railway cut through the interior of continents, allowing quick transport of goods to shipping ports, and goods could now be refrigerated during lengthy voyages, a process that brought meat and dairy products literally across the world from Argentina, Australia and New Zealand to the United Kingdom. New Zealand's first shipment of frozen lamb and mutton left Port Chalmers in February 1882. Troops, too, could be moved more easily as transport options multiplied, and new long-range rifles and machine guns increased their firepower. Yet as late as 1931, the Indian census showed less than 10 per cent of the country's population working in industrial occupations.

Although in the long term technological innovations cut prices, in the short term they were often costly, and while Britain wanted a large empire, it wanted it as cheaply as possible. The revival of the chartered companies and the use of new forms of governance such as Protectorates requiring less administration were strategies designed to minimize the Empire's cost to Britain. Year after year, budgetary discussions in parliament focused on the expense of colonialism, and this is another of the reasons that historians have seen the British as only reluctant conquerors. Even given the many penny-pinching tactics employed, the Empire was not cheap to run, for it necessitated a large body of troops and a smaller but still sizeable body of administrators in the colonies and in Britain. But the burden nonetheless lay disproportionately with those colonized rather than with the colonizers, for the principle, as we have seen, was always that the colonies, other than militarily, should be self-financing. In most colonies outside the white settler arenas, little substantive economic development occurred under colonial rule, and in many places the encouragement to produce goods for the British market helped the British more than it did the producers. The export back to India of cheap finished cotton goods hurt the indigenous textile trade, for example, and in Africa and Malaya products valuable for the growth of British industry were exported in huge quantities, but there were few attempts to locate those industries more locally.

A good example of this inequality at work can be seen in the development of the railway in India. Private investors in Britain, who were offered a return of 4.5 per cent to 5 per cent on their investment, grew wealthy as the railways expanded in India, but little of the wealth produced stayed in India. Even the equipment and the stock used were more likely to have been exported from Britain and Europe than produced locally. For all this, the railways were nonetheless a huge success, not only in facilitating more effective colonial rule but in their widespread use by local peoples as well. Indians took to the new form of transport enthusiastically.

White settler countries, by contrast, actively encouraged industrialization, especially those outside Africa. Though these colonies were encouraged to cater to British markets and needed that trade for their own economic well-being, they experienced industrial and economic development on a scale utterly unknown in the dependent non-migrant colonies. Here, in lands more and more peopled by an influx of British and European whites during the course of the century, we can see the development of all the trappings of nineteenth-century industrial capitalism, opening ever wider the gulf between colonies of settlement and dependent colonies, as well as between settlers and increasingly marginalized indigenous peoples in the settler lands.

The effects of colonization were, then, as varied and diverse as the forms of colonialism that took root in this period. More often than not in the nineteenth century the experience of colonization was deeply affected by race, as much in settler as in other colonies. Whereas white migrants intent on making a new life in places such as New Zealand or in Canada might feel they had a stake in this new land, indigenous peoples mostly experienced colonization as upheaval. Land use and ownership, occupational prospects, laws and customs, language and culture were all changed by the white colonial presence. This was as much the lot of Aboriginal Canadians and Australians, New Zealand Maori and many Southern African peoples as it was of those in non-settler environments. In both instances, for example, the zeal for social reform already so fashionable in Britain was imported to address the alleged savageries of local culture. Alongside reforming politicians, scores of lobbyists demanded reform in a wide range of activities from customs regarding dress to the treatment of newborn children, from sexual mores to religious rituals. Missionaries, feminists, humanitarians, doctors, teachers and a host of others called on colonial governments to end what they saw as barbaric practices and to encourage Christian and western behaviours. This was the 'civilizational' model of imperialism, the common and popular argument that allegedly backward peoples were well served by good colonial administration that would educate and Christianize them, help them curb disease and poverty (neither of which the British were showing much sign of controlling at home), and fit them for a place in the afterlife. These were powerful and deeply felt arguments and many people genuinely believed in the good they felt colonial rule could do in improving 'backward' and difficult lives.

The nineteenth century, then, was a time of tremendous change, expansion and experimentation in colonial terms. The land mass of the Empire was massively augmented, the range of export and import goods considerably broadened, and the types of rule employed hugely expanded. British imperial interests were not confined to a particular region, though certainly later in the century Africa and the islands of the Pacific were actively colonized and at a quickened pace. The entire century was a period of major global expansion in which the British Empire guaranteed Britain a prominent role in world politics and trade out of all proportion to an island of Britain's size, commodities and production. In the nineteenth century, and despite fears over cost and complex negotiations, a British future without the Empire was an impossible notion.

FIGURE 7 *Thomas Onwhyn,* Mr and Mrs John Brown's Visit to London to see the Great Exposition of All Nations, *1851* (The British Library)

References

1   J. R. Seeley, *The Expansion of England* (London: Macmillan, 1883), p. 8.

2   See, for example, Bernard Porter, *The Lion's Share. A Short History of British Imperialism, 1850–1995* (Harlow, Essex: Longman, 1996), pp. 11–12, 28–29.

3   Peter J. Durrans, 'The House of Commons and the British Empire 1868–1880', *Canadian Journal of History,* 9, no. 1 (1974), pp. 19–44; Ronald Hyam, *Britain's Imperial Century, 1815–1914. A Study of Empire and Expansion* (Basingstoke: Macmillan, 1993, 2nd edn), p. 116; Timothy Parsons, *The British Imperial Century, 1815–1914. A World History Perspective* (Lanham, Md.: Rowman & Littlefield, 1999), p. 15. In their *Colonialism and Development. Britain and its Tropical Colonies, 1850–1960*

(London: Routledge, 1993) Michael Havinden and David Meredith see such reluctance as a 'passing phase' (p. 24).

4   Ronald Robinson and John Gallagher, 'The Imperialism of Free Trade', *Economic History Review*, 2nd series, 6, no. 1 (1953), pp. 1–15.

5   Christopher Bayly, 'The British and Indigenous Peoples, 1760–1860', in Martin Daunton and Rick Halpern (eds), *Empire and Others: British Encounters with Indigenous Peoples, 1660–1850* (Philadelphia: University of Pennsylvania Press, 1999), p. 37.

6   W. H. Mercer, *A Handbook of the British Colonial Empire* (London: Waterlow & Sons, 1906), p. 2. Mercer was a career civil servant in the Colonial Office.

7   Frederick Lugard (1858–1945) was a soldier turned politician whose lengthy career in Africa was divided mostly between Uganda and Nigeria. His many years in India (where he was born and lived as a child, returning in the late 1870s as an army officer) clearly influenced his philosophy of indirect rule.

CHAPTER 7

Ruling an empire

Ruling a colony was serious business, and though, as we have seen, it has sometimes been fashionable to represent the British Empire as something inadvertently acquired, neither accident nor serendipity could get the job done once a territory became British. Consider the scope of the enterprise: by the start of the twentieth century, Britain administered 47 territories, of which a mere 12 were self-governing. As already noted, the population in this vast swathe of land numbered some 400 million, and the range of languages, religions and cultures was huge. Maintaining order in such a diverse array of regions and among such different peoples required something more than merely muddling along.

There were key moments, mainly crises of rebellion, when British administrations needed to stop and take stock, to consider with all possible seriousness what empire was and what it was not. And, of course, the answer to such questions did not remain the same over time, for imperial rule and attitudes changed with the times, moving in tandem with other cultural and political developments. In the 1780s, the loss of America, a major turning point for the Empire's future even if mainly in psychological terms, led Britain to explore more fully other regions of the world, while in the mid-nineteenth century the Jamaican and Indian uprisings took Britain's leaders in a different direction, imposing more direct and autocratic forms of rule in some regions. Many factors – economic, racial, cultural, strategic – help explain these varied tactics and responses: this chapter will explore those factors in the context of the lives, experiences and attitudes of those charged, whether in Britain or stationed in the Empire, with ruling a colony.

Many Britons firmly believed that imperial supremacy was the national destiny, a sentiment that certainly in both the nineteenth and the twentieth centuries peppered the public utterances of politicians, the writings of

PAPAGALLO, N°50   ALLEGORIA SULL'IMPERO INGLESE   Anno. VI.

OMBRE Progresso e civiltà rigirano il mondo. Molti credono l'Inghilterra una piccola isola, e ben vediamo che è un serpentone.

FIGURE 8 *Allegory of the British Empire strangling the world, 1878. Not everyone shared the view that British Colonialism was necessarily a good thing.* (Bibliothèque Nationale, Paris, France/Archives Charmet/The Bridgeman Art Library)

historians and journalists, and the teaching of British schoolchildren. This patriotic reading of expansion and colonization saw British law and govern-ance as the finest and noblest expression of humanity. Britons were kinder and more just as colonists, according to this view, and their colonial power was used to benefit the colonized. Englishmen, claimed a school textbook from the start of the twentieth century, 'are especially fitted by nature' to be colonists because they are 'persevering, unflinching . . . patriotic . . . [and] love order and justice'.[1] According to Sir Lepel Griffin, an experienced and long-term Indian civil servant, the 'secrets of govern-ment . . . in the modern world' belonged 'to the Anglo-Saxon race alone'.[2]

Fiction for children and for adults was saturated with this point of view from the later nineteenth century. Much of the impetus behind the new scouting movement established by Robert Baden-Powell in 1908 derived from this imperially suffused patriotism. It was a powerful rallying call that often worked well for politicians. Yet it was by no means the only or always the dominant attitude within Britain and among the British. As Britain's economic and political dominance came to be challenged in the mid-nineteenth century by new industrial and imperial competitors, many saw the Empire as a means of political and economic survival rather than

a blessing for the less fortunate. In 1906, Viscount Milner, one of the leading pro-imperialists in Britain, told the Manchester Conservative Club
that if Britain did not remain 'a great Power . . . she will become a poor
country'. Britain was too small to compete alone but 'Greater Britain may
remain such a Power . . . for ever', guaranteeing future prosperity.[3] His
colleague, Cecil Rhodes, thought civil war likely if settler colonialism were
not there to absorb population and to buy British goods.

This was clearly more a pragmatic than a moral stance, less concerned
with Britain's duties than with its political and economic success. It shared,
nonetheless, with the promoters of progress a strong belief that those colonized by the British were weaker and inferior. Whereas the moralists saw
it as a duty of imperialism to take civilization to lesser peoples, those more
concerned with British survival in a competitive arena saw the failure of

Diagram showing the time at various places in the Empire
"on which the sun never sets."

FIGURE 9 *The Sun Never Sets: the idea that the Empire was so huge that
somewhere in it the sun was always high, was a common image. Unusual here
is that New Zealand and not Britain is at the centre.*

63 'The sun never sets', Craven Mixture Tobacco advertisement, *Punch*, 22 July 1931

FIGURE 10 *Craven Mixture Tobacco advertisement, 'The Sun never sets', 1931. The same motif of the never-setting sun, here put to commercial use.* (Punch Photo Library)

those they colonized to use their resources productively as the principal justification for empire. Both camps of colonial boosterism, then, saw the colonized as lacking intelligence, social organization and, of course, civilization.

The distinction between those who ruled and those who were ruled took many different forms within the Empire, as we have already seen in tracing the contrasts between forms of governance in settler colonies and in the various types of dependencies. These differences, however, became much more visible in the nineteenth century as the Empire expanded and as the non-settler colony became more typical of British imperialism. In much of the world in the eighteenth century, settler and non-settler colonists alike lived in closer contact with indigenous populations, and in many instances were dependent upon them. In India, Mogul rule dominated much of the area where Britain's growing commercial interest lay, and throughout the eighteenth century the British often needed permission to trade, to live and to build there. In the American colonies, relations with Native Americans were far more central than they would become later when indigenous peoples were pushed to the margins. The early settlers traded with, bargained with, and learned from local peoples, and often had no choice but to accommodate local needs. Gradually, as British power and wealth spread across the globe, compromise and negotiation became less common than conquest and autocratic rule, and increasingly the alleged savagery and lack of civilization of other cultures became a major justification for this slow but palpable change of overall policy. Even in those areas where Britain's imperial influence was informal, in Latin America, for example, a strong sense of British superiority was discernible. This hierarchical self-confidence was typical of the western and Christian world, and was clearly buttressed by Britain's constant and mostly successful colonial expansion.

At the same time this pride in British worth was also invariably undercut by anxiety. Would the Briton abroad 'go native' and be tempted to behave in un-British ways that would undermine British rule? Would the effects of 'lesser' cultures corrupt Britain at its centre? These were fears that beset Britain's ruling class throughout the years of imperial rule. In the eighteenth century, West Indian planters and returning East India Company employees (the so-called 'nabobs') were often regarded with mistrust and satirized in print and in cartoon for their distance from 'proper' English behaviours and their fondness for 'native' customs. In the nineteenth and twentieth centuries, colonial governments as well as the central imperial government moved to limit marriages between local women and colonizing men in an effort to keep colonizer and colonized separate. Assimilation at the height of Britain's imperial power was very much a one-way street. It was colonized peoples who were expected to conform to British behaviours and values: movement in the other direction was considered contamination, not assimilation.

Imperial anxiety was not limited, however, to the fear of contagion or pollution. The immense sense of difference and alienness experienced by Britons living abroad in other cultures is something many memoirs of imperial service mention. Sir John Strachey, who spent his career in India, wrote in 1903 that the colonial official 'has to wage constant warfare against strange barbarisms, horrid customs and cruel superstitions, ancient survivals, ready, at any moment to start into activity'.[4] Because of this sense of strangeness and incomprehension, there was too an undercurrent of uncertainty about whether and, sometimes, when those being ruled might refuse to submit. The fear of rebellion and resistance was no fantasy; violence underpinned imperial might but worked in both directions. Slave rebellions, wars, mutinies and riots litter the history of the Empire. Even in settler colonies, imperialism could be fraught with uncertainties. Frontier societies (such as those in Canada, South Africa and Australia) proved hard to domesticate into a British image of respectability. Men striking out to tap gold deposits or to work in mining and logging had little interest in, or opportunity for, a settled, demure lifestyle that empha-sized religious duty, marriage and family. The existence of disorderly white communities in outback territories made the claims of empire as a civilizing mission fragile.

Migration, so important to British colonialism, fed many of these fears, as more and more Britons moved to imperial locations, permanently as settlers or temporarily in colonial employment. Whereas the eighteenth century saw a vast number of people moved within the Empire by force as slaves, the nineteenth century was characterized by voluntary migration, although the many indentured labourers who criss-crossed the Empire after the end of slavery often made constrained choices and, in some instances, were the victims of kidnapping (see Chapter 8). Likewise, a large percentage of free migrants were prompted by poverty at home, though they journeyed freely enough to new lands. Almost 23 million people left Britain between 1815 and 1914, and although the United States absorbed the greater proportion (62 per cent), until around 1870 the Canadian colonies were the most popular destination. Those headed for the Empire went mostly to white settler lands, attracted in large part by the prospect of owning land. In the twentieth century settler options expanded as large tracts of Southern and East Africa, notably in Rhodesia and Kenya, were given over to white migrants. In Kenya, there were two principal classes of migrant, poorer whites from South Africa, and an upper class, about 3,000 strong by 1905, who came out from Britain. The less affluent were given parcels of cheap land, around 1,000 acres each, while the wealthy settled on vast estates in the highlands of central Kenya where their lifestyle became legendary for its decadence. By the mid-twentieth century changes were afoot, and many of the white migrants moving to Africa and other colonies were skilled workers and profes-sionals rather than poorer, unpropertied folk looking to start anew.

Outside the settler lands, British populations in the colonies tended to be small and often quite scattered. Colonial Office staff posted abroad numbered around 6,000. The Colonial Office had one of the smallest staffs among major government departments. With numbers on the ground so thin, there was a good deal of room for improvisation, especially in minor matters that might not attract attention in London. In Africa imperial rule was for the most part a loose and highly decentralized business, depending very heavily on a very localized prefectural administration. The two largest groups of Britons in the non-settler colonies were almost always civil servants and troops. There was also invariably a smattering of medical workers, teachers, missionaries and business people. In the early years of colonialism, men had been prohibited or severely discouraged from bringing their families to live in the Empire; in India, for example, for most of the eighteenth century, the male to female ratio would easily have approached 50:1. By the mid-nineteenth century, changing attitudes meant that wives more frequently accompanied husbands appointed to colonial positions. Children often spent the first few years of their lives in the family home, but anyone who could afford the expense had their children educated in Britain from quite a young age.

Children were sent back to Britain for a host of reasons: to ensure they were schooled in the British way and to root out any local culture they may have picked up, but also because in many colonial environments they were vulnerable to diseases unknown or uncommon in the British Isles. Neither the cities nor the countryside of Britain were free of disease in the eighteenth and nineteenth centuries, and epidemics of many dangerous illnesses coursed through the country well into the twentieth century. There was, however, a deep fear that tropical colonies were unhealthy environments for whites, where they would be susceptible to fevers and melancholy, to lassitude and sickness. In places such as northern Australia and the West Indies, fears that manual labour for whites would prove physically impossible prompted the use first of slaves and later of indentured labourers. In the eighteenth century, parts of Africa were known as the 'white man's grave' since mortality rates among Europeans were so high. This vulnerability was not, of course, limited to colonists, as earlier chapters have shown, but the devastation wreaked on local populations was often deemed a regrettable part of bringing civilization to savage lands, whereas white mortality was a danger to be guarded against. Colonial medical practice, not surprisingly, was concerned more with protecting white colonial populations than with the health needs of those they colonized. It would be inaccurate to suggest, however, that indigenous peoples were clamouring for western health care – on the contrary, they were often suspicious and even resentful of it. Still, the discrepancy between access to medical care of colonist and colonized was always substantial, and is certainly suggestive of the relative value in which their lives were held under imperialism.

The inequalities so typical of colonial health care are just one example of the gap that divided the colonist and the colonized in imperial settings. Life for colonists was often an uneven mix of the domestic and the foreign, more especially in places where groups of colonists gathered. A civil servant or plantation overseer posted to a remote location might be the sole Briton for miles, but most colonists lived in or close to towns and cities where racially exclusive neighbourhoods sprang up to service them. The distance between colonist and colonials was both spatial and social in most cases. Whites lived in enclaves where their social life revolved around a racially exclusive club, a Christian church, and a set of neighbours of mostly similar background, experience and attitude. Such neighbourhoods were less crowded than those where indigenous populations lived, and the architecture was often intended to evoke Britain, adjusted for the local climate but distinct from the usual building styles of the region. To this day one can visit typically Victorian churches in the cities of India, and grandly appointed hotels and official buildings in a European style in many former colonies.

Frontier conditions for white settlers were considerably less comfortable. In British Columbia in the Canadian north-west, labourers lived in basic conditions in logging and mining camps. Less well-to-do settlers in Rhodesia and Kenya often lived isolated and harsh existences on rural farmsteads, though they would have employed black servants and farmhands from among the local population. Class played an important role in the colonies as it did in Britain itself, and working-class colonists (loggers in Canada, soldiers and sailors in Asia, farmhands in New Zealand, to name just a few) were separated from the wealthy whites of the colonies as firmly as were the locals. There was some slippage in the middle ranks, and those of humble background could sometimes rise further in a colonial than a British setting. Yet colonial white society was almost always governed by rigid social hierarchies even after some of these social barriers had begun to be relaxed in Britain. The humbler commercially employed whites in India, sneeringly known as 'box-wallahs' by those above them in rank and station, were as fully removed from the higher rungs of the colonial social world as were the Indians.

Though local labour was cheap and plentiful for white colonists in most locations, the social hierarchies of colonial life often increased expenses considerably. Many of those who went to the colonies did not

FIGURE 11 *Bovril advertisement, 1902* (Illustrated London News)

possess a private income, and colonial pay was seldom generous. Doctors in the colonial medical service, for example, were very jealous of their right to engage in fee-paying private practice alongside their government duties. On occasions when that right was under threat, they pointed to the low pay of their official positions. In government service, promotion could be slow and often depended upon a death or retirement to free up a position. Since men were expected to provide for wives and children as well as to keep a retinue of household servants, keeping up appearances could severely tax a family's income, and many juggled constant debt in their effort to lead a 'proper' colonial life. In the earlier years of the Empire this acted as a discouragement to marriage. Goods imported from Britain, which remained always fashionable among and sought-after by colonials, were costly but socially necessary expenses for middle-class colonists.

That it was men who governed the Empire is a well-established fact, but how did they do it? Few colonies supported a large contingent of British troops. Even in post-Mutiny India, the sheer size of the Indian soldiery, and indeed the Indian population of British India, could without much trouble have rebelled successfully. Some have argued that because the British governed in a less violent fashion than their European rivals, they had the consent of local populations for their presence.[5] This benign picture of a kindly Empire is hard to sustain, however. Britain had no compunction about resorting to violence when necessary, and violence in the Empire took a bewildering variety of forms. In the first half of the twentieth century, for example, a significant weapon of colonial governments against political dissidents was incarceration. In India, in Africa and elsewhere, nationalists were in and out of jail, locked up for delivering rousing anti-colonial speeches or for urging disobedience against the government. Courts of law frequently meted out light sentences for whites convicted of violence against local peoples, whereas harsh punishment awaited the non-white offender convicted of violence against a colonist. In India in 1883, huge controversy was precipitated by the introduction of the Ilbert Bill, a law that would have permitted Indian judges jurisdiction over British subjects in criminal cases. The uproar from whites living in India was such that considerable modifications were made to the law before it could be passed; the provisions of the original law were much watered down by a new clause that permitted whites to demand a trial by jury in which at least half the jurors were either British or American.

Overt violence was not uncommon either. Colonial governments were seldom shy about sending military detachments to persuade obstinate and

FIGURE 12 *Thomas Joshua Alldridge (1874–1916), a district commissioner in Sierra Leone, in the 1890s. Alldridge's sense of authority and superiority comes through vividly in this picture.* (Royal Commonwealth Society. Photo Collection by permission of the Syndics of Cambridge University Library)

nominally independent rulers to back down on issues deemed critical by the British. As we shall see in Chapter 11, British authorities were reluctant to use their armed forces against white insurgents in the tumultuous years of decolonization, but much less fussy about deploying troops and police in non-white arenas. Violence, in short, though not always visible, was nonetheless a key feature of ruling a colony.

Yet there was far more to the success of the Empire than the gun and the sword, or even the navy frigate. The age of empire was also an age of collecting and of classifying, an age in which the very boundaries of knowledge seemed almost limitless, and the Empire played a substantial role in the intellectual confidence that bolstered these typically western views. Britain in the eighteenth and nineteenth centuries became an avid exponent, as did Europe more generally, of what we might call the knowledge trade. Changes in western scientific practice led to a new emphasis – in botany, in anatomy, in geography – on classification and ordering. As we have seen, eighteenth-century expeditions always included scientists who were there to collect data and specimens. For many colonists the lands and the peoples of the Empire were also specimens to be listed, categorized

FIGURE 13 *Execution at Kowloon, 1891: photographs such as this were intended to drive home the 'natural' cruelty of the Chinese towards one another* (Getty Research Institute/Los Angeles, California (91.R.5))

and labelled. Just as the poor in Britain became objects of official scrutiny in the age of reform early in the nineteenth century, colonies and colonial subjects were counted, described, given classifications. Some were seen as warrior-like, others as passive. Some were regarded as cruel, and others indolent. All, of course, were regarded as inferior to the British colonizers.

By the late eighteenth century, western opinion took seriously a quasi-scientific hierarchy that argued for a racial ladder of development that placed white northern Europeans at the pinnacle of reason and progress. Ideas about the developmental difference between blacks and whites found an especially fertile medium of culture in the self-congratulatory and dominantly Christian environment of Victorian Britain, a place well convinced of its moral and political superiority over not just its own colonized peoples but over its local European rivals as well. Newly developing disciplines such as anthropology and sciences like physiology emphasized racial difference rather than similarity, and it was a simple step from marking difference to equating it with moral development. Even in books aimed at British children, this difference was underlined. Agnes Baden-Powell, sister to Robert of Boy Scout fame, informed her young audience in 1912 that in Britain's 'magnificent Empire . . . The territories are there, but the people are only coming'.[6]

Opinions about the effects of western education and western rule on colonial people went back and forth over time, and different interest groups clearly had markedly different stakes in this debate. In the North American colonies, many people of European origin feared that Native Americans were degraded by exposure to whites, picking up only their bad habits and eschewing their better values. Their counsel was to isolate Amerindians from contact with the west in order to preserve their 'noble savagery'. In the early 1830s, as mentioned in Chapter 5, Thomas Macaulay made a now-famous and impassioned plea – which nonetheless attracted a good deal of scepticism – for educating elite Indians in English ways in order to produce brown-skinned replicas of the 'superior' English through proper education. Evangelicals fervently believed in the civilizing propensities of Christianization, while others thought the changes brought about by empire and proselytizing could never be more than superficial. These debates were, of course, the flip side of the concerns about the colonist corrupted by exposure to lesser societies. Here, the terms of the thinking were all about measuring how far towards a western norm the colonized could be brought, and out of these concerns grew the new social sciences of anthropology and sociology, firmly rooted in the assumptions of imperialism.

FIGURE 14 *'A Group of Hausa', 1901: a typical photograph taken by an anthropologist at the turn of the century. The one white figure stands out against a seemingly impersonal mass of Africans.*

Both in Britain and in the colonies there were groups who saw a troubling gap between these rather fervent expositions of the moral good of empire and actual practice. The Aborigines' Protection Society (APS), founded in London in 1836, constantly lamented the degradations visited upon aboriginal peoples by British colonists. They too saw the colonized as weaker and inferior, and it was in imperialism's failure to protect the weak that their protests against colonialism lay. The APS held that 'in proportion to their inherent feebleness is the strength of their claim to the paternal care of the Government'.[7] It was the action of those living in the colonies that, they argued, required control. Humanitarians mostly failed in their efforts to control the course of colonization, but their voices form nonetheless an important part of the landscape of imperialism.

In reality, all such concerns were as much class-specific as they were palpably racial. The larger mass of the people, whether in Egypt or Singapore, India or the West Indies, were faceless and, in this reckoning, irrelevant or irredeemable. It was the elites within colonial societies to whom colonizers turned much of their attention, and who they worked hard both to control and to accommodate. Lord Lugard's policy of indirect rule in early twentieth-century Africa looked to tribal chiefs to maintain stability and keep the colonial state ticking. In British India the landowning classes had been steadily strengthened since the days of the East India Company as a bulwark against rebellion. The rulers of independent states in India were carefully monitored by British officials. The Chinese merchant class in Hong Kong and in the Malay peninsula were accorded a limited measure of participation in local government to ensure their loyalty to the British state. When they did as they were told, all remained pleasant; if they took on their colonial masters, they were liable to lose the tenuous privileges they had.

Technology, as Chapter 6 has argued, was another growth area vital to Britain's conduct of the Empire, for new and deadly weaponry such as the Gatling gun were hard to counter. Technology was not limited, however, to military purposes; it was a hugely important factor in many ways in the ruling of colonies. The development of extensive railway systems allowed the swift movement of goods as well as of soldiers, and while the impetus for building the rail networks was as much military as it was economic, as a passenger and goods service it changed the face of the Empire profoundly. In India, some 24,000 miles of track had been laid by the end of the nineteenth century, in British East Africa almost 600 miles of track. The huge Trans-Pacific Canadian railway was completed in 1885.

Neither can the development of telegraphy be underestimated as a factor in colonial success. Wars against the Ashanti in Africa (1873–4) and the Malays at Perak in 1875 were directed in large part by telegraph. By the 1870s, the telegraph had become the standard mode of communication between the Colonial and India Offices in London and far-away governors; secret codes were developed for transmitting sensitive materials, and quicker decisions than had previously been possible became standard. Throughout the Empire, the application and introduction of western technology was always a piecemeal affair, designed more to serve the colonial state than those it colonized, despite the persistent rhetoric of munificence. Recall, for example, how eighteenth-century sugar production (as we saw in Chapter 3) was strictly divided between the West Indies and Britain, the bulk of the refinement done after shipping to the United Kingdom. The colonies were restricted, in this case by mercantilist considerations, as to what they could undertake without British consent. The same was true in the Indian textile trade, for the British state would not countenance serious colonial competition with the fragile but important textile industries in Britain. The needs of the colonized remained in all such instances subservient to those of Britain, at the centre of the Empire.

Science, technology and medicine were routinely depicted as the beneficent bringers of modernity and prosperity to the colonies. Furthermore,
they were also always seen as above the fray of politics, as neutral ideals
with invariably positive results. In 1924, at the newly built Wembley
Stadium in north-west London, a huge British Empire Exhibition celebrated the enterprise of empire. A two-roomed 'pure science' display at
the exhibition boasted of the benefits that western science and medicine
brought to Britain's Empire. The various items on display illustrated
how medical and scientific knowledge was changing the face of colonies,
making them healthier and more productive environments. The political
message was not hard to read in this celebration of a technology-driven
western model of development.

Policing was another arena where colonial resentment could be strong,
and here colonial practice departed significantly from the domestic.
Police forces in the colonies were far more military in character than those
that operated in England, Scotland and Wales. Not insignificantly, colonial policing was often modelled on the Royal Irish Constabulary, a body
created specifically to quell nationalist unrest in Ireland. Unlike British
constables, colonial police officers carried guns and were organized into
military garrisons. There were two kinds of colonial police: a higher
paid, more senior white rank and a 'native' force consigned to lesser or
sometimes more brutal tasks. In many colonies beyond the white settler
domains, it became standard practice by the mid-nineteenth century to
import police from other parts of the Empire. In Hong Kong, in Singapore
and in Perak, Sikhs from British India were commonly employed as police
officers. Barbadians were brought into the Trinidadian police force. As
outsiders to the community they policed, they were thought to be more
intimidating to the local population and less corruptible. In times of crisis
the colonial police forces, with their quasi-military background, were
liable to be called upon as part of the defence services alongside the full
military. This was common in India and during the Kenyan Emergency in
the 1950s as well as in the treaty port of Shanghai during the 1930s.

The colonial military, like colonial police forces, was frequently divided
along racial lines. Senior military ranks were reserved for whites, although
the larger proportion of white military men in the colonies were working-
class men. A spate of substantial British military reforms in the 1870s
allowed men to sign up for shorter periods of service, making military
service a more practical and attractive option. In a colonial posting, a
working-class recruit from Britain was amazed to find himself no longer at
the bottom of the social pecking order. Still subject to military discipline,

he could nonetheless lord it over native men who did his bidding. He might also feel quite wealthy for he was likely stationed somewhere where even the meagre pay of the soldier went a long way.

The soldier and the sailor were regarded by many as the ultimate line of defence, the bulwark against colonial insurrection. Year after year, when the military budget was debated in the British parliament, this was the rationale offered to those who protested against the high cost of defence. In 1867, the Indian commander-in-chief, W. R. Mansfield, described the British troops in India as the Empire's 'bullion deposit', vital for security and continued colonization.[8]

The soldier, at least, was in the field, unlike the staff of the Colonial Office, about whom there was often a great deal of resentment. Those living in the colonies regarded as unwarranted and certainly unwanted any interference from the imperial centre. It was common for colonists to argue that London officials could not properly appreciate local conditions and that they should therefore cede decision-making to those who lived and worked in the colonies. Colonists argued that officials stationed in Britain could not begin to understand the manners of the Chinese or the Fijians or the Nigerians as well as they, the colonists, could from years of observation and interaction. The Colonial Office returned the compliment, frequently scornful of the work done by colonial officials. After a series of reforms in the 1850s and 1870s, jobs in the British civil service were highly competitive and based in large part on examination scores; the colonial service, however, selected its recruits on a much more informal basis, often based on family ties or personal connections as the civil service had done prior to the reforms of the 1850s. Clearly, those in the colonies and those in Whitehall saw expertise and qualification for the job in profoundly different ways. The brief tenures of most colonial governors and colonial secretaries – the most senior of the Colonial Office positions – fuelled all of these mutual suspicions. It was rare for a Secretary of State for the Colonies to serve more than a two-year term, and colonial governors seldom stayed more than six years in any one colony, although they often moved from colony to colony in the course of their careers. During Joseph Chamberlain's unusually long tenure as Colonial Secretary (1895–1903), selected Colonial Office staff were seconded to a colonial setting for a year to learn at first hand about the colony and about the conditions of work there. Officials from the colonies were simultaneously sent to London to fill the positions left vacant. The principle was that each would learn to appreciate the other's work and responsibilities. Despite Chamberlain's best efforts, however, the constant tension, not only between those with local experience and those without, but between the potential for continuity and the need to respond to changing politics in Westminster, made imperial governance a sometimes unwieldy and unpredictable business. Although there were over-arching rhetorics (and sometimes even principles), much imperial rule as it was imposed was of a pragmatic and immediately responsive turn. Writing in 1906, Sir Augustus Hemming recounted the tale of his asking permission to make an official visit to the Gold Coast while he was head of the West African department of the Colonial Office. The request, he recalls, was 'refused on the ground that there appeared to be no necessity for the visit'.[9]

A substantial and important group of Britons living and working in the Empire was the missionary contingent; by the end of the nineteenth century there were around 10,000 British missionaries dotted across the globe. It was in the late eighteenth century that British missionary work in the Empire really began to grow. Each of the major Christian denominations in Britain founded missionary societies in the 1790s. The missionary enterprise was, however, neither exclusively nor originally aimed at the colonial poor. In the early North American colonies, missions worked largely among the settler populations. It was in his missionary work in colonial Georgia in the 1730s that John Wesley garnered the ideas that would lead to one of the world's most successful branches of Christianity, Methodism. In British Canada, missionaries were mostly concerned with the wanton behaviour of the miners, prospectors, loggers and trappers who had emigrated from Britain and who lived – and drank – hard in frontier communities. However, even when attending to colonial populations, missionary work began with the never successful intent of converting ruling groups, and not the lowly. The emphasis on non-settler colonies thus came quite late in missionary history, burgeoning at the end of the eighteenth century.

In these early years, colonial officials in both London and the colonies were often suspicious of the missionaries, who had to fight for permission to work in the colonies. They often faced suspicion and resentment not only from those they sought to convert, but also from colonial officials, for the missionaries were frequently critical of colonial practice and expert at making public their often unflattering opinions of colonial governments. Missionaries had been in the forefront of anti-slavery protests and were seldom reluctant to criticize what they saw as colonial exploitation of indigenous peoples. In the nineteenth century, missionaries spread across the colonial globe and could be found in the West Indies and the Pacific, in Africa and in India, in south-east Asia and the Chinese treaty ports, and

FIGURE 15 *A missionary's wife and child seated on a hippopotamus, c. 1910–20*
(School of Oriental and African Studies/Council for World Mission/London
Missionary Society)

in North America. Over time, governments and missionaries came closer
together, but missionaries nonetheless often had a quite complex role in
the colonial world, promoting western values through conversion but
often vocally critical of imperial policy and practice. In the case of particularly active critics among the missionaries, colonial governments shared
information about their whereabouts, travel and activities so as to minimize
any political damage to government that might ensue from their work.

Missionaries, perhaps more than any other class of colonizers, lived
and worked among local peoples, building schools and hospitals and
shelters, all designed to bring the gospel of Christianity to Britain's
colonial subjects. Yet despite their distance from the state, and despite
the disapproval and hostility they often experienced from the colonial
bureaucracy, missionaries were nonetheless a part of imperial conquest
for they mostly saw the populations among whom they worked as children in need of saving from their own ignorance and moral poverty. This
is not to suggest that missionaries could not make a material difference
to the lives of their charges. They were often the only conduit for western

health care and for education in remote areas, and mission schools certainly improved literacy rates in many places. But the price was steep in some ways, for embracing Christianity to the full meant adopting a new way of life. Converts were often given 'Christian' names, a practice that emphasized their social and cultural distance from the non-converted. They were often unable to maintain close links with their families and communities, and missionary disapproval of local customs often stood in the way of converts making good marriages or partnerships within the local contexts in which they lived. It was not imperialism as a philosophy that missionaries criticized; their disapproval was reserved for imperial politics that to them did nothing to consolidate and extend Christianity into non-Christian environments.

The missionary success rate overall was low. Only small numbers converted, and many of them did not sustain the change in the long term, not least because missionary practice, despite a rhetoric of equality, could be rigid, hierarchical and unforgiving. Equality remained more a theological principle in the missionary world than a social practice. As we shall see in the next chapter, there was also a very significant trend among converts in adapting Christianity to a variety of colonial customs and traditions, an un-expected and, to the missionaries, mostly unwelcome outgrowth of their efforts.

Unflattering portraits of missionaries dot the pages of Victorian novels: the unbending St John Rivers in Charlotte Bronte's *Jane Eyre* or Charles Dickens's redoubtable Mrs Jellyby, whose grimy and hungry children are ignored by her in her zeal to collect tracts and bibles for the 'savages' abroad. Imperial themes, characters and backgrounds are common, not only in nineteenth-century literature and art but in earlier periods too. Satirical cartoons in the eighteenth century and the popular comedic dramas of the 1770s and 1780s constantly poke fun at ingénues made wealthy by the Empire and at the antics of those who desire to part them from their new-found wealth. By the late 1800s, satire as well as the realism of the nineteenth-century novel yielded in popularity to colonial romancing. By the late nineteenth century, the empire became for fiction writers, for poets, for artists, a place of adventure and secrecy, of bravery and individualism. Henry Morton Stanley's *In Darkest Africa* was an instant best-seller when it appeared in 1890. This new genre of what was effectively a literary and visual form of pro-imperial propaganda coincided with political efforts to drum up imperial support and interest in the British population at large. The introduction early in the twentieth century of Empire Day (24 May) as a celebration, the increasingly colourful pageantry in Britain around Empire (as well as in the Empire itself), and the concerted effort to turn the school curriculum into an education for imperial longevity all mark a new centrality for the Empire by the start of the twentieth century. Shifts such as these are useful reminders of the way in which empire had different meanings in different eras, with distinctive and time-sensitive political resonances that cannot be lumped under a single heading. And just as ruling a colony was nuanced by time and place and form, so too were the reactions, responses and experiences of those who lived under British imperial rule. It is to their concerns and interests that we next turn.

References

1   J. Hight, *The English As a Colonising Nation* (Christchurch, Wellington and Dunedin: Whitcombe & Tombs, ?1902), pp. 19, 20.

2   J. H. Parry, *Trade and Dominion. The European Overseas Empires in the Eighteenth Century* (New York: Praeger, 1971), p. 40, quoting Lepel Griffin.

3   Alfred Milner, *Imperial Unity: Two Speeches delivered at Manchester (14 December 1906) and Wolverhampton (17 December 1906)* (London: National Review Office, 1907), p. 18.

4   John Strachey, *India: Its Administration and Progress* (London: Macmillan, 1903), p. 432.

5   A good example of this genre is Niall Ferguson's *Empire: The Rise and Demise of the British World Order and the Lessons for Global Power* (New York: Basic Books, 2003).

6   Agnes Baden-Powell, *The Handbook for Girl Guides, or How Girls Can Help Build The Empire* (London: Nelson, 1912), p. 405.

7   *The Colonial Intelligencer; or Aborigines' Friend*, vol. II, no. XXIV, new series, April 1850, p. 408.

8   W. R. Mansfield to John Lawrence, 21 January 1867, British Library, Oriental and India Office Collections, Mss. Eur. F.90/30, no. 91.

9   Augustus W. L. Hemming, 'The Colonial Office and the Crown Colonies', *The Empire Review* 11, no. 66 (July 1906), p. 504.

CHAPTER 8

Being ruled

Freedom has always been a cherished idea within British politics and culture, and the vision of Britain as a nation devoted to, and a champion of, freedom has a long history. In the years of imperialism, the concept of civilization was often yoked to that of freedom, as colonizing Britons imagined themselves preparing colonial subjects for their eventual freedom. The sentiment that colonial peoples required careful nurturing and proper education such that they might one day enjoy the benefits of freedom was a commonplace of journalists, politicians, explorers and travellers, and a good portion of Britons overall. However, central to that argument was that freedom was some distance off, a future dream towards which colonial peoples might aspire and towards which they were expected to work. It was an elaborate justification not only of colonial rule but of colonial unfreedom, and its effect on all aspects of the lives of those who lived under colonial rule was huge. What, then, did it mean to live as a subject of the British Empire? Were the daily lives of Malays, Andamanese, Tamils, Zulus or Creoles directly affected by a distant if powerful country that claimed so much power over them? Although the consequences and experience of people in different places, and of different ranks, were rarely the same, the effects of imperial rule were nonetheless potent, affecting every aspect of people's lives, livelihoods and relationships. Where one might live, job opportunities, property ownership, marriage laws, religious practice, education, entertainment: all these and more were affected by the presence and impact of colonialism.

In political terms, the colonized experienced radically different forms of government from those that would emerge in Britain during the era of colonial expansion. By the late 1920s all adults in Britain were entitled to a vote in national as well as local elections, while Crown Colony and

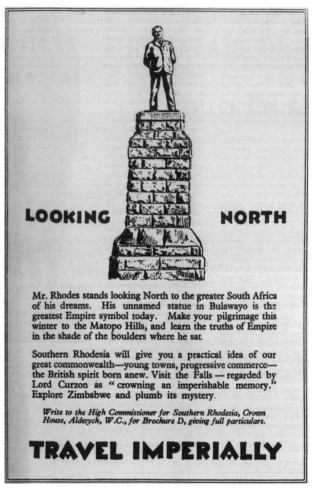

Mr. Rhodes stands looking North to the greater South Africa of his dreams. His unnamed statue in Bulawayo is the greatest Empire symbol today. Make your pilgrimage this winter to the Matopo Hills, and learn the truths of Empire in the shade of the boulders where he sat.

Southern Rhodesia will give you a practical idea of our great commonwealth—young towns, progressive commerce—the British spirit born anew. Visit the Falls — regarded by Lord Curzon as " crowning an imperishable memory." Explore Zimbabwe and plumb its mystery.

Write to the High Commissioner for Southern Rhodesia, Crown House, Aldwych, W.C., for Brochure D, giving full particulars.

FIGURE 16 *Travel advertisement for Southern Rhodesia, 1931* (Illustrated London News)

Protectorate administrations were not even elected, but appointed from the top. The key roles in government were held by Britons, not local peoples, a pattern repeated in other official arenas such as the courtroom and among the police. As we shall see in Chapter 10, this top-down and undemocratic rule played a large part in fuelling anti-colonial nationalist movements across the Empire

As we have seen in earlier chapters, in the white settler colonies the principle of responsible self-government had given settler men over the age of 21, and who owned property, the right to vote for the legislative assemblies. Other than in New Zealand and the Cape, indigenous non-settler locals were denied these rights of political participation, their lives being much closer to that of colonial subjects in the Crown Colonies and Protectorates. In New Zealand, four seats in the legislative council were reserved for Maori from the 1860s, and at the Cape the 1910 Act of Union reconfirmed the vote for male Africans and Cape Coloureds who met property and education qualifications. In 1936, African men lost that right. For a brief period from the mid-1880s, Canadian natives living east of the Great Lakes were entitled to vote; that right was withdrawn in 1898. The pattern for indigenous peoples was routinely one of loss rather than gain.

In Jamaica, as we have seen, governance went in a reverse direction from local representation and decision-making to dependent status. Though the shift to non-elective government came only after the 1865 rebellion at Morant Bay, Jamaican politics had been significantly affected by the abolition of slavery. As early as 1839, soon after abolition, the British parliament had considered suspending the Jamaican constitution for five years. The ensuing controversy forced the resignation of the prime minister, Lord Melbourne, and the plan was abandoned. Though it would be more than two decades before Jamaica lost its political independence, parliament's earlier consideration of the change illuminates how differing colonial situations could shape the debate over political representation, and how far Britain's needs rather than those of the colony dictated colonial decisions.

As the previous chapter demonstrated, British policy generally sought a degree of collaboration with those who they saw as the elites among locals. This tactic helped preserve conservative traditions, as these elites recognized that their invitation to a limited form of power-sharing depended on their acceptance of Britain's ultimate power. Both Britons and colonial elites manoeuvred such liaisons to maximize their own power. In India princes who, in the days of the East India Company, had been criticized and sat-irized as wilful, spoiled and tyrannical became, under direct rule, close associates of the British Indian authorities. Cooperation with the British ensured a local prince's power. The same was so in twentieth-century Africa where the growing use of 'indirect rule' looked to local chiefs and rulers to do much of Britain's work for it. The effect was often to make local rulers more responsive to the needs of the colonial government than to their own people, especially since the British rewarded such alliances with land and wealth as well as power. The British also cultivated wealthy merchants and traders. In the Malay Peninsula Chinese businessmen enjoyed the ear of the colonial powers, a favouritism much resented by the indigenous locals and by poor Chinese. These favoured elites were anxious to distinguish themselves from their poorer compatriots whose labour built such economically successful cities as Singapore.

Politics aside, the economic needs of colonialism led to huge changes in landscape, land use and building. The urbanization that had so drastically and yet so unequally altered the British Isles in the late eighteenth and early nineteenth centuries had similarly striking consequences in the colonies. Port cities became critical for the Empire, for through them people, manufactures and material were shipped to and fro. As in Britain, cities, whether inland or on the coast, offered new job opportunities and in the nineteenth and twentieth centuries mass urban migration was common-place, producing new classes and communities, new styles of buildings and a more urgent attention to questions of sanitation and public safety. Kingston on the south-east coast of Jamaica was, in the eighteenth century, an affluent and bustling city occupied mostly by white planters and merchants and their retinues. After the abolition of slavery, and as former slaves moved there in search of work, the white population diminished dramatically and Kingston became a black and a much poorer city. In South Africa it was rich veins of gold and diamonds that prompted the founding of the cities of Kimberley and Johannesburg in the nineteenth century. The commercial importance of these areas led to the transforma-tion of ragged, poverty-inflicted mining camps into major metropolitan areas in just a few decades. When Maori began to move in significant numbers to New Zealand cities in the second half of the twentieth century they tended to be crowded into poorer, less attractive neighbourhoods that rapidly became associated with danger, squalour and poverty.

Colonial cities strictly segregated 'native' and 'European' residential areas. India's urban centres had long had a separate 'white town' and 'black town'. Delhi, which would become British India's capital in 1911, is a good example of how urban development mirrored the broad inequalities of colonialism. Old Delhi, which pre-dated British rule considerably, was 'local' territory. The buildings reflected Asian living styles in which shared dwelling space was common, and no strict division between residential and commercial usage was readily apparent. By contrast New Delhi, designed by British architects Edwin Lutyens and Herbert Baker in the early twentieth century, was an area where fenced-off single-family bungalows, wide streets and a strict division of functions gave the city a wholly different feel from the crowded lanes of the old city. Increasingly, the parts of cities where local people lived came to be seen by colonial officials as spaces of criminality, disease and political dissent. In many colonies, urban curfews restricted the movement of locals after dark, and those found in European areas of the city were subject to challenge and surveillance. In Victoria in western Canada, for example, aboriginal Canadians were forbidden from being in the city at night from the 1860s.

Curfews were just one way in which the changes wrought by a colonial presence constrained the mobility of colonial subjects. In Canada and in Australia especially, indigenous peoples were increasingly encouraged, if not forced, to live on reservations. Aboriginal Protection Ordinances in the Australian colonies gave the office of the Protector of Aborigines widespread powers to dictate the contours of Aboriginal lives. Throughout Southern Africa, Africans were required to register with local authorities and to carry identification certificates; pass laws in many colonies allowed the prosecution of those found away from their locale without an employer's permission. In East and in South Africa, rural reserves intended for African residence were established. In Indian military towns (cantonments), Indian women were often banned from work that brought them into contact with soldiers, for fear that they would prostitute themselves and disease the soldiers. The rules, which assumed widespread prostitution among Indian women, narrowed both women's freedom of movement in such towns and the range of jobs open to them.

Wandering and nomadic peoples became a particular target of colonial scrutiny. In the early years of imperial rule, mobile peoples had served an enormously important purpose in helping the British understand and control unfamiliar terrain. Whether it was learning how to trap animals for their pelts, or to find waterholes in the parched Australian desert, in the eighteenth century indigenous peoples were invaluable guides to the local landscape. In later years, however, whether through isolation on reservations or through criminal legislation, the lifestyles of nomadic peoples came under fire. From the 1820s onwards, the military in India moved increasingly against nomadic groups. Drastic 'criminal tribes' legislation in the 1830s sought to domesticate and settle them, often (as in Australia) on land unwanted by white settlers. Similar suspicion hung over nomadic peoples in Malaya and Sarawak. They were regarded as lacking proper systems of rule or land usage, a judgement used to justify their exclusion from lands they had traditionally exploited and denying them any prospect of ownership of such lands.

These distinctive and often impoverishing changes in land use and landscape were intimately linked to massive upheavals in the pattern, as well as the availability, of employment. Menial household work that in Britain was done largely by women was, in the subject colonies, frequently dominated by local men, a peculiarity suggestive of the ways in which both race and gender were entangled in hierarchical social structures. Cooks, servants and cleaners (all of whom in Britain would have been over-whelmingly female) were – in India, in the African colonies, in the Straits Settlements, for example – mostly indigenous men. The use of colonized men in household jobs was simply one important and highly visible way in which the powerlessness of subject men could be demonstrated. Using men as servants, in kitchens and in laundries embodied in daily life and routine the power of British colonialism. This did not mean that there were no jobs for colonized women, nor that labour opportunities did not remain gendered. On the contrary, the sexual division of labour, if differ-ently applied, was critical in colonial settings: women's sexual labour – as prostitutes as well as bearers of children – had been fundamental to successful colonization since the days of slavery. Manufacturing and building work in the colonies often employed women as well as men, even as women in Britain were increasingly pushed out of such jobs. There was a far larger female manual labour force in the colonies than would have been acceptable in Britain by the nineteenth century.

Urbanization and the building of railways in Asia and Africa produced work opportunities for indigenous men, as did the growth of large-scale agriculture, the exploitation of mineral resources (diamonds in South Africa, a variety of gemstones in Ceylon, copper, gold and tin in Australia) and the development of manufacturing. Their wages were far lower than those of white workers, and they were frequently assigned to the nastiest and the most dangerous of the jobs available. Ports and shipping also created jobs, and much of this new work profoundly altered existing social structures by housing workers in male-only barracks close to their work and away from their kin. Railway work also forced men to live apart from their families for long periods, as they moved across a country laying track.

In British colonies, and especially in British Africa, master and servant legislation governed relations between white employers and their colo-nized employees long after the equivalent British legislation had been abandoned in 1875. These laws favoured the employer over the employee, on the grounds that Africans, unused to 'modern' labour discipline, needed greater surveillance than British workers. Leaving a job 'without lawful cause', drunkenness, careless work or insulting a master could all lead to formal prosecution, with penalties ranging from the withdrawal of wages to imprisonment. In Kenya, registration laws formalized the prosecution of desertion from a job, since the identity certificate adult men were required to carry noted their current employment alongside name, fingerprint, ethnic group and even past employment details. Employers had to notify the police that they were letting a worker go before he could be hired elsewhere. Without this formality, men could be prosecuted for deserting their jobs. The key principle of master and servant legislation was a breathtakingly unequal one that made employers at fault on labour contracts liable to civil action, but their workers liable to criminal prosecution. Labourers frequently ignored or challenged these laws, though they could pay dearly for such infringements. Passes (called *kipande* in Kenya) and identity certificates were illegally altered, were shared to help others get around or find work and, of course, were constantly lost.

Colonial employers in Africa consistently used floggings and beatings to discipline their workforce. Courts could also impose whippings, a practice that began to decline in East Africa only in the 1940s. It was not uncommon for serious injuries to result from the beatings inflicted by employers, which helps explain the high rate of desertion. When their native workers died from such assaults, colonial employers might occasionally find themselves arraigned in court. It was rare, however, that they would be found guilty, for the judge, the lawyers and the juries in such colonies were their peers and reluctant to punish or harm those they saw as their own.

Danger at work came not just from direct physical violence but also from poor working conditions. In the colonies of Southern Africa where diamonds and gold were extensively mined from the second half of the nineteenth century, and on the coalfields of India, the work reserved for local men was enormously dangerous as well as poorly remunerated. Mining companies, many of which in the early years of the trade were small and had insufficient start-up capital, were notorious for their lack of attention to safety measures. Accidents were common, as were fatalities, and miners risked a host of work-related respiratory and other diseases. When they were not working – though hours were long – the workers lived in crowded compounds with inadequate sanitation, further exposing them to disease and disharmony as well as separating them for long periods from family and friends.

In Dominion colonies, mining was a very different business. It was still a dangerous as well as an all-male work area, but at the silver mines at Broken Hill on the New South Wales/South Australia border and in the copper mines of South Australia, labour was white and was often in the vanguard of unionization, which forced better working conditions as well as higher wages. White workers mostly refused to work alongside indigenous people in settler colonies, so the range of jobs was often greater for local peoples in areas of sparse white settlement. Their situation was always tenuous, and as white populations grew all but the most arduous and unpopular of jobs were closed to the indigenous population.

In India, textile manufacturing attracted large numbers of migrants from rural areas to work in factories. Owners and managers exploited existing divisions of language and religion to keep the workforce from uniting, often adding to the tensions that would spill over into communal violence in British India. Conditions were routinely poor and dangerous, and wages low. Although master and servant legislation in Africa claimed that colonial workers needed to be trained in modern work habits and discipline, the factories in India instead played up what were seen as traditional Indian relations based on reverence for family authority (ma-bapp). Workers were expected to revere the manager as an authority figure who would have the unit's best interests in mind. It was a system that was often violently interrupted by workers' frustrations at the inequalities it attempted to obliterate.

Work experience and opportunity in the colonies also owed much to changing patterns of landownership and land usage. Plantations in Ireland, the West Indies and colonial North America were among the earliest large-scale reallocations and apportionings of land affecting work in immediate and significant ways. Intensive sugar cultivation radically altered the countryside of many Caribbean islands over the course of the eighteenth century. The Highland clearances in Scotland in the mid-eighteenth century and the changing patterns of agricultural taxation in India in the same period proved disastrous for the majority, for the shift to an English model of single (or corporate) ownership robbed small cultivators of a stake in the land, reducing them to tenants with very few rights. Demanding levels of taxation, even in years of crop failure and famine, denuded the assets of much of rural British India, forcing people to migrate in search of work or to face starvation, as thousands did in famine years. In 1912, peasant landholders in parts of Malaya were prohibited from growing rubber for sale for fear they would undercut the larger corporations. In Kenya, the railway cut deep through the territory traditionally farmed by the Kikuyu people, adversely affecting their ability to earn a living from the land. The Kikuyu lost more than 60,000 acres of fertile land to white settlers, further impoverishing them and laying the groundwork for anti-colonial resistance in the twentieth century.

In Egypt, the consolidation of landownership took its toll on an agrarian population unable to compete with large landowners. The emphasis on producing crops for the British market forced many small proprietors to sell their land, but rather than profiting from these sales, spiralling land costs impoverished many since renting land became prohibitively expensive. Many were forced into low-wage labour in the cotton fields in the late nineteenth and early twentieth centuries. Large-scale cotton required constant irrigation of the land, resulting in a significant increase in the water-borne parasites that caused the blinding affliction bilharzia. Those who worked in the fields were the most vulnerable to disease, produced in large part by changes in the environment related to economic demand. Irrigation schemes throughout the colonies also, if unintentionally, created an easy environment for the spread of malaria, by providing good breeding grounds for its carrier, the *anopheles* mosquito.

In Australia, too, the landscape was profoundly altered by the coming of colonialism, changes that pressed sorely on the capacity of Aboriginal peoples to survive in a changing outback. The introduction of sharp-hoofed animals to the continent had an adverse impact on the soil, native plants were crowded out by English flora, and many local animals were hunted, sometimes to extinction, as pests to settled agriculture. The creation of pasturelands for cattle and sheep created fire and flood hazards as well as soil erosion. Aboriginal responses were increasingly desperate, and increasingly subject to severe punishment, but the ability of the indigenous people to live off the land was fast vanishing in the wake of a settlement not of their choosing.

As in India and Egypt, it was the colonists' ideas of proper land management and ownership that prevailed in the Australian colonies. It would be 1889 before *terra nullius* (discussed in Chapter 4) was fully confirmed in law, but long before then it had resulted in a denial of any Aboriginal rights to land. Aboriginal settlements and sacred spaces could be erased without obligation or repayment, destroying lives and culture at a stroke. The indigenous Canadians also saw their traditional lands appropriated without consideration. White settlement pushed local peoples further and further to the margins. By 1911, indigenous Canadians made up less than 1 per cent of Canada's total population, down from about 20 per cent only a century earlier. The disappearance of the buffalo from over-hunting affected the provision of food, clothing and transport. In Southern Rhodesia, as late as 1937, Africans without work on white-owned lands were required to move to reservations where overcrowding and insanitary facilities made life miserable, uncomfortable and often short-lived. In some areas local farmers were prohibited from growing certain crops so they did not compete with settler farmers.

In both settler and dependent colonies the best and most attractive land was reserved either for European use or concentrated in the hands of the local elite whose profits and wealth depended on their cooperation with colonial demands. Moreover, it was not only land devoted to commercial use, agricultural and industrial, that was cordoned off in this way. Just as the European areas of Indian towns and cities boasted wider streets and larger dwellings, the new hill stations in India created a series of exclusive resorts where whites could escape the ferocious summer heat. Indians in hill stations, however, were employees, never vacationers. These 'little Englands' in the hills became the model for similar resorts in other tropical areas, and it was no accident that the highest portion of Hong Kong island, The Peak, was also the colony's most exclusive address. Likewise, the fertile, cool, hilly region of central Kenya, known as the White Highlands, was an exclusively white enclave, its name reflecting its racial demography as well as its geography.

Colonial populations in the earlier eras of colonialism had often turned colonial commerce to advantage. In West Africa, in New Zealand, in North America, trade between locals and colonials by no means always disadvantaged the non-Europeans, and European objects were often put to uses unforeseen by traders: items considered utilitarian by western traders were folded into local religious rites or became fashion statements. Similarly, local knowledge could be a prized commodity, making trading relations not always unequal. Although British commentators liked to write off colonial trading transactions as a case of fobbing off primitives with cheap baubles, colonized peoples often turned trade to their advantage and profited by it. Such opportunities visibly and quickly diminished as the large-scale economics of capitalist Europe took off across the imperial world. Mass production, manufacture and a growing attention to what were seen as universally applicable economic 'laws' disadvantaged those with non-capitalist economic systems.

These kinds of inequalities produced a significant movement of labour not just within colonies, but across them too. Penal transportation saw convicts moved forcibly across the globe, and slavery shifted huge numbers of workers. As those forms of labour waned, indenture was revitalized. In the nineteenth century plantation owners sought alternative sources of labour to replace their freed slaves, but they looked not to Britain but to the Empire. Half or more of those who migrated under indenture in the seventeenth and eighteenth centuries were European in origin, but the new indentured labour from the 1830s onwards was overwhelmingly Asian. Some 60,000 south Asians went under indenture to work in Fiji between 1879 and 1920, when indenture was abolished in the

Empire, while Fijians were moving under indenture to Queensland and other Pacific destinations. By 1838 there were some 25,000 indentured south Asians working on the sugar plantations of Mauritius. Some 30,000 south Asians built Kenya's railways in the late 1890s, over a third of whom were killed or seriously injured in the process. Altogether more than a million south Asians worked under indenture in the British Empire. Their numbers forced the Indian government to get involved: in 1871, the government regulated the indenture business by licensing recruiters and instituting medical examinations and protectorates.

Though Indians formed the bulk of the colonial indentured workforce in the nineteenth century, there was also a large community of Chinese indentured labour, of Pacific Islanders and of Sierra Leonians. Some 18,000 Chinese indentured workers mined phosphate, gold and copper and worked on sugar plantations in the Pacific between the mid-1850s and the mid-1880s. After the Boer War, Chinese indentured labour was common for a brief period in the early years of the twentieth century at the Transvaal gold mines in Southern Africa. Their presence was hugely controversial and many anti-slavery activists accused the British imperial

FIGURE 17 *Indian slaves, or 'coolies', brought to work in the British colonies of the West Indies: an idealized depiction of the 'coolie' in the nineteenth century* (Mary Evans Picture Library)

government of revitalizing slavery, while white settlers in the colony opposed them, wanting to keep non-white migrants out of the country altogether. In 1913, South Africa imposed restrictions on non-white immigration, as New Zealand had done in 1899, Australia in 1901, and Canada in 1910.

Working conditions for this new class of indentured workers were almost always poor, but the terms of labour could vary quite significantly from colony to colony. Five-year contracts were standard, although before 1862 contracts in Trinidad were for three years and in Mauritius the contracts initially issued were for one-year periods. Almost everywhere, workers could choose at the end of their term of indenture either to reindenture or to return home. In Malaya workers were required to repay the cost of their passage, whereas in Trinidad there were financial incentives for those who chose to stay on in the colony. British Guiana allowed workers in the early years of indenture to change employers after a certain term, taking their original contract with them.

Regulation of indenture was mostly ineffectual, but there was nonetheless good reason for it. When, in the 1860s, the western Pacific became an active ground for labour recruitment, Melanesians and other Pacific Islanders were sometimes kidnapped for work on the northern Queensland sugar plantations, a practice known as 'blackbirding'. Britain and Queensland both implemented legislation to prevent such kidnappings, but poor and desperate workers throughout the Empire knew little of the conditions they would face under indenture even when they voluntarily agreed to go.

Employers favoured indenture because it guaranteed a stable labour supply, and fixed the rate of pay for the duration of the contract. This, of course, helped drive down the overall cost of labour anywhere indenture was common, and it tended to make those under indenture unpopular with locals. While some employers paid money wages, others paid in rations. Most had rigorous systems in place to punish absenteeism. In some colonies a day's sickness meant the labourer owed the employer a day's work; on the expiry of a worker's contract, she or he had to work off sick or absent days with no further pay. In some colonies, Mauritius among them, pass laws similar to those seen in Africa led to the arrest of indentured labourers found outside permitted areas.

Mortality rates were high on the plantations. Crowded and unhealthy conditions spread disease easily, and violence was a constant feature of life. News that Chinese mine workers in the Transvaal were being flogged for infractions in the early 1900s by mine officials provoked a massive outcry in Britain. Workers everywhere were easy prey for violent overseers since they could not change jobs, and both the murder and suicide rates were far higher among indentured than other workers. The tensions on plantations were not eased by the imbalance between the numbers of men and of women. Sexual jealousies flared easily in these conditions and women were vulnerable. Other than among the indentured Indian populations there were few women labourers, and even in the Indian communities there were many more men than women. Among the licensing requirements demanded by the government of India was a quota of women; ships that did not meet the ratios required by the government were not cleared for sailing. Where Indians were not the major source of indentured labour, the workforce was overwhelmingly male. Accompanying the Chinese indentured workers in the Transvaal gold fields, about a fifth of whom claimed to be married, were only five wives.

Many workers chose not to return home when their contracts expired. Queensland forced indentured workers to leave, and in parts of Africa taxes and fees were employed as a disincentive to Indians to stay on. Many nonetheless did stay on, not just in Africa but in the West Indies, in Fiji and in Mauritius. Over 600,000 Indians were living in Malaya in 1930. As Chapter 11 discusses, in the 1960s and 1970s the Indian presence in East Africa became a political flashpoint. African anti-colonials resented the Indian populations as a colonial legacy, part of the diaspora of cheap labour that had sustained British imperialism. In Kenya and Uganda, in particular, the process of 'Africanization' led to the wholesale and hasty expulsion of south Asians from the former colonies. Many chose to settle in Britain rather than in India, which had ceased over time to be home. In recent years the impact of Indian indenture has been felt in Fiji where native Fijian political movements have sought to concentrate government power in native hands, stirring up violence against the long-standing Indian population. In 1933 leaders of the Fijian population asked to live apart from the migrant Indians, creating a racial and cultural segregation of these populations with lasting consequences.

Although both the imperial and some colonial governments intervened on occasion to regulate the worst excesses of the indenture system, colonial governance tended to be light in the arena of economic control, allowing private investors, corporate and individual, considerable freedom. In Fiji, the largest single employer was the Australian sugar manufacturer CSR (the Colonial Sugar Refining Company, founded in 1855, and even now Australia's largest sugar company). In Africa, companies such as the African Lakes Corporation controlled literally millions of acres. Private investment was typical in colonial settings, leading inevitably to distinctive imbalances in the economy, as profit and not local need dictated development. Essential infrastructure such as transportation was privately controlled, giving private corporations enormous power. Land could be and was seen solely in terms of profitability in most colonies. The effect was often devastating for residents who did not share in the profits, and not only in terms of their labour opportunity. Changes in land use alongside natural changes in weather patterns often helped produce droughts and their grim relative, famines. From at least the late eighteenth century, famines and crop failures in India were intensified by the forms of agricultural taxation, and therefore crop cultivation, introduced under British rule. A famine in northern India between 1860 and 1861 killed around 2 million people. More than 6 million died in famines that spread through the country in the 1870s, and in the late 1890s famine took another 5 million or so lives. A serious famine occurred in East Africa in 1919 as droughts and a plague of locusts devastated the crops. In the 1930s parts of southern Africa once rich in grain were importing food to cope with severe shortages. In addition, where famine struck, disease almost inevitably followed. The monsoon failures of 1896 and 1897 in parts of India brought severe famines exacerbated by a simultaneous outbreak of plague in 1897.

Disease was helped in its spread by the lack of medical facilities available to local peoples. Indigenous practitioners facing diseases they had never before witnessed were unable to cope, and cholera, plague, influenza and a host of other, often fatal, diseases swept through vulnerable populations. A cholera epidemic that devastated the West Indies in the early 1850s killed almost 50,000 people. Fiji hosted virulent epidemics of measles, TB and influenza in the years of indenture. In Hong Kong and in India, plague and cholera outbreaks in the late nineteenth century took a damaging toll. Smallpox was a major killer among Australian Aboriginal populations. These diseases affected local and colonizing populations, but it was when they affected white populations that research and action to stem epidemics were initiated. Even where colonial authorities did act to reduce the spread of diseases their methods were frequently unattractive to their colonial subjects. European doctors complained frequently about the suspicion with which they were regarded by colonized peoples, and about the unwillingness of local populations to undergo western treatments, and especially hospitalization. Given that diseases and doctors often arrived in the colonies simultaneously, such suspicions were not unreasonable. Nor was the resentment felt by practitioners of non-western therapies, who were often regarded by their European counterparts as superstitious quacks when, in practice, the western medical arsenal was often not much better or that different from local treatments. What did differ radically were the western practices of hospitalizing the sick and isolating the infectious. The rise of compulsory isolation tactics in India and in Africa in the late nineteenth and early twentieth centuries severely damaged relations between British doctors and indigenous patients; doctors quickly encountered resentment and resistance to their approaches. Colonial medical authorities took a pragmatic approach, seeing such measures as practical responses to an urgent problem, particularly in crowded environments that facilitated the swift spread of pathogens. They were frequently unaware of, or unsympathetic to, the effects such policies had on families, economically as well as psychologically. Their application of western ways of tackling problems did not help persuade subject peoples of the benefits of colonization.

Doctors saw local patients as not only superstitious but also uneducated, but they usually failed to appreciate the huge difference in the education available to British and to colonial children. Most of the education available to colonized children was provided by missionaries, who were also the main purveyors of medical treatment other than during

FIGURE 18 *Colonial authorities disinfecting the bedding of plague victims at Poona, India, 1897, as local people watch* (Getty Research Institute/Los Angeles, California (96.R.81))

epidemics. The education the missionary schools offered was mostly quite basic, producing for the most part limited literacy and numeracy. Whereas Britain in the later nineteenth century moved slowly towards compulsory education, at least at the elementary level, for all children, the only equivalent laws in the colonies were, not surprisingly, in white settler lands. In 1921, only 3 per cent of Indians were formally educated, and less than 1 per cent had been English-educated. The early nineteenth century had in fact seen considerable debate in British India about the appropriate education for the local population. The East India Company had long supported education in Sanskrit and in Arabic, but in the reform era of the 1830s 'Anglicists' pushing for English-language training and in western subjects had the upper hand. For the sons of the urban elite, government schools provided a training for young men who would join the Indian civil service. By the 1860s, both in British India and in Ceylon, English-language schools had their own overseeing body, the Department of Public Instruction. An English-style education was reserved, of course, exclusively for a male elite, not just in India but in Egypt, Hong Kong and the Straits Settlements, among other colonies, where wealthy business communities recognized the benefits of an English-language schooling for their sons.

There were also schools and colleges devoted to maintaining the local cultures and languages that drew on much the same affluent client base. In south-east Asia and in India, Muslim schools offered elite males an alternative curriculum to that of the colonial authorities. Nonetheless, over time English became not just the language of colonial power, but of economic and political success. The switch in modern Canada to a dual language system is a direct result of the colonial period, when French was the minority language of a non-dominant population within a British colony. The modern practice aims to redress the balance by putting Francophone Canada on an equal footing with Anglophone Canada, especially with respect to official documents.

Yet English, the language of power, also adopted vocabulary from the colonies, much of which has survived in modern speech. The Aboriginal 'boomerang' has supplied an English verb, while the Indian 'bungalow' has given us a distinctive architectural style now seen in many countries around the world. In the islands of the Pacific, local peoples developed a language for communicating with the colonists, sometimes known as 'pidgin', incorporating local and English vocabulary. It was the islanders who instructed the English in this highly adaptive language. In India, in the West Indies, in Australia, distinct forms of English emerged, significantly different from that heard in England. English was dominant, but not by any means uniform, whether as a written or a spoken medium of communication.

This phenomenon of adaptation or syncretism, in which the customs, practices and beliefs of the colonial power were altered in the light of local knowledges and uses was by no means confined to language. We have seen how locals found unexpected and unanticipated uses for items they traded or received as gifts from colonizers, and it is equally visible in the uses to which mission-taught Christianity was sometimes put.

The continued flourishing even now of varieties of Christianity in many former British colonies suggests that the missions enjoyed some degree of success in their work, yet the adaptation of western Christianity to non-western belief systems was common. Many saw the missions not as a source of spiritual inspiration but as a practical and often wholly secular source of training and education, housing and health care. Others reshaped their newly acquired beliefs into a more familiar mould. By the eighteenth century, Jamaican Baptists had forged a hybrid religion that would horrify the missionaries who observed it. It combined Christian belief with West African myalism, involving communication with the spirits of the dead, often through dance ceremonies, and ritual sacrifice as a means of exorcizing harm.

After the abolition of the slave trade, it was common for recaptives rescued from slaving ships to be settled in and around Freetown in the colony of Sierra Leone. The governor, Charles MacCarthy, envisioned a community of African Christians who could help 'civilize' Africa, and missionary attention was encouraged early in the nineteenth century. In many respects it was a highly successful conversion exercise, with many adopting not just a new religion but many of the trappings of British life: a Christian name, western clothing and so on. Yet religious practices, as in Jamaica, took on an identifiably local flavour in a syncretism not always to the taste of the missionaries and the white colonists.

In 1862, and further south, the British Bishop of Natal, John William Colenso, published his misgivings about prevailing interpretations of the Old Testament Pentateuch as a document written by Moses, and protesting against the limitations imposed on ministers in preaching these first five books of the Bible. Colenso was unorthodox in his beliefs, and always sympathetic to the Zulu peoples among whom he lived. His challenge to a literal reading of the Bible had been shaped in no inconsiderable measure by the questions posed by African colleagues working with him on a translation of the Bible for use locally in Natal. A huge furore followed his publication and the Bishop of Cape Town promptly excommunicated Colenso. The excommunication was overturned in London in 1865 and Colenso stayed on in Natal, although a second bishop sent out to the diocese, and supported by the white settler population, competed with him thereafter and until Colenso's death in 1883. Colenso was certainly unusually outspoken for a man in his position, but his actions show how local opinions and challenges could have considerable effect in shaping the work of the missions.

Colonial peoples used such syncretism to their own advantage, and one unexpected but inevitable adaptation that emerged out of colonial rule was the emergence of what one early twentieth-century anthropologist, C. G. Seligman, called the 'professional primitive'. Anthropologists, explorers and officials as well as tourists all encountered colonial peoples who, increasingly familiar with what colonists expected of them, played up to the images of savagery and primitivism that were the bread-and-butter depictions of the colonial world. Exhibitions and books that offered western viewers a snapshot of African and Pacific societies (in particular) as composed of scantily clad and brightly ornamented 'primitives' squatting in front of mud huts primed such expectations, and locals quickly learned to act the part where necessary. It could be a lucrative performance on occasion.

FIGURE 19 *Anthropologist Tom Harrisson learning first-hand about local traditions – he is being initiated into Sakau manhood by a chief's wife, who cicatrizes a permanent pattern across his chest (1933)*

Nonetheless, colonial expectations could significantly alter social structure and the forms of identity that colonized peoples themselves understood. Where once there were people of different cultural groupings living in proximity, under colonialism there were 'Africans' or 'Native Americans', labels unknown in pre-contact times and reflecting how colonists saw both regions and peoples. In slave colonies, people from widely differing cultures and societies were thrown together and finding more in common with other slaves than with their masters, a homogenized idea of 'African' cultures unknown in Africa developed from those encounters. The assumptions so often made by missionaries and officials (both civil and military) about leadership and authority patterns in other societies helped create new forms of rule and indeed of dissent. The British emphasis on caste distinction in India reinforced and often strengthened these social divisions, while the search for tribal chiefs in Africa and elsewhere often led to their actual creation. In some instances the statelessness of peoples was what most confused the British, who simply could not understand how a society could function where there was no one with whom the colonists could formally communicate as a leader. The East African Kikuyu and the West African Igbo both fell into this category. These were not societies with chiefs, but the British need for identifiable rulers on whom they could devolve certain duties made them set about creating tribal chiefs where none had existed. The massive changes wrought by these assumptions could be deeply disruptive to social and political stability.

The British Empire, then, was a place of deep inequality between colonizer and colonized. A few small elite groups, useful to the British, were encouraged and pampered, but the vast majority of those affected by colonial rule were almost certainly worse off as a result. Their lands were appropriated, their access to employment limited and prescribed, their movement often restricted, and their communities redefined and sometimes literally moved from their locations. Although the argument was made that colonialism was a beneficent force, an exercise in enlightened development allowing the entire world to enjoy the benefits of western living, the reality was often one of limitation, constraint and oppression. The growth of anti-colonial movements throughout the colonial world was critically fuelled by this uneven distribution of wealth, power and privilege; Chapter 10 will chart the growth of this local resistance to colonialism.

CHAPTER 9

Gender and sexuality

It will be obvious by now that the Empire, throughout its long history, was dominated by the concerns of colonizing men. In Britain, the Empire was represented as a place of masculine proving and of adventure in which white women and indigenous peoples were, at best, incidental, and more often detrimental, to good rule. This perception was grounded in a ruler-oriented view of the Empire that regarded it as a dangerous and difficult environment to be tamed.

In Britain, the Empire was depicted as populated predominantly by men, an image that frequently left local populations as well as women invisible and uncounted. It was, however, among migrant populations that dramatic imbalances in sex ratios in the colonial world were mostly to be found. Among colonizing whites and labouring groups such as slaves, indentured workers and convicts, men vastly outnumbered women. Permanent colonized populations, despite the severe losses from disease or violence they sometimes suffered, had gender ratios close to those found in Europe. Local practices, particularly in relation to the disposing of unwanted children of one sex or the other, might skew the ratio slightly but those populations where men massively outweighed women were artificial creations of imperial expansion.

In many colonies British women were thin on the ground, but this was not the case everywhere. British America before the War of Independence had a more equitable gender balance than British India at the same moment. The circumstances and type of colonization as well as the period affected gender balance everywhere. In settler lands there were often far more men, especially in the early stages of colonization. In 1861 there were 150 men for every 100 women among white settlers in Australia, and 160 men for every 100 women in New Zealand. In most of Africa and in the Malay archipelago there were roughly twice as many British men as British women into the 1920s, and it was only after the coming of direct British rule in India in 1858 that the numbers of white women there began to climb in any significant way.

It was no surprise, then, that the most general impression of the Empire was of a man's world. This perception directly affected the shape and the history of the Empire for both colonizer and colonized. The numerical dominance of men was associated directly with imperialism, and this helped reinforce the idea of the Empire as a gendered and masculine domain. Some colonial jobs actually demanded that men remain single: men employed by India's Forest Service, for example, could not marry until they had completed their probationary period, and regions considered particularly dangerous were often off-limits to women – married men posted to such places had to be willing to leave their wives behind. It was not only men in government service who faced restrictions such as these: many trading companies required their employees to seek company permission before marrying, and in some sectors marriage was permitted only after a man had served a set number of years on the job and for that company. Doctors and others argued that women's natural frailty and delicacy made them unfit for the rigours of colonial climates, hot or cold, while others saw dangers at every turn, whether from wildlife with a taste for human flesh, from disease or from unfriendly locals.

Gender is, however, about far more than numbers. The desire espoused by imperialists to prepare colonized societies for future western-style freedom drew strength from the belief that the social structures of the colonizing power were superior. Colonial administrators, settlers and other Britons seldom left their values and beliefs wholly behind when they moved from Britain to its colonies. Although a few moved to the colonies expressly to leave British attitudes and customs behind, most went convinced of British superiority and keen to extend British values. One of the most powerful and far-reaching of western ideas they brought with them focused on the idea of separate public and private worlds inhabited respectively by men and women. It was in the eighteenth century that the gendered belief that men were best suited to the public and women to the private sphere really began to grow in influence in Britain, at much the same time as imperial expansion was high on the British political agenda. Though this principle of the 'separate spheres' was always and everywhere unrealistic, it was nonetheless powerful as an ideal and as an organizing social principle. Clearly, it reflected a highly specific – and privileged – class position in which there was sufficient money for women not be engaged in paid labour, a luxury well beyond the reach of many in Britain. It became increasingly difficult in Britain for married women to find formal paid work, and sentiment followed practice, with men defining their masculinity through the stay-at-home wife. Within both Britain and the colonies the effects of this thinking were significant.

This division of public and private was potent well beyond the economic sphere. Behaviour, especially sexual behaviour, was increasingly regulated by considerations of what was proper in the different spheres. The respectable person understood the requirements and limits of these boundaries and acted accordingly. Sex was an entirely private business, not to be talked about in public; commerce and politics were public functions, better suited to male conversation. Child-raising was a domestic and womanly activity. The heterosexual family in which father paid the bills and mother raised the children and created a calming environment, in contrast to the hustle and bustle of the public arena, was key to this vision of the separate spheres.

When colonists arrived on other continents they often found drastically different social and sexual arrangements. Frequently a distinction between the worlds of public and private simply did not exist. Attitudes to family, women or sexuality were sometimes radically different from those in the west. Among many African peoples, for example, the idea of sexuality as a private affair made no sense, because the key social group was not the nuclear family but a bigger and broader collective. One's responsibilities and ties were not to a spouse, but to this wider kin. In south Asia, marriage was mostly a family business, and certainly not centred on a personal attraction between one man and one woman. In situations such as these, the roles occupied by men and women could be very different from those familiar to colonists, and colonists mostly criticized these variations rather than seeing them as viable alternatives. The disapproving descriptions of native sexuality that dominated earlier periods of the Empire gave way in the twentieth century to apparently scientific explanations for the 'hypersexuality' accorded to colonial peoples. Sigmund Freud, the renowned pioneer of modern psychiatry, argued that there was an identifiable difference in the psychological make-up of Europeans and what were thought of in his time as 'primitive' peoples. His 1908 essay 'Character and Anal Eroticism' argued that Africans, Pacific Islanders and Australian Aborigines were characterized by an absence of the period of sexual latency he saw as moderating the sex drive among Europeans.[1]

Gender relations became a mainstay of colonial criticism alongside a disapproval (sometimes mixed with envy!) of the sexual behaviours of colonized peoples. In particular, colonized societies came, quite early on, to be defined by the apparently vast number of ways in which women were degraded and brutalized. Brushing aside the huge inequalities suffered by women in Britain itself, one of the characteristics seen to define colonial peoples and to relegate them to a lesser status was this apparent lack of respect for women.

The list of perils allegedly visited on women by barbarous and savage men was huge. The mistreatment of women came to be seen as definitive of primitive societies, and one of the many reasons justifying the need for colonial authority. Colonial peoples, claimed colonizers, sold their girl children into prostitution or domestic servitude, or married them off at alarmingly young ages without a qualm. In many places 'natives' were said to kill female children at birth, because the expense of rearing them was not worth it. Those girls allowed to live were often kept in seclusion, restricted in movement and education, forced to hide behind heavy clothing and barred windows. When married, it was often in polygamous arrangements, and if they had the misfortune to survive their husbands they might be expected either to commit ritual suicide or to live singly and modestly after his death and not remarry. Their genitals were said to be subject to mutilation, their delivery of children was threatened by the use of unclean and untrained midwives, and colonial women led, by British reckoning, miserable, brutal and wretched existences in the shadow of their menfolk, who thought nothing of bartering women's bodies as commodities.

All of these practices undoubtedly existed among some groups in some places, just as in Britain itself women endured restricted access to education, arranged marriages, loss of property rights upon marriage, domestic violence, little control over their children, minimal right to divorce and virtually no political power well into the nineteenth century and beyond. These parallels were seldom recognized, and instead colonial female perils came to spell the problems that made colonial rule imperative. These evils pointed not only to the misfortunes of women but to the misbehaviour of men. It was the failure of colonized men to do right by women that many in Britain saw as justifying the need for British governance.

Emphasis on the oppression of women often involved selective reporting too, ignoring instances in which women enjoyed freedoms beyond those of women in the west. Missionaries in eighteenth-century North America, for example, found the matrilineal practices of the Huron peoples disturbing; the birth of a girl was celebrated more than that of a boy. Instances such as this were, throughout the colonial period, played down while female oppression at the hands of men was seen as widespread and characteristic of what was wrong with colonized societies.

In many places the colonial state began in the early nineteenth century to curb practices seen as detrimental to women's well-being. Laws banning suttee and female infanticide and regulating age of marriage were passed in nineteenth-century India (see Chapter 5), and in the twentieth century there were attempts to tackle the custom of female circumcision in parts of Africa. In some instances, the influence of westernization led to changes in local practice, as was the case among the middle-class intellectuals of Calcutta and other urban areas of India who began to move away from purdah (the seclusion of women) in the mid-nineteenth century. In twentieth-century Iran, similarly, modernization was effected in large part through reforming the position of women. The Iranian reformist ruler, Reza Shah, banned the veil and chador in 1937, and opened universities to women. (The Islamic revolution of the late 1970s would, of course, reverse much of the shah's work.)

The dilemma – for local reform groups as much as for the colonial state – was that imposing the values of another society seldom sat well with a large portion of the population. In the case of reform groups and organizations, that problem was part of the wider question of whether wholesale westernization was the right direction for the future, a point to which the next chapter will return us. Colonial governments, on the other hand, had no such qualms. Officials might believe that local populations would resist change, but this did not on the whole make them doubt the superiority of the reforms they sought to enact. When things went wrong, as they almost always did, it was local resistance and not colonial policy that was invariably faulted.

As we have seen in earlier chapters, colonial rule relied on collaboration with some portion of the indigenous population, and relying on (and often creating) local elites distorted colonial understanding of indigenous customs and practices. Yet the enforcement of laws addressing intimate behaviours was invariably difficult, not only because of local resistance or subterfuge, but because enforcement often relied on western practices. Age of consent legislation, for example, which laid down the minimum age at which girls could be married (or could legally have heterosexual relations), assumed that age could definitively be established, something that became possible only where and when birth certificates were routine. The lack of birth certificates affected campaigns against female infanticide too, although some of the earliest instances of birth certification in India in the 1860s were the result of the state's concern with the death of infant girls. In all these instances colonists blamed men: it was the perverted appetites of men that victimized young girls exposed too early to conjugality, and it was men's carelessness and faulty authority that allowed infanticide to occur. The critique of colonial masculinity offered an implicit and flattering comparison with the chivalrous masculinity of the colonizers.

Many of the practices abhorred by colonial observers were also targeted by local critics, although the colonial state only occasionally joined forces with these reformers. Locals were not unaware of their own problems, just as critics in Britain found plenty at home in need of reform. The rich literary tradition of Bengal contains many a tale of the lonely child bride torn from her parents and mistreated by the mother-in-law who now ruled her every waking moment. The *mui tsai* of Chinese communities, the girls sold into domestic and sometimes sexual service at a young age and often in perpetuity, were commonly pictured in Chinese literature as powerless and exploited victims.[2] Yet colonists bent on reform seldom chose to work in tandem with concerned locals to improve conditions.

For the colonized, social reform was also bound up with questions about whether changes to women's lives would require westernization, not always a popular option among colonized peoples. While some welcomed western influence, many in colonial societies were critical of the west preferring the traditions with which they had grown up. There was no wholesale yearning for western ways, but rather a critical reckoning of the benefits and disadvantages the west bestowed.

If the colonized woman was most typically held up as epitomizing all that was wrong with other cultures, the British woman in the colonial world has taken much of the blame for the intolerance and hierarchical nature of colonialism. Some historians argue that the increase in women living in the Empire radically altered the practices and routines of colonial life, introducing snobbery, rigidity and formality, and aggravating and even creating racial tensions.[3] The literary critic Edward Said has pointed out that for Kim, the eponymous hero of Rudyard Kipling's famous novel set in British India and all about political intrigue, the biggest hindrance he faces is not physical danger but being 'eternally pestered by women'.[4] In Kim's world, women did not belong in the male arena of risk, and were simply a nuisance. They distracted men from the business at hand. They required protection. They demanded polite society and sexual fidelity. They drew sharp racial lines between whites and others, and poisoned the earlier harmony of colonial conquest.

The arrival in parts of the Empire of greater numbers of women certainly coincided with some distinctive social changes in colonial rule, but the growth in the female population generally came about because changes were already under way. The nineteenth-century expansion of Britain's colonial holdings, along with the growing complexity of colonial rule, required a more settled British presence. Asking ever larger numbers of British men to forgo participation in family life was not feasible, and so instead family moved to the Empire. Most British women in the Empire were there because of their family circumstances; they were the sisters, daughters, mothers and wives of men posted to, and living in, the Empire. There were solo British women in the Empire too, but their numbers were far smaller, and many of them married soon after arriving. With the increase in married women, the previously widespread taking of mistresses and concubines by British men began to recede, at least in its public form. Marital infidelity was hardly unknown in Britain, and the mistress was neither a new nor a singularly colonial phenomenon. However, since women were leaving their families behind and moving to strange and far-removed settings to be with their husbands, their tolerance for such behaviour within marriage may well have waned in proportion. Since so many more men were married and living with their wives in the later colonial years, these non-marital arrangements now competed with recognized marriages rather than substituted for them.

With the growing presence of British women in the Empire came also a greater number of young children living with their parents in the colonies. New living conditions emerged from that singular change. British residential communities began to develop more fully, making racial exclusivity (which was by no means a new phenomenon) much more visible. Women's presence was seen by many parties as a means of softening and domesticating dominantly male environments. In the settler context, officials hoped that by encouraging single women to migrate to the Canadian and Australian colonies these tough, male-dominated pioneer societies would become respectable and conformist. The Indian government's insistence on a female quota on ships carrying indentured labourers paralleled the policy of encouraging women's migration to the prairies and forests of Canada and the sheep and cattle runs of Australia. Officials believed that a greater female presence among indentured workers would help stabilize these populations and therefore increase economic productivity. In the mining camps that began to spring up in Southern Africa in the late nineteenth century, the presence of women close by, selling food, sex and companionship to the male workers, was tolerated and indeed sometimes quietly encouraged as a stabilizing force in otherwise volatile conditions. Worried about the restlessness of the Indian male convicts serving time in the isolated Andaman Islands, out in the Bay of Bengal, officials introduced family immigration schemes in the mid-nineteenth century designed to rehabilitate criminals. In 1890 the authorities took the extraordinary step of allowing husbands to require that, even if the women's own sentences had expired, convict wives remain in the penal settlement with them.

The conception of the Empire as a man's world, for the colonizers at least, guaranteed that masculinity was always important, if also always beset by uncertainty. That the Empire was an unsuitable environment for women was a tenacious maxim that continued well into the twentieth century, and it depressed opportunities within the Empire for women. When the Colonial Service began appointing women to Colonial Service positions (in tiny numbers) in 1937, many men in the service were unhappy. Those women who did rise to the senior ranks recognized the barriers imposed by sex. Margery Perham was perhaps the most notable of the small group of women who, by the mid-twentieth century, had made a name for themselves in colonial policy work. Perham's expertise on Africa made her a respected figure in both political and academic circles, and she was sufficiently eminent that she was invited to deliver the British Broadcasting Corporation's prestigious annual Reith Lectures for 1961. Yet crossing the Pacific as a young woman in 1929, she had remarked on the accidental and gendered good fortune of a fellow passenger on his way to take up the governorship of American Samoa. 'I envied him,' wrote Perham, 'his job – and his sex.'[5] Though Perham never allowed gender discrimination to deter her, she always recognized how the Empire system made working there easier for men than for women.

Even after the mid-nineteenth century, when women's presence grew, the Empire was a world dominated by men, and this had massive and broad consequences for both ruler and ruled. Since colonialism involved some form of domination, whether by military conquest, economic power or cultural ascendancy, it was easy to imagine maleness in terms of authority and power. The subjugation of men from the colonies under British rule made the assumption of weakness an easy one; their submission, for the rulers, was proof of a lesser manliness, for the manly would never concede defeat. Yet at the same time there were groups among the colonized who Britons saw as admirably masculine: some of the African peoples, such as the Ndebele who had fought vigorously against colonial intrusion, and the northern Indians who the British called the 'martial races'.[6] Newspaper and journal articles often described such men in almost erotic physical terms, emphasizing height, muscularity and gait. They likewise derided colonial men they regarded as effeminate and insufficiently manly.[7] Descriptions of such men tended to focus on their unhealthy pallor, weedy frames and air of constant exhaustion. There was always an undercurrent of fear that colonial effeminacy, brought about by luxury and indolence, might transfer to British men. Cartoons of the returning 'nabobs' in the late eighteenth century often showed them bedecked with jewels more suitable for women, a clear sign of their corruption that was at once economic, moral, physical and cultural. Effeminacy was not the only danger to beset manliness. Homosexuality loomed large as a concern, and it was a widely held British belief (based on very little evidence) that male–male sexual relations were common and acceptable in many colonized societies. Colonial Office memoranda carefully noted such proclivities among wealthy and influential colonial men, more proof in British eyes of colonial inferiority. Ignoring the considerable male homosexual activity in Britain – made visible by the trial of the playwright Oscar Wilde in 1895 – the assumption of widespread homosexuality in the colonial tropics 'proved' colonial inadequacy. Although some colonies certainly had more fluid sexual rules than Britain, just as many of the places the British colonized had belief systems that matched those of Britain with respect to same-sex relations. The tendency to lump together non-white colonies as tolerant of practices outside the contours of British sexual respectability allowed a more wholesale condemnation of what was seen as typical of colonial sexuality.

In practice, of course, imperial environments were frequently homosocial for white men. In the earlier years of imperial expansion especially, white men lived, worked and socialized largely among men. Prostitution and concubinage, serviced by colonial women, flourished but men lived mostly among other men. Such profoundly male environments, in which a female presence was temporary, provided fertile ground for same-sex liaisons that, though frowned upon and frequently hushed up, were not uncommon among British men.

The most exclusively male of all colonial environments was the military. Below the officer corps, army and navy men were discouraged from marrying. Only a tiny percentage of the rank and file was permitted to marry, a decision prompted in part by a fear that marriage would divert a man's loyalties from his regiment to his family, and in part by economic concerns. Particularly as a bulwark against homosexuality, prostitution was seen as vital to army stability, and in many places informal regulation of military prostitution existed from an early date. In India, Lord Bentinck took an active interest in schemes that required women working in the sex trade to submit to frequent genital examination and to compulsory treatment for sexually transmissible diseases (STDs). Such schemes, funded out of municipal and company coffers, were operating in the Indian presidencies from at least the 1790s. These regulatory experiments identified women but not men as the source of STDs. In the mid-nineteenth century, more systematic attempts to regulate the sex trade criss-crossed the empire, and included a system of regulated brothels designed (unsuccessfully) to protect soldiers and sailors from STDs. These 'contagious diseases' laws tried to stem the high levels of sexually transmitted diseases among colonial soldiers and sailors by genitally examining women sex workers at regular intervals. For a host of reasons, the laws failed: women avoided and resisted regulation, men visited unregulated women, the pathology of these diseases was only poorly understood, and the available treatments were at best partial. In addition, these laws attracted massive protests both in Britain and in the colonies in the late nineteenth century, especially from women outraged at the double standard they enshrined that held women but not men responsible for the transmission of disease. By the century's end they had been formally abandoned, though they often lived on in informal schemes seldom policed by the state.

Although they failed in their goal of reducing STDs, the contagious diseases laws tell us much about both gender relations and about sexuality in the Empire. That Victorian politicians could so easily pass laws legalizing prostitution, an activity regularly deplored as immoral as well as uncivilized in the press, in parliament, in churches and on the streets, is in itself significant. Soldiers, as we have seen, were regarded as the ultimate defenders of the Empire, the force that, if and when resistance erupted, was always called upon first: they were the face and the frame of imperial masculinity, the final enforcers of rule through brute force. Women – in this case, colonial women – were expected to service them, to provide the necessary sexual outlet that masculinity was understood to require. It was, even for the squeamish Victorians, preferable that a man visit a prostitute than that he have sexual relations with another man. Colonized women as mistresses and prostitutes, and British women as colonial wives and companions, were vital components in maintaining a gender structure that allowed for a clear distinction between men and women, masculinity and femininity, proper and improper forms of sexuality.

It is for this reason that we see so much regulation of sexuality in the Empire, especially in the nineteenth and early twentieth centuries. Laws of this sort kept both sexual behaviours and the boundaries between manliness and womanliness properly distinct. It was, of course, also axiomatic among the British that those they colonized were sexually promiscuous and unheeding of the idea of moderation. There is also no question that explorers and other colonists often encountered locales where sexuality was very differently viewed than in Britain. Needless to say, many among the British took advantage of freer sexual mores while simultaneously deprecating the societies offering them this opportunity.

This contradictory and indeed hypocritical position demonstrates British ambivalence about the gender structures and social organization encountered in the colonies. The imperial period was one of deep Christian orthodoxy, with its bifurcated understanding of sexuality as either sinful or procreative. There was already a long tradition in the Christian world of regarding women as dangerous temptresses, easily reinforced when British men encountered women unencumbered by the religious association between sin and sexuality. In such environments there was inevitably a fascination with women who differed so palpably from the representations (if not always the reality) of British womanhood. This ambivalence often paired desire and disgust: descriptions of colonized women frequently veer between enthusiasm for their beauty and sexual freedoms and horror at their ugliness and promiscuity.

In the summer of 1810, Londoners who could afford the steep 2s. 6d. entrance fee could view in the flesh the woman the papers were calling the 'Hottentot Venus', shipped for display from the Cape of Good Hope. Sara (or Saartje as she was known in South Africa) Baartman was a Khoisan woman who had made the long and perilous journey from South Africa to London by ship. Displayed by white entrepreneurs in fashionable Piccadilly on account of her allegedly vast buttocks, breasts and labia, Baartman has come to symbolize the early nineteenth-century European obsession with an abundant and exotic colonial sexuality. The hugely popular exhibition of Baartman's body in London, and later in Paris, was a colonial act, a display that illuminates both the European fascination with what they saw as excessive African sexuality and the ways in which women, almost everywhere subordinate to men in this period, were a key element in the power relationship that defined the Empire.

The depiction of colonial women as animalistic and beastly, even if also sometimes comely and erotic, dates back at least to the early days of navigation and European travel in the sixteenth century. Descriptions of women's bodies were a standard element in early travel writings, and these descriptions routinely emphasized sexual attributes, often remarking in particular on women's breasts. It was an article of faith that childbirth was inconsequential for these naked and primitive women, in stark contrast to the sufferings endured by 'civilized' women in labour. This was a belief with huge geographical spread. Observers claimed this enviable trait of easy childbirth for the women of the Americas, of Australia, Africa and the Pacific. It was one of the hallmarks of 'primitive' sexuality and served to differentiate the heathen from the Christian. According to the Old Testament, after Adam and Eve sampled the forbidden apple, God's punishment included the vow that 'in sorrow thou shalt bring forth children'.[8] Widely interpreted as visiting pain on women during parturition, Christian women experienced God's curse on Eve while the heathen remained untouched.

In the eighteenth century, when naturalists began in earnest to seek for the origins of humankind and Carl Linnaeus argued for a commonality between apes and humans, the theme of bestiality crept into writings about non-western peoples. Claiming a greater resemblance between Africans and apes, Edward Long, writing in the 1770s, suggested that the 'oran-outang' passion for 'Negroe women' was 'a natural impulse of desire, such as inclines one animal towards another of the same species'.[9] The African and the ape were thus elided into one species. Such musings – and Long was not atypical in his lurid imaginings – allowed sexual behaviour, real or imagined, to become the sign of cultural and moral inferiority, bolstering the justifications for colonial rule.

It is within such a climate of disapproval and misunderstanding that the remarkable political attention paid to the regulation of sexuality is best understood. Britain also saw an increase, particularly from the late nineteenth century, in governmental incursions into these professedly private areas of life. However, in the colonies we see a wider range of such laws and much earlier than would have been acceptable in Britain. The contagious diseases laws discussed earlier were already operating in a number of British colonies in the 1850s, yet were not introduced into Britain until 1864, and the British version was much less comprehensive than the colonial laws. In the colonies, laws dictated not only the contours of paid sex, but also marriage, abortion, infanticide, non-marital sex, age of consent, interracial sex and more. Always prominent was the tension between what the British considered proper behaviour and the behaviours of the peoples they ruled.

The western definition of marriage that came increasingly to dominate in the colonies was particularly influential because it covered such a wide range of practices, from age of marriage to the status of widows, from authority within marriage to what legally constituted a marriage and, of course, how many people one could be married to simultaneously. Christian ideology, which saw marriage as exclusively a covenant between one woman and one man, could not countenance many of the practices Britons encountered in their colonies.

Concubinage (the keeping of a mistress) received a decreasing level of encouragement over time, not only because more women were moving from Britain to the Empire, but because of a growing concern about the mixed-race offspring such relationships produced. The children of these mixed-race intimacies often experienced considerable discrimination. In the early years of North American settlement, they were mostly raised within native families, while in India a large and distinctive Eurasian community grew up over time. Eurasian children were sometimes sent to institutions founded specifically to train and raise mixed-race children, but their likeliest future was in the tight-knit Eurasian community, set apart from both Indians and the English. In the West Indies there was also a large mixed-race population separated from both the black community and from the planters alike.

By the early twentieth century colonial officials began to make it known that government men involved in sexual relationships with colonized women could not expect promotion, though the effect was probably to push these arrangements further to the margins rather than to reduce their frequency. Women would have been forced to live separately from their male partners, but would still be expected to provide them with sexual and other services. The loss of income or housing would all have been, of course, on the woman's side. The advantages of concubinage were always almost all on the male and British side.

Yet for both free and enslaved women liaisons with colonizing men could and often did spell some economic improvement in their lives, even if only temporarily. The security of these arrangements was always tenuous. Men ended such relationships at their own convenience, often because they were marrying a white woman or had been posted to a new location. Most colonial concubinage was among the less well off, although the stories of glamorous liaisons with wealthy princesses are those we generally hear. Few women were kept by wealthy foreigners, most instead servicing men of modest means and always aware that their arrangements could end abruptly. Unlike formal marriages, there were no responsibilities or duties expected of the men; in practice, some did support any children they had fathered or would settle a sum of money on the woman. It was a rare man who would recognize a mistress as a legitimate wife, and the children of the alliance as his heirs. All the responsibilities were centred on the woman for whom concubinage was a form of paid work. These 'temporary marriages' so typical of the colonies are best understood as a type of gendered labour.

Work more broadly is another key area where the operation of colonial gender divisions was often markedly different from that in Britain. Poor women who had to earn a living worked, whether they lived in Britain, on the African continent, in Hong Kong or in Egypt. The work they performed, however, could be strikingly different and, not surprisingly, we can trace the very substantial effect of colonization on the gendered division of colonial labour. As in Britain, much of the heavy manual labour associated with manufacture and mining was male. In India, where a tradition of manufacture pre-dated heavy industrialization, it was women workers who lost their livelihoods, in an eerie echo of the changes in the British textile industries that replaced a predominantly female with an overwhelmingly male labour force by the middle of the nineteenth century. In Britain, women's removal from the factories was widely hailed as a social and moral reform that improved the family even though the loss of women's wages was often devastating to the family in reality. In India, rather differently, the insistence of British merchants that Indian textiles did not compete with British led to the deliberate slowing of Indian textile manufacture, and the consequent loss of huge numbers of traditionally female jobs. Agriculture became increasingly feminized as women sought to feed themselves and their families. Plantation work in India, especially in tea and coffee picking, became an increasingly female world whereas, by the early twentieth century, men occupied around 90 per cent of industrial jobs.

Nonetheless, a British observer moving between the colonies and Britain would have been struck by how many more colonial women worked in jobs that at home would long have been reserved for men. Their numbers diminished over time but the observer would have found women in the factories and underground in the mines, in the building trade working at heavy manual labour, and in many other industries long closed to British working women. Thomas Alva Edison, the early American film entrepreneur, shot a series of films in the British West Indies in 1903 that registered the amazement of a western onlooker at the heavy manual labour done by women. Three of the five films in the series showed women coaling ships docked in the Caribbean harbours, the women carrying baskets of coal on their heads into the boiler room of the vessels; the other two depicted more traditional scenes, a woman washing a baby and washing clothes.

Protective labour legislation that had begun to restrict women's manual work in Britain from the 1840s came to India only in the late nineteenth and early twentieth centuries. As in Britain, these laws were focused largely on manufacturing and mining, skirting the main employment areas in which women could now find jobs. In 1911 women working in Indian factories were prohibited from night work, a restriction that in Britain dated much further back to 1844. In 1928, women's participation in mining in India was limited, a law that had passed in Britain in 1842. The shift out of heavy manual labour thus came far later in the colonies than in Britain, although it everywhere reduced women's chance of economic independence.

The distinctive movement of women into agriculture was by no means limited to India. Africa too saw the male workforce increasingly occupied in mining and manufacture, often far from home, leaving women with the immediate burden of providing for families. Subsistence agriculture became women's work while large-scale corporate cash-cropping made increasing inroads into the land available for such work, further impoverishing rural women. As a result women began to move in search of work, though in smaller numbers than men. They worked on agricultural plantations or moved to the cities as petty traders, as domestics, as sex workers, often combining these skills to make ends meet. As opportunities arose they might sell cooked food to men living in barracks, or brew beer, or offer sexual services, combining these as necessary to maximize their earnings.

White women also worked in the colonies, both in the settler lands and in the dependent colonies. In white settler environments, they occupied much the same place as in Britain, working principally in domestic service in the nineteenth century, and expanding into the sales and service sectors over time. The same domestic sentiments – that women, especially once married, belonged in the home raising children – restricted white women's labour opportunities. For indigenous women in settler lands, there was, of course, even less opportunity. Domestic and sexual services were their likeliest means of supporting themselves in the white colonial world, and they could expect even lower remuneration than white women.

In non-settler colonies white working women were unwelcome to officials, despite their small numbers. Only a limited range of jobs was available, and white women were thus often clustered in hotel and bar work as well as in the brothels. Although by the later nineteenth century white nurses were a reasonably common sight in the colonies, other single white working women were suspected of being prostitutes, selling sex to those who could afford to buy. A single woman working as a barmaid in a city such as Singapore may have been in a typically female if morally ambiguous job, but her obvious independence mocked the idea of the Empire as a man's world. And the lack of respectability implied by her occupation was regarded by officials as putting 'proper' white women at risk. Unwaged white women in the colonies mostly agreed. In Southern Rhodesia, petitions calling for a prohibition on the employment of women in bars and hotels, and presented to the legislative council in 1915, were signed by most of the white women in the colony. The petitions were unsuccessful, but they demonstrate the intensity of feeling about the topic and about the unstable status of white women in colonial settings. Even nurses, so much more respectably feminine, were kept on a tight rein, their free time and leisure pursuits carefully policed.

Whereas white women, however limited the opportunities, might find work in a British colony, it was far harder for a woman from the colonies to find work in Britain. There were colonized women working in Britain for returned colonial families mostly in domestic positions, but their numbers were small and there were few alternatives for them. In the colonies, women certainly experienced a huge increase in mobility as a result of imperial rule, but their work choices remained more constrained than those of men. They could sometimes move within the Empire, but it would have been under indenture or with families. For men from the colonies, residence in Britain was a little easier. Those who worked, as many did, on ships that docked at British ports were quite likely to stay on in Britain for periods of time, working mostly in manual labour. Further up the social scale, it was not uncommon for elite colonial men to visit Britain, even sometimes to live there for long periods, as did Dadabhai Naoroji who was sufficiently integrated into British society to serve as the member of parliament for a London constituency in the late nineteenth century.

White women of wealth, meanwhile, could move reasonably freely around the Empire. Many activist women visited imperial sites to investigate social conditions, while in the nineteenth century something of a cult developed in which wealthy women travellers visited spots off the tourist trail and published accounts of their adventures, many of which sold very well indeed. Although such women generally travelled without white male companions, they did not travel alone. Like the European male travellers and explorers of the era, these women travelled in the company of carriers, cooks and guides with local knowledge. This was very much a pastime of those with money to spare, and some amassed major collections of colonial art and artefacts. Mary Kingsley, who travelled extensively in West Africa in the closing years of the nineteenth century, collected widely. After her death from fever in South Africa in 1900 her uncle, the novelist Charles Kingsley, bequeathed her considerable collection to the Pitt Rivers Museum in Oxford.

Women such as Kingsley always remained anomalous, however. Women's contribution to empire-building was much more commonly seen through the lens of domesticity, and this helps explain why so many people continued to see a fundamental disconnection between the idea of the Empire and the presence of colonial women. In the early years of the Empire, life was anything but domestic. Though the situation changed significantly, particularly over the course of the nineteenth century, there were still plenty of rugged frontier outposts (memorialized over and over again in fiction and in film) seen as masculine territory. Representations of the Empire in Britain tended to play up this dimension; it was more newsworthy and more exciting. Reading late nineteenth century accounts of the Empire would have conjured a world of camel-riding, jungle-clearing, back-breaking labour in intemperate weather and always with danger close by. It was, then, only a place suitable for women when men had first civilized and tamed the land and those who lived on it. Women's part was to maintain this hard-won advance by rearing future colonists, by maintaining order and cleanliness, and by setting a civilizing example. Writing in 1905 in the *Contemporary Review*, Liberal politician T. J. Macnamara declared that 'Empire cannot be built on rickety and flat-chested citizens'.[10] Fears of diminishing working-class heath and hygiene in the early twentieth century stimulated greater attention on women's role as mothers in the white settler colonies as well as in Britain. Declining birth rates also triggered alarm for the future of the Empire. Increasingly, governments investigated schemes for infant welfare and for the promotion of family life, aided by a willing press that painted a picture of women's purpose in life as selfless devotion to the higher causes of family and Empire.

Missions in particular worked hard to promote Christian family models. Evangelical support for the abolition of slavery had often stressed that emancipation would permit Africans to live more easily in western family formations where men would head households and women raise the children. Schooling for girls in mission schools frequently emphasized gendered skills such as sewing and homecraft, and missionary support for convert families could be swiftly withdrawn if the family stepped out of line. Missionaries often struggled with their colonial congregations over control of children, for the missionaries regarded an education in

Christianity as vital for securing the permanence of conversion. It was legal in many Australian colonies in the nineteenth century to remove Aboriginal children from their natal families to institutions at the whim of local authorities, an unsettling trace of the 'stolen generation' years in the mid-twentieth century when part-Aboriginal children were forcibly placed in residential schools hundreds of miles from their families. Child removal in twentieth-century Australia (and, to a lesser extent, among Canada's First Nations peoples) has become one of that country's greatest political scandals; by the late 1960s, 18 per cent of Aboriginal children in the Northern Territory were in care, removed by the state from their parents.

The growing female presence in the Empire created in some instances an inflated alarm about sexual danger. The long-standing prejudices entertained about the sexual looseness of 'lesser' peoples fuelled a fear that colonized men would be unable or unwilling to control their sexual appetite for white women. The attack by Indian sepoys on English women and children at Cawnpore in 1857 quickly became in the British press a narrative of rape and sexual abuse as well as disloyalty. Although the evidence for those charges is flimsy, more than a half century later, when Indian soldiers fought alongside the British in the First World War, those convalescing from battle wounds in Britain were barely allowed off the hospital grounds for fear they would seduce British girls. The War Office fought strenuously to ensure that British nurses were not involved in work that necessitated their even touching these men, for fear this would inflame Indian passion.

In some colonies this exaggerated vision of uncontrollable sexual desire led to punitive laws that made the sexual assault of a white (but not a local) woman a capital offence. In parts of Southern Africa and in Papua New Guinea indigenous men were liable, from early in the twentieth century, to execution if convicted of such assaults. The first of these laws was passed in Southern Rhodesia in 1903, and copied in 1926 in Papua New Guinea where the law was explicitly named the White Women's Protection Ordinance. It remained in force there until 1958. In Southern Rhodesia related laws also made it an offence for white women to engage in sexual relations with African men, or even to invite sexual attention from them. Nonetheless it was black men who were likeliest to find themselves in court on sexual charges. 'Black peril' scares of this sort were common in a number of colonies at the end of the nineteenth and the start of the twentieth centuries, and reflect a colonial anxiety about sexualized dangers to white male power. The thought that white women might choose sexual liaisons with men of colour was, if anything, an even more

FIGURE 20 *Indian Mutiny (1857) memorial at Cawnpore. Memorials to the English dead were common in India.* (Getty Research Institute/Los Angeles, California (96.R.84))

alarming prospect than that of their being coerced by such men. Fears that white women might willingly stray into this sexually charged territory affected both colonial and domestic arenas. In the First World War, newspapers as well as official documents revealed qualms not only that Indian soldiers would fascinate British women but that impressionable teenagers were being sexually lured by Chinese men. The race riots that rocked many British cities in 1919 were at least partially precipitated by white male resentment over white women's relationships with men of colour.

When a 'Savage South Africa' exhibition opened at London's Olympia in 1899, there was considerable controversy over the fact that the Zulu actors shared the stage with white women actresses. When one of the Africans became engaged to a white woman, the show was forced to close its doors to women. Critics saw the mixing of black men and white women as itself productive of the 'evil' of mixed-race marriage.[11]

The gendered dangers that attended colonized peoples were, if less enthusiastically policed by the colonial state, a critical feature of the experience of the colonized. Conflicts and jealousies over women were endemic in frontier societies where men outnumbered women; in these instances local women were highly vulnerable to rape, kidnapping and sexual coercion, and the penalties for colonizing men were minimal. In the Australian outback in the nineteenth century it was taken for granted that white men could have their pick of the Aboriginal women they encountered, a practice commonly justified by claims that Aboriginal peoples were in any case promiscuous. It was not uncommon for Aboriginal women to be taken against their will by white settlers and kept in chains to prevent them from running away. The huge number of mixed-race children who resulted from decades of exploitation would become in the mid-twentieth century the subject of an attempt to 'breed white' in Australia by removing them from their Aboriginal mothers and raising them with western and Christian values in residential schools. Never equal to white Australian children, these mixed-descent children were trained for work in domestic service if they were girls, and as farm and station hands if they were boys. At the same time, however, Aboriginal men accused of sexual violence against white women in colonial Australia were unlikely to obtain a fair trial, for their actions were considered, as in non-settler colonies, a dangerous threat to the ruling white race.

In some cases it was the after-effects of colonial rule that heightened the incidence of sexual and gendered violence. When the British withdrew from India in 1947 (see Chapter 11 for details), the resulting violence between Hindu and Muslim groups led to the rape, assault and abduction of some 100,000 women by men of opposing religious factions. In many families, as news of the sexual violence spread, women were killed before they could be abducted, as a means to save the honour of the family. Women became the symbol of the anxieties produced by partition, and they died in huge numbers on a battlefield produced by colonial rule and not of their own making. Whereas white fears of sexual danger were in most cases grossly out of proportion to reality, sexual violence and danger were common experiences for colonized women, subject to colonialism's sexual coercion and its tendency to dehumanize the lives of colonized peoples.

The likelihood of colonial violence should not, however, blind us to the considerable efforts made by women to promote gender equality. Women in the colonies fought similar battles to those fought by British feminists to extend women's rights. As noted in Chapter 4, women in the white settler colonies of New Zealand and Australia won the right to vote early, although the extended franchise did not bring it with greater employment opportunity or many other major changes in women's lives. In Australasia, women's suffrage (achieved in New Zealand in 1893, and by 1908 in all the former Australian colonies) was intended to stabilize and conserve the status quo, since it was widely assumed that women would either vote as their husbands did or be 'natural' conservatives. It is no coincidence that women's gains in Australia came at much the same moment that governments there were looking for ways to reduce the political influence of the predominantly male labour movement.

The question of suffrage was academic, of course, in colonies where legislative bodies were appointed and not elected. As this slowly changed, women showed themselves ready and eager for political participation. In India women demanded representation when, at the end of the First World War, the limited opening of the political system to indigenous peoples was inaugurated by the Government of India Act of 1919. These cautious reforms gave Indians a say in provincial (but not central) government, and India's first elected woman took office on the Madras legislative council in 1927. In 1935 Indian women over the age of 21 and qualified by virtue of property or an education gained the right to vote; it was a symbolic victory for it enfranchised only some 6 million women in India's vast population. Yet women used their new rights vigorously; of the 1,500 or so seats in provincial legislatures for which elections were held in 1936 and 1937, women won 56 of them. Indian women were not alone among colonial women; in Palestine, during the British Mandate, Jewish women fought for political representation (though not for Palestinian women), a right they gained in the mid-1920s. Women were also active in the fight against colonialism, especially in the twentieth century. In Kenya a detention camp for women Mau Mau supporters began imprisoning women in 1954. Everywhere, colonized women joined the struggles for freedom from colonial rule: in Palestine, in Africa, in south-east and south Asia, anywhere where colonialism met local resistance. The next chapter will return us to their efforts.

Despite this long history of women's activism, the most common stance of British feminists towards colonial women has been, in many ways, more akin to the theme of 'feminine peril' than to the building of common threads and unity. British feminists have routinely portrayed women from the colonies as helpless and degraded, enslaved and in need of help rather than as partners in a broader enterprise aimed at equality. Western feminists frequently enunciated their role as one of rescue, not so different from the aims of missionaries and reformers. In the late nineteenth century, the feminist press ran innumerable articles on the 'downtrodden' Indian woman kept behind high walls and deprived of an education. In the 1920s and 1930s women politicians in Britain pressed the imperial government to intervene in colonies that practised female circumcision, or where girls could be sold into domestic servitude. It was rare that these campaigners would seek alliances with local women's groups. They saw themselves rather as pioneers in places where women were too brutalized to fight on their own behalf.

The tendency to view colonized women as needing guidance and protection was often the result of a pro-imperialist politics within feminism. Many feminist activists were, in the nineteenth and early twentieth centuries, committed imperialists and their critiques were aimed in large part at Britain's failure to improve the lot of women rather than at the principles of colonialism. Yet even among those identified as anti-imperialist, the tendency to assume that colonized women could not speak for themselves has remained common.

There were always, of course, women who rejected the idea that non-western and colonial women were subordinate or more oppressed than their western sisters. One woman who thought that gender systems in other countries were certainly no worse than in her native Britain was Lady Mary Wortley Montagu who, as wife of the British consul to the Ottoman Emperor, lived in the eastern Mediterranean in the early 1700s. Montagu thought that the veiling of women, so widely regarded by the Europeans as a sign of female oppression, was liberating since it permitted women to go about disguised and invisible to their husbands. While women like Montagu were rarities in the eighteenth and nineteenth centuries, when women were commonly enthusiastic in their support of Britain's imperial project, the twentieth century began to see changes as a considered anti-imperialism among westerners slowly grew. Yet even among women aligned with anti-imperial western politics, the tendency to assume that women's experiences and problems could be universalized remained strong, a stand that tended to minimize the particular coercive structures of a system that relied so very heavily on gendered distinction for its successful operation. Masculinity and femininity, defined according to western norms, were central planks in the management of the Empire. This is not to suggest that the societies Britain encountered were somehow gender-neutral. On the contrary, they too often had their own notions of manhood and womanhood and, as we have seen, it was common for the colonizers to deprecate those ideas. Not only did the colonizers largely see their own gender structures as superior, but they frequently failed to notice where similarities existed, emphasizing difference in a hierarchical fashion.

Gender, defined as the social roles differently imposed upon men and women, shaped the worlds of colonialism deeply and in myriad ways. The expectations and the values of the multitudes of peoples involved – whether by choice or by force – in the colonial enterprise frequently clashed in this critical but slippery arena. The imbalance in sex ratios so often produced by the demands of the colonial economy, the differing outlooks on sex roles and on sexual behaviours, on the definition of the family, on what men and women could and should do, meant that gender considerations were always a point of negotiation and a critical issue within the colonies. This was no side issue, but a key and central organizing principle by which colonial rule was shaped and maintained.

References

1 Sigmund Freud, 'Character and Anal Eroticism', in J. Strachey (ed.), *The Standard Edition of the Complete Psychological Works of Sigmund Freud*, vol. 9 (London: Hogarth Press, 1953), pp. 169–75.

2 For excellent examples of this literature, see Sarah Paddle, 'The Limits of Sympathy: International Feminists and the Chinese "slave girl" Campaigns of the 1920s and 1930s', *Journal of Colonialism and Colonial History*, 4, no. 3 (2003), pp. 18–20.

3 In her book *White Women in Fiji, 1835–1930. The Ruin of Empire?* (Sydney: Allen & Unwin, 1986), Claudia Knapman discusses this argument at some length.

4 Edward Said, *Culture and Imperialism* (New York: Alfred Knopf, 1993), p. 137.

5 Margery Perham, *Pacific Prelude: A Journey to Samoa and Australasia, 1929* (London: Peter Owen, 1988), p. 77.

6 Heather Streets, *Martial Races: The Military, Race and Masculinity in British Imperial Culture, 1857–1914* (Manchester: Manchester University Press, 2004).

7 Mrinalini Sinha, *Colonial Masculinity. The 'manly Englishman' and the 'effeminate Bengali' in the late nineteenth century* (Manchester: Manchester University Press, 1995).

8 Genesis 3:16.

9 Edward Long, *The History of Jamaica. Reflections on Its Situation,
   Settlements, Inhabitants, Climate, Products, Commerce, Laws and
   Government* (London: 1776; reprint edition, Montreal and Kingston:
   McGill–Queen's University Press, 2002), vol. 2, p. 364.

10 T. J. Macnamara, 'In Corpore Sano', *Contemporary Review* (February 1905),
    p. 248, quoted in Anna Davin, 'Imperialism and Motherhood', *History
    Workshop Journal* 9 (1978), p. 17.

11 Annie E. Coombes, *Reinventing Africa: Museums, Material Culture, and
    Popular Imagination in Late Victorian and Edwardian England* (New Haven,
    Conn.: Yale University Press, 1994), pp. 91–2.

CHAPTER 10

Contesting empire

Britain's Empire was at its largest following the end of the First World War, augmented by the mandated territories ceded to it by the new League of Nations. Yet we might just as reasonably emphasize not growth but contraction as the most characteristic feature of the twentieth-century British Empire. The specifics of the process of decolonization will be found in the next chapter; here, and as the backdrop against which we may understand decolonization fully, we shall discuss the slow and patchy but nonetheless critical growth of anti-colonial nationalist movements within the Empire.

Nationalism already had a lengthy history by the time it began to appear among colonized peoples in the Empire. Historians of both the early modern and the modern periods have claimed that the rise of the 'nation state' was peculiar to the age they study. In the nineteenth century, significant changes in European boundaries created the modern countries of Italy and Germany, and the First World War redrew the map of central and eastern Europe in significant ways. Much of this change was achieved as a result of military and imperial activity, but there was also a considerable groundswell of popular sentiment about consolidating national identities. Colonial versions of these nationalist leanings often differed quite radically from those seen in Europe, but they too emphasized a distinction between legitimate and illegitimate rule. In an era in which western imperial powers were embracing ever more democratic forms of government, the profound lack of indigenous representation in most of the colonies looked more and more out of step with the political tenor of the age. This is not to suggest that the forms of nationalism that took hold in British colonies were purely western imports. There were certainly western influences at work, but shrewd activists were also skilled at reinventing nationalist

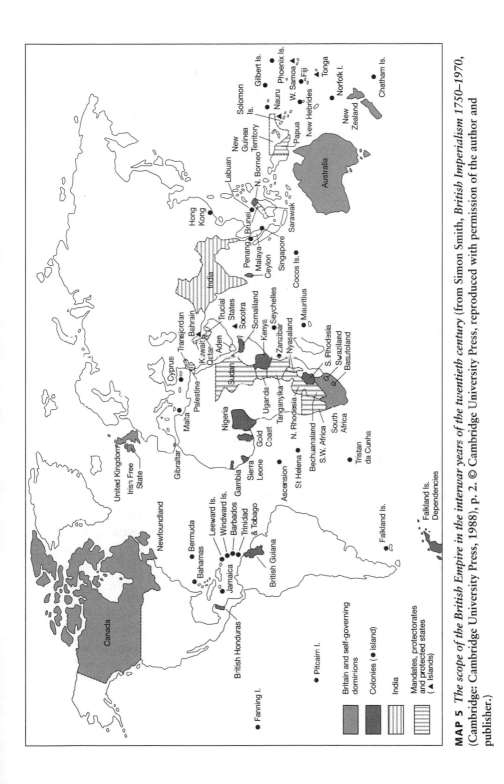

MAP 5 *The scope of the British Empire in the interwar years of the twentieth century* (from Simon Smith, *British Imperialism 1750–1970*, (Cambridge: Cambridge University Press, 1988), p. 2. © Cambridge University Press, reproduced with permission of the author and publisher.)

sentiments in an idiom more likely to appeal in their own populations. As a result, we see a lively variety of nationalist movements in different parts of the Empire: what linked them, for the most part, was that they increasingly challenged the validity of British colonial rule. Anti-colonial nationalism was a specific form of nationalism yoked to a critique of colonial governance, but though it often helped move the process of decolonization along it was by no means the only factor in that process. British officials took anti-colonial nationalism very seriously, and responses to it were often vigorous and punitive.

To place a beginning date on anti-colonial versions of nationalism is no easy task; it is obviously a form of nationalist sentiment closely tied to the experience of being colonized by outside forces, and protests against such authority can be found early on in the history of the Empire. It was in the twentieth century, however, that protests spread – and spread quickly – such that very large segments of the Empire experienced sustained protest on a significant scale. Although the British had largely dismissed colonial resistance in the nineteenth century as local and tribal, it became much harder to deny nationalist leanings in the twentieth century as movements in the colonies learned new political strategies and organized even more vigorously. Christopher Bayly points out that the 'big' names in imperial administration at the turn of the century – Curzon in India, Milner in South Africa and Cromer in Egypt – prompted a rise in resistance to colonialism with the tactics they employed for 'heading off, diverting, or suppressing demand by the educated intelligentsia for greater freedom and political representation'.[1]

At the very start of the twentieth century, Britain's two major wars – the South African (or Boer) War of 1899–1902 and the First World War (1914–18) – had shaken loose a significant number of imperial ties. In the first of these conflicts, in South Africa, it had been by no means certain that Britain would win, and it was only as the British endorsed increasingly ruthless tactics that they gained the upper hand against the Boers. The use of detention camps and of a 'scorched earth' policy to wreck the productivity of Boer farms did not gain the British much approval around the world. Both internationally and from critics at home there was a strong outcry against the tactics they used, yet similar policies would re-emerge later in areas such as Kenya and the Malay peninsula where the British fought resistance to their rule.

The First World War likewise destabilized a number of imperial relationships within the British Empire. The British relied heavily on colonial troops, since the war dragged on for so very much longer than expected and took a far greater toll on soldiers than anticipated. This was a highly labour-intensive war requiring large numbers of troops in all theatres. Dominion and dependent colonies alike provided both fighters and labour corps to bolster the British effort, but not without protest and dissension. Australia, for example, twice rejected the policy of conscription, sending only a volunteer army. New Zealand (in 1916) and Canada (in 1917) introduced a military draft, although French Canada protested vigorously against the Military Service Act of 1917. Canada led the Dominions in criticizing the British handling of the war, and demanded a greater role in determining wartime policy. In 1917 the Imperial War Conference, made up of Dominion leaders alongside Whitehall politicians, was founded in response to the demands of the settler colonies, although the daily operations of the war remained firmly in British hands. The fledgling navies that Canada and Australia had so recently formed were brought under the authority of the British Admiralty with very little consultation.

These colonial criticisms of Britain were seldom grounded in opposition to the war itself. The leaders of the Dominion countries supported the war as did the larger proportion of their populations. Their frustrations were over their own role in its conduct, and over what they saw as British mismanagement. Among white population colonies, only Ireland boasted a strong anti-war faction. Ireland had the lowest rate of military recruitment among the white settler colonies: only 6 per cent of adult Irish men fought, compared with 19 per cent of white New Zealanders and 13 per cent of white South Africans, Australians and Canadians. Conscription, introduced in Britain in March 1915, was not applied in Ireland, arriving there only in April 1918 but barely implemented before the war ended.

For the dependent colonies, the degree of representation granted the Dominions during the war was not considered appropriate. Other than the inclusion of India at the Imperial War Conference, the Crown Colonies and Protectorates were wholly unrepresented in wartime decision-making. With the exception of Indian soldiers, colonial troops from the dependent colonies were used as labourers, loading and unloading ships and transports, and were not issued with weapons. These soldiers and labourers enjoyed far less freedom than their white counterparts. Their leaves were more constrained, and they were often not permitted to leave their military camps unless escorted by their officers.

The Indian army provided a significant fighting force for the British, unlike other non-white colonies. Indian soldiers were frequently deployed in trouble spots around the Empire, but this was the first time they had been called upon to fight in Europe. When war broke out nationalism was already widespread in parts of India, and activists expected that the help India afforded Britain would be repaid after the war with greater political representation and a move towards self-government.

Closer to home, in Ireland, nationalists chose to pursue their goals during the war. The first measure of self-government for Ireland since the union of 1800 was passed in 1912, but the outbreak of war had led to its suspension; by the time the war ended in 1918 the plans for Home Rule were in tatters, and Ireland was on the brink of civil war. Taking advantage of the fact that military attention was focused elsewhere, a small cadre of Irish Republicans had proclaimed a provisional government in Dublin in 1916. In what became known as the Easter Rising, some 1,600 Republican supporters occupied major buildings in Dublin, declaring a provisional government independent of Britain. Within a week troops brought in from English garrisons had regained control of the city, but not before considerable damage had been done to public buildings. Around 3,500 people were arrested, about twice as many as were known to have been involved – the British government was anxious to send a stern message to Irish nationalists. In doing so, however, the government made a critical error that increased support for their nationalist antagonists: 80 rebels were sentenced to death for treason and in May 1916, shortly after the rebellion had been quelled, 15 were executed. Rather than quieting or frightening nationalist feelings, this quick and harsh response alienated the Irish public, pushing many who had not supported the rebellion closer to the nationalist camp.

Ireland was not the only colony where hostility and protest erupted in the war years. Serious uprisings in South Africa in 1914 and in 1915 demonstrated that the hostilities that had erupted there during the Boer War were by no means contained. Britain also faced disturbances in Egypt, Turkey, Afghanistan and Iraq, as well as in India soon after the end of the war.

The forms that nationalism took in settler colonies and in dependent colonies were quite distinctive. The partial but considerable self-government enjoyed by the white populations of the Dominions, along with their strong sense of racial and cultural unity with Britain, deeply influenced their articulation of nationalism. They could, after all, argue that their capacity to govern themselves had been proven over and over by this time, and their elective political systems did indeed mean that their demands were, in critical ways, less far-reaching than those that would characterize colonies demanding independence from a far more autocratic system of government. The self-governing colonies, already autonomous in many respects, were not shy in pointing out why practices beneficial to Britain might nonetheless be too risky for them to endorse. This national assertiveness was accompanied by a growing pride in local culture distinct from that of Britain and by no means always in thrall to it. At the Peace Conference in 1919 (where the former colonies of the German Empire were divided among the Allied powers) the Dominions insisted upon and won representation separate from the British. Although the white settler colonies were largely uninterested in breaking away in all respects from the Empire, they were mostly committed by the early years of the twentieth century to expanding the principles of self-determination. In 1917 the Imperial War Conference passed a resolution proposed by Jan Smuts of South Africa that called for a special conference to be held when the war ended to discuss full political and diplomatic autonomy for the Dominions. Britain could no longer dictate policy without discussion and

ADVANCED AUSTRALIA!

AUSTRALIA. "IF YOU PLEASE, MOTHER, I WANTED A LITTLE MORE FREEDOM, SO I 'VE HAD THIS LATCH-KEY MADE. YOU DON'T MIND?"
BRITANNIA. "I 'M SURE, MY DEAR, IF ANYBODY CAN BE TRUSTED WITH IT, YOU CAN."
[Clause 74. "Australasian Federation Bill," abolishes appeal to Privy Council.]

FIGURE 21 *Advanced Australia!* Punch *cartoon, 25 April 1900: the wry comments of the satirical magazine,* Punch, *on the occasion of Australia's federation as a single nation.*

negotiation. In the years after the war, the Dominions continued to assert this kind of nationalist agenda: in 1923, for example, Canada signed a fishing rights treaty with the United States, completely bypassing Britain, and did so almost as soon as Britain had formally acknowledged Dominion rights to negotiate treaties without imperial input.

Ireland alone took a rather different political path among the white-populated colonies. Deeply divided at the end of the war, the Home Rule plans of 1914 were all but impossible. Faced with nationalist agitation elsewhere, Britain was anxious to hold on to Ireland. Its secession from the Empire would clearly loosen more ties than merely those between Britain and Ireland. In 1918, the republican Sinn Fein party won 73 seats in the general election and quickly set up its own assembly, declaring, as the nationalists had done in 1916, a republic that the British refused to recognize. In an effort to appease both Republicans and Unionists, the 1920 Government of Ireland Act created two separate parliaments, divided broadly along Republican/Unionist as well as Catholic/Protestant lines. The 6 counties of Ulster in the north-east, largely Protestant and Unionist, were to become Northern Ireland, while the larger 26-county Catholic area would be renamed Southern Ireland. This plan for self-government failed, for while the Ulster counties had by 1921 embraced their new status, the Southern Irish activists refused to swear an oath of allegiance to the British Crown, a requirement upon which the British government insisted. Civil war and bitter conflict led to the eventual granting of Dominion status in 1921 to Southern Ireland, which was now renamed the Irish Free State. The partition of the country, however, spelled trouble. Fighting between disappointed Republicans and committed Unionists in Ulster disrupted people's lives long after the separation of the two Irelands.

The Irish troubles, closely watched by the Dominion powers in particular, raised critical questions about the limits of autonomy for self-governing entities within the Empire. The declaration of war in 1914 by the British monarch had been a declaration on behalf of the whole Empire: there was no need nor provision for consultation. During the war, Dominion leaders not only felt free to criticize British handling of the conflict but pressed for a greater and more influential role in policy-making. That push was maintained after the war, and the conflict in Ireland was in no small measure influential in applying that pressure. In 1931, the Statute of Westminster created the modern Commonwealth, formally acknowledging the Dominion (or Commonwealth) countries as independent states no longer bound, other than by choice, by past or future British laws. It is worth noting, however, that the dominant sentiment in these colonies remained pro-Empire. The majority did not seek to sever ties with Britain, but rather to approach equality within an imperial framework. Complete separation was not the goal in Dominion countries.

The significant changes in the relationship between the imperial centre and the Dominions did not extend, as we have already noted, to Britain's other and more numerous colonial possessions, and in these latter the aim of complete separation from Britain was rather more developed. Though India had attended both the Imperial War Conference and cabinet, as well as the 1919 peace negotiations, its post-war history was markedly different from that of the Dominions. Nationalism was already a factor in Indian politics long before the First World War. The Indian National Congress (INC, known as the Congress) founded in 1885 was by no means the only organization committed to the promotion of nationalism, although its lengthy and influential history makes it prominent in any account of anti-colonial nationalism in India. In its early days it drew largely from the same urban middle-class intelligentsia who had flocked to reform societies in India throughout the nineteenth century. Its base of support would broaden considerably in the twentieth century, but it was in the cities, and especially in Calcutta, that its early promise was nurtured. But the INC was not unique and nor was nationalism always an organized force. In 1913, Indian film-maker D. G. Phalke released what he called the first Indian film made for an Indian audience with an entirely Indian production team. His films, which were grounded in Hindu mythology, were hugely successful and often openly nationalist.

The resurgence of a militant Hinduism also fed anti-colonial nationalism in the late nineteenth and early twentieth centuries. The reassertion of non-western values and a strident critique of the west's role in India offered nationalist thinking a non-western model quite different from that promoted by the INC, and one that was also sometimes productive of significant tensions between Hindus and Muslims. The British encouragement of the formation of the All-India Muslim League in 1906 as a counter to the Hindu-dominated INC was regarded by many in India as a deliberate manipulation of religious divisions designed to undermine the growth of nationalist solidarity.

In the years before the First World War, nationalist challenges to British rule in India were common, and both violent and peaceful tactics were employed. The concept of *swaraj* (self-government) was firmly in place among Indian activists by the early years of the twentieth century. There were boycotts of British-manufactured goods, and from 1908 (at about the same time that militant suffrage activists in Britain turned to violent protest) radical nationalists resorted to bombings and assassination attempts. In 1906, the INC declared a formal commitment to self-government for India. Faced with these disturbances, the Indian government offered some small measure of political representation in 1909 in the form of a limited electorate. This minimal concession was drastically undercut by a draconian press censorship Act instituted a year later in 1910. This pattern of parallel concession and repression by the British authorities, each round of which sparked further anti-colonial militancy, would endure for decades.

The outbreak of war in 1914 further stoked discontent with colonial rule. The fiscal implications of the war were, for India, serious. Land revenue, the staple form of colonial government revenue, was augmented by customs and income taxes, the latter having been introduced in the cities in 1886; Indians were paying for this distant war both with bodies and with money. By 1917 nationalism was once more growing in India, and political discontent among soldiers fighting in the war had the colonial authorities sufficiently worried that they carefully monitored the letters sent home to India by those fighting on the Western Front.

The protest movement known as *satyagraha* (truth-force or soul-force) had begun to gather steam in 1917. *Satyagraha*'s dual intent was to demonstrate Indian fitness for self-rule and to show respect for the enemy. Its most famous advocate was, of course, Mohandas 'Mahatma' Gandhi, who had returned to India in 1915 after 20 years abroad. Between 1915 and 1917 Gandhi travelled extensively in India, disseminating the principles of non-violent resistance, passive civil disobedience, and a rejection of western values. Faced with growing unrest, the Secretary of State for India, Edwin Montagu, announced in 1917 that Britain intended to move towards responsible self-government for India, but the actions of the government did little to persuade Indian nationalists of the sincerity of this commitment. The INC had supported India's participation in the war, imagining that self-government would be the reward for participation. They were to be deeply disappointed by what Britain offered.

The year 1919 in particular was a dark one for anti-colonial nationalism in India. The Rowlatt Acts of that year kept in place emergency measures usually reserved for wartime, and which substantially curtailed ordinary civil liberties. Trial without jury and internment without trial were legitimated and led to widespread and serious protests in cities throughout British India. It was at one such protest that one of the most notorious events in twentieth-century colonial history occurred. In the Punjabi city of Amritsar a large but peaceful crowd of protesters gathered in April of that year in an enclosed area, the Jallianwalla Bagh. Without warning, the local military commander, General Reginald Dyer, ordered his troops to disperse the crowd by gunfire. Dyer sustained the firing for ten minutes, killing some 380 Indians and wounding more than 1,100. The firing came at a tense moment, shortly after the murder of a number of Europeans in and near the city, and after the assault of a white woman missionary. Dyer had not only ordered public floggings in retribution but had issued the now-notorious 'crawling order' forcing Indians to crawl on their hands and knees at the site of the missionary woman's beating. Relations between the British authorities in Amritsar and the Indian community were thus particularly tense when the firing occurred, and not helped by the reputation of the local lieutenant governor, Michael O'Dwyer, who made no secret of his distaste for Indian political activism.

FIGURE 22 *The Crawling Order, Amritsar, 1919* (National Army Museum)

Dyer was officially censured and forced to step down from his position, but no legal action was ever pursued against him and in some quarters he was treated like a hero. Reminiscent of the split in British opinion over Governor Eyre's handling of the Morant Bay rebellion in Jamaica in 1865 (see Chapter 6), Dyer attracted both ebullient support and fierce criticism in Britain. The British community in India wholeheartedly supported him, and the House of Lords made clear its refusal to see Dyer punished in any significant way; on his return to England a sum of £30,000, raised by supporters, awaited him.

The failure of the British government meaningfully to punish Dyer's actions bolstered Indian anti-colonial nationalism and made Britain's claims to be a civilizing colonizer seem rather hollow. By 1920, a major campaign of non-cooperation was in full swing, just as the British unveiled the latest round of political reform for India. The Government of India Act instituted a system of dyarchy in which both Indians and Britons served in ministerial offices. Three of the seven ministers on the executive council were to be Indian, and Indians would serve as ministers in the provincial councils. The law also increased the size of the electorate, but the changes were largely cosmetic, and the nationalists knew it. Legislation from the provinces could be invalidated by the governor general and new Indian ministers were largely assigned to the 'softer' portfolios – education, health, agriculture – rather than being entrusted with key and controversial issues such as revenue or policing. The Indian princes were brought into the new system via a chamber of princes, which the British saw as a conservative counter to radical nationalism.

Discontent and nationalist activism, far from being quelled by these reforms, swelled in the 1920s and 1930s. Urban rioting increased as did the Gandhian tactic of civil disobedience. Calcutta suffered 40 riots in 1926 alone. The response of the imperial authorities was increasingly military and punitive. Violence, despite Gandhi's stand, was common. The economic hardships of these years of rising prices and uncertain harvests also radicalized the countryside. Attacks on landlords and on property were common, and in the factories trades unions began to strengthen and grow. Class-based protests, urban and rural, added to the foment of unrest aimed in large part at colonial rule and its consequences. Congress boycotted the opening of the legislative assembly in 1929, and a new campaign of civil disobedience began in 1930.

Out of this crisis came the 1935 Government of India Act, which sought to placate nationalists, maintain cordial relations with the Indian principalities, and sustain the support of the pro-imperialist wing within British politics. It failed on every count. The principle of dyarchy intro-

FIGURE 23 *Indian National Congress poster, 'The Right Path to Liberty'* (The Art Archive/British Library)

duced in 1919 was extended to central government while the provincial councils were awarded full self-government. The electorate remained limited (about 30 million people), and defence and foreign policy were reserved to the governor general. The Act nonetheless produced extraordinary election results in 1937, with the Congress Party securing an absolute majority in six of the eleven provinces and forming a government in seven of the eleven. The outbreak of war only two years later brought this political experiment to an abrupt end as Congress leaders resigned their posts in protest as the British once more declared war on behalf of India without any consultation. The contrast with the Dominions, where leaders had the right to declare war (or not) on their own behalf, hammered home the different treatment of white settler colonies and of India. This inequality was deeply damaging. In 1942, the widespread 'Quit India' campaign led to the swift banning of Congress and the jailing of its leaders. These tactics fanned

FIGURE 24 *The Indian police dispersing a crowd in Bombay (Mumbai), 1931*
(Illustrated London News)

nationalist anger and the Quit India campaign spread from the city of
Bombay into the countryside and across the vast expanse of British India,
leading to violent riots and attacks on government property and on the
police.

But the campaign was only one of the wartime nationalist crises Britain
faced in the Indian context. Led by Subhas Chandra Bose, a contingent of
Indian soldiers, aided by the Japanese, formed the Indian National Army
in opposition to British colonial rule. By 1943 Bose had some 11,000
soldiers ready, and was training another 20,000. Although Bose's campaign petered out, the INA demonstrated quite clearly that nationalist
desires now far outweighed loyalty to the British in many quarters. British
efforts to court-martial some of the leaders stirred protest in India after
the war, in much the same way that the execution of rebels after the Easter
Rising in Dublin made nationalist policies more attractive to many in
Ireland. The imperial government, it seems, learned few lessons when it
came to relations with their nationalist opponents. None of their actions
suggest a state anxious to divest itself of its colonial possessions and uninterested in its Empire. On the contrary, the reaction of British governments to nationalist protests suggests that neither Labour nor Conservative
governments were ready to abandon the Empire. Among the most prominent of pro-imperialists was Winston Churchill, who had been vocal in his
fears that the establishment of the Irish Free State and the prospect of a
Dominion India would weaken Britain's hold on its Empire. Anti-colonial

nationalism (in Ireland and in India especially) was, by this measure, successful: it forced the imperial centre to debate the very nature of its colonial enterprise.

By the summer of 1945, when Congress leaders were released from jail, it was clear that independence for India was inevitable. Growing violence between Hindu and Muslim Indians alongside nationalist agitation speeded the transfer of power, and the end result (detailed in Chapter 11) was the momentous partition of the former British India into India and Pakistan in August 1947, both as British Dominions. The subsequent violence was immense, but the two new states survived.

In the second volume of her autobiography, the white Rhodesian novelist Doris Lessing described the moment in 1956 when she could no longer see Britain in a sentimental light. 'How very careless, how lazy, how indifferent the British Empire was, how lightly it took on vast countries and millions of people.'[2] Lessing's disappointment with what she saw as a cavalier and heartless Empire was unusual for a white African, but large numbers of black Africans shared her opinion. Colonized peoples could not but be aware of the growing gap between their own economic and political condition and those of the west; even during the years of the depression, when severe unemployment and considerable hardship struck many in Britain, the contrast between the developed and colonial world was still stark. In the West Indies, the suffrage was extended during the Second World War, and new constitutions granting limited self-governance were introduced, but the limitations on self-rule were palpable. Moreover, labour conditions prompted the growth of trades unions, and these proved fertile ground for the growth of nationalist leaders such as the Barbadian nationalist Grantly Adams. In places such as Kenya where a wealthy white settler class lived in style while indigenous people found themselves on ever more marginal land, such contrasts yielded growing resentment of colonial rule. It was to protect African land rights that in 1928 Jomo Kenyatta (who would be the first president of Kenya after independence) and Harry Thuku launched an organized political campaign among Africans in Kenya. Severe economic hardship in interwar Africa helped anti-colonial sentiment gain a foothold, and the labour migration that saw thousands of men moving in search of work enlarged urban populations, which were the earliest and most successful home for nationalist recruiting.

India and Ireland are perhaps the most famous arenas of interwar anti-colonial nationalism (and probably the easiest to reduce, however wrongly, to questions of religious division), but campaigns in these countries form only one small segment of the increasing opposition faced by the Empire in the twentieth century. Nationalism in its anti-colonial form was a force to be reckoned with in many other parts of the Empire too, both in older and newer colonial possessions. Problems in India and Palestine demanded instant attention while, not long after, the British found themselves fighting a lengthy and daunting war against nationalists in Malaya. Serious eruptions of long-term violence followed in Kenya and in Cyprus, while riots and strikes rocked western Africa in particular in the late 1940s.

Throughout the Middle East as well, the British faced significant opposition to their influence and rule. Nationalists watched with concern when Muslim lands were given, without consultation, to the European colonial powers as the Ottoman Empire was broken up after the war. This new consolidation of European colonialism in the Muslim Middle East revealed that the voices of colonized peoples were of little importance and that the era of European imperialism was far from over. Self-determination was more theory and vision than practice. In Egypt, the British colonial authorities ruthlessly suppressed nationalism, tightly controlling what the local press could publish. When riots broke out in 1919 (as they did in so many British imperial arenas) the British offered minor concessions to the Egyptian nationalists. Despite bitter opposition from pro-imperial politicians such as Churchill, Britain declared Egypt independent in 1922 yet maintained control of the Suez Canal and of foreign affairs. It was a situation guaranteed to raise ire among Egyptian nationalists, deprived of genuine control of Egyptian affairs. Britain also managed to upset the Dominion countries in that year, and along similar lines. There was no consultation with the Dominions over war with Turkey, yet Britain expected them to provide troops as they had in the 1914–18 war. The refusal of support by Canada and South Africa signalled a growing gulf between Britain and the Dominions. In the end, war with Turkey was averted but the 1922 crisis, known as the Chanak Crisis, revealed that the strains within the Empire were varied and deep.

Another area where British failure helped kindle nationalism was in Palestine, whose administration Britain had formally acquired in 1920 but that had in practice become British in 1917 when military action forced the Turks out of the region. Zionist settlers in Palestine had been assured in 1917 that 'His Majesty's Government view with favour the establishment in Palestine of a national home for the Jewish people, and will use their best endeavours to facilitate the achievement of this object.'[3] However, the British had also promised the Palestinians that their lands would not be compromised, and these promises were clearly incompatible despite a dividing of the territory at the River Jordan into Jewish and Arab zones.

Growing Arab–Jewish violence resulted from the continued Zionist migration to the region. In 1926 about 150,000 Jewish settlers lived in Palestine; by 1936, as fascism in Europe became more boldly anti-Semitic, those numbers had risen to around 400,000, representing one-third of the total population of the area. Serious rioting in 1929 saw more than 200 deaths. The continued influx of Jews in the 1930s precipitated Arab attacks on British troops and Jewish settlements. The restriction on Jewish immigration that Britain then imposed in 1941 could not have come at a worse time, given the massive scale on which the detention and killing of Jews was now in force in Germany. Arab Palestinians felt betrayed by the influx; Jewish settlers were frustrated by what they saw as Britain's dilatoriness in formalizing a homeland. Both sides saw Britain as failing to fulfil promises. In Iraq too, Arab rebellions against the British defined the 1920s, but the economic and strategic importance of the region was more important to the Empire than was the placating of anti-colonial nationalist demands. It would only be after the 1939–45 war that any substantive independence would come to the region, as the next chapter will show. Even after Iraq gained its independence in 1932, the British insisted on the use of Iraqi airfields for quick response in the region, and in return helped the new regime to silence Kurdish nationalism.

Further south, in sub-Saharan Africa, anti-colonial activities were also on the rise. The African Association, founded in 1897, allowed only those of African descent to become members, including both Africans and Afro-Caribbeans among its members. In the 1890s the West African writer Edward Blyden was touring the USA and Britain, as well as West Africa, advocating African nationalism. What would in 1925 be renamed the African National Congress (ANC) was founded in 1912 as the South African Native National Congress. Influenced in its adoption of passive resistance tactics by Indian nationalism, and especially by the Indian National Congress, the ANC illustrates how nationalists in different countries learned from one another in their struggles against the British. Both the INC in India and the ANC in South Africa would play major roles in securing independence from colonial rule. More radical organizations were also active: the South African Industrial and Commercial Workers Union organized successful strikes in 1919 and 1920, and the interwar years saw growing links between African-Americans, especially by Marcus Garvey and his followers in the West Indies, and South African nationalists.

Rioting and rebellion against British rule in Africa gathered steam throughout the early years of the century. Dissatisfaction over working conditions and economic inequality often helped fuel early nationalist sentiment. The years prior to the First World War saw violence in and beyond British Africa, including in British Guiana, Nigeria, Kenya, Natal and elsewhere in Southern Africa and, though not all of this protest was explicitly anti-colonial, the widespread unhappiness with imperial rule spurred the growth of nationalism. A revolt among the Nandi people in Kenya in 1905 over taxation and land had prompted a military sortie by the British that left over 1,000 people dead. Later nationalists claimed the Nandi leader, Koitalel Samoei, as Kenya's first freedom fighter for his resistance to imperial encroachment in East Africa. Death rates among local protesters were often high in these riots, although this did little to deter rioting that, by 1918, had spread to Kenya and Northern Rhodesia, then to Aden out in the Red Sea, and to Somaliland in the 1920s. Rail strikes crippled Sierra Leone in 1919 and again in 1926, and Nigeria in 1921. Strikes hit the Rhodesian copper mines in 1935. Economic depression in the 1930s fuelled discontent, and by the 1930s many political organizations in Africa advocated self-government. The Nigerian Youth Movement, founded in 1934, moved from advocating higher education to promoting self-government.

The marked difference in lifestyle that indigenous peoples in colonies such as Kenya and Rhodesia witnessed between their own poverty and the privilege of white settlers kept anti-colonial resentment very much alive. Although not all white settlers in these colonies were wealthy (many struggled to stay afloat in the mid-war years), they nonetheless lived on land appropriated from local use, and they employed black workers at low wages to do their bidding. These social and political inequalities produced impoverishment as well as social and economic disruption among displaced and relocated local peoples, which in turn encouraged the growth of nationalist organizations. It was organizations such as the Kikuyu Central Association in Kenya (banned in 1940 as subversive) that helped mobilize rural peasant populations and transform anti-colonial nationalism from a largely urban to a mass movement that incorporated rural peoples. It was a key issue, for Africa in the interwar years remained largely rural.

By the mid-1940s, African nationalism was far more than the collection of disparate regional dissatisfactions that British officials claimed it was. Nationalist leaders in different colonies saw similarities in their goals, and in 1945 the fifth in a series of Pan-African Congresses, held in the northern British city of Manchester, pledged itself to a non-violent socialist goal for the African colonies. The first of the congresses where a majority of the delegates were African rather than Caribbean, it was also the first to put African independence centre stage. The Pan-African movement had close ties to black liberation politics in the United States, and as the Cold War began to dominate world politics in the 1950s its commitment to socialism would, as the next chapter discusses, have important consequences. Violence, despite the non-violent goals of the 1945 conference, did not end in Africa. The Gold Coast (which would be the first of the British colonies in Africa to gain independence, in 1957) saw rioting in 1948. Buganda in eastern Africa experienced anti-colonial riots in 1945 and again in 1949 and, as in the 1930s, the depression of the post-war years was a major factor. In the 1950s nationalism began to spread in earnest to rural Africa, and even harsh repression could not suppress its growth. By 1960, as the next chapter will show, more than half of British Africa was independent: the press dubbed it 'Africa Year'.

Another key imperial site where significant anti-colonial nationalism occupied British attention, and indeed personnel, was on the Malay peninsula where the nineteenth-century importation of non-native labour, and in particular the growth of a Straits Chinese community, had long divided the population. In this region, forms of nationalism unassociated with British imperialism complicated the situation. In the 1920s the nationalist Kuomintang, which had ousted the Chinese imperial family, had made considerable headway among the Straits Chinese population, as had their rivals, the communists, although neither ever exercised much influence outside the Chinese population. In 1926 (four years before the establishment of the Malayan Communist Party), the Singapore Malay Union began to organize among the indigenous Malay community. In the interwar years, anti-British strikes and risings erupted. The most intense period of nationalist activity came after 1938 and was met with severe repression from the British, who sent some 40,000 troops to police the region in a futile attempt to stave off independence.

One of the distinctive features of Malay anti-colonial nationalism was that there was never much common ground between the large ethnic Chinese population there and the indigenous Malay population. It was, of course, imperialism that had created this diverse and divided population and that exploited the differences that emerged between the different groups, just as in India the British had encouraged divisions between Hindu and Muslim nationalisms.

In Burma, too, colonial actions helped structure the particular form that anti-colonial nationalism took there. Nationalist organizations in Burma did not share a common vision of what Burma's post-independence future should look like, but they did have in common a desire for political separation from India. Shortly after the First World War, the exclusion of Burma from the political changes applied in India (from where the colony was governed), which had given Indians a greater if still limited role in governance, precipitated riots among Burmese nationalists. Britain hastily extended the new system of dyarchy to Burma in 1921, but although Burmese nationalists shared an anti-colonial agenda the new system provoked markedly different readings of how nationalism should subsequently operate. Riots in the 1930s saw attacks on both Britons and Indians living in Burma.

In common with many other colonies, there were important differences in the goals of urban and rural activists, but it was perhaps the difference between those who emphasized Burma's Buddhist legacy and those who favoured a more westernized and secularized nationalism wedded to modernization that ran deepest in Burmese nationalism. As in other colonial settings, the divide between those who wanted to embrace a more western style of politics for the future and those who rejected what the west offered was a strong and a divisive factor. Rural rebellion, student strikes and riots were common in Burma in the interwar years, and in 1935 the Government of Burma Act separated Burma from India (as of 1937) and extended its self-governance considerably. As elsewhere, the key policy areas of defence, foreign affairs and finance remained under British control, a move that only encouraged and deepened anti-colonial beliefs. As among some Indian nationalists in the 1940s, some in Burma also allied with Japan in an anti-western political gesture.

These alliances with Japan highlight not only the anti-western element that was an inevitable by-product of imperial rule, but also the factors external to the specific rule of Britain and of the Empire. In particular, the two world wars had massive repercussions. We have already traced the impact of the first of these conflagrations, visible perhaps most vividly in Egypt, India and Ireland. The Second World War was no less influential in sustaining, creating and sometimes transforming anti-colonial nationalisms throughout the Empire. In part this influence arose from the simple fact that so much of this war was fought on imperial soil, and the collapse of British rule in east and south-east Asia suggested the potential weakness of the British. The Japanese invasion of Hong Kong, Singapore and much of the British Pacific, as well as the war in Burma and the Pacific, exposed Britain's military and political vulnerabilities. Existing hostility to colonialism was certainly amplified by Britain's wartime failures. Just as Irish nationalists had seized the opportunity of rebellion in 1916 when

British troops were occupied elsewhere, so in the 1940s did anti-colonial nationalists foment disturbances and seek allies against the British. The war escalated nationalist demands and exposed British weaknesses as well as betrayals, and the aftermath of the war did little to undercut these destabilizations of colonial authority. Britain's reliance after 1945 on American aid and the growing division between capitalist and communist regimes worldwide, sharpened nationalist conflicts.

For subject peoples, nationalism spelled the prospect of independence and self-governance, free from colonial authority, but anti-colonial senti-ment could also be found at the heart of the Empire and among those associated with the imperial power. Some western critics of the Empire were committed to ending imperialism, others to reforming it. In the nineteenth and early twentieth centuries the Liberal Party had been publicly associ-ated with opposition to the Empire, although its policies never reflected that position consistently. The Liberal Party sponsored the principles of Home Rule in Ireland but it was a compromise policy that won the party few friends among either Irish Republicans or Unionists opposed to separ-ating Ireland and Britain. These efforts led, moreover, to a major breach within the Liberal Party. Many Liberals who favoured union with Ireland switched political allegiance in the late nineteenth century when the Irish question dominated parliament.

In the twentieth century, the Liberal Party was eclipsed by the newer Labour Party, also for the most part associated with opposition to imper-ialism, but equally inconsistent in its practical approach to the issue. Though the parliamentary parties, invariably torn by competing interests, were at best dilatory in their colonial policies, there were anti-colonial organizations separate from the major political parties at work in Britain. A few parliamentarians, activists and missionaries in the interwar period drew attention to brutality in the Empire, but were quickly marginalized. In the 1950s left-of-centre MP Fenner Brockway established the Movement for Colonial Freedom. The group acted as a watchdog, protesting against the repressive tactics employed by both Labour and Conservative govern-ments in the post-war years of colonial rebellion. Brockway was particu-larly vocal, as was fellow Labour MP Barbara Castle, about the cruel tactics employed in the Kenyan emergency in the mid-1950s. Brockway, Castle and their supporters vigorously opposed detention without trial and protested against the poor conditions of the detention camps hastily set up to contain Kenyan nationalists.

Also in the 1950s the Reverend Guthrie Michael Scott founded the Africa Bureau, an organization committed to advising anti-colonial

Africans whose tactics against colonialism remained constitutional. Where Brockway's group could thus work on behalf of groups such as the Mau Mau – who did resort to illegal measures and to violence – Guthrie's support was reserved for those of more cautious and limited tactics. There was as much heterogeneity in domestic anti-imperialism as there was in anti-colonial nationalism in the colonies themselves.

Marxist politics offered another anti-colonial perspective. European critiques of imperialism in the twentieth century often argued that capitalism and colonialism were critically linked, and in the Cold War years many anti-colonial nationalist groups were aided and funded by the USSR as part of its broader anti-capitalist strategy. In 1927, the Anti-Imperialist League, based in Berlin, was created as a satellite organization of the Comintern, the Soviet office designed to promote communism internationally, and European communist parties established organizations for colonial students. Many anti-imperialists in the west were disillusioned when the USSR embarked upon its own imperial quest. In 1956 and again in 1968, as Soviet tanks crushed rebellions in Hungary and in Czechoslovakia, membership of European communist parties plummeted. For nationalists on the ground in colonial arenas, however, the luxury of such principled dissociation was not possible. Just as some in Burma and India were willing to embrace Japanese fascism in the 1940s in order to oust Britain, in the Cold War years the aid offered to anti-colonial nationalists by the Soviet Union was often vital to a group's survival. Despite its own actions in eastern Europe, the Soviet Union continued to encourage and to fund anti-colonial nationalist movements in regions where European colonialism was strong and where they could thus offer a thoroughgoing critique of the relationship between capitalism and imperialism, long a mainstay of Marxist economic and political analysis.

While Marxist readings of colonialism stressed class and economics, other divisive factors were also at work. The gap between rich and poor, between propertied and propertyless, was clearly critical in fomenting discontent in the colonies. Just as important, however, were racial distinctions, which gave rise to considerable anger. In the African settler colonies, whites had rights to the best land available, often employing the very people they had dispossessed to work it for them. As we have seen, in every colony, whites – even the working-class troops who at home had little social standing – could dominate the local population, order them around, restrict their movements and demand obedience. This division by skin colour was unmistakable and relentless, and common throughout the Empire. Not surprisingly, these characteristic colonial behaviours based on race shaped, in turn, a corresponding racialization of anti-colonial nationalisms. Anti-Indian agitation in Burma and anti-Chinese attacks in Malaysia are good examples of how racial divides created by British rule could be translated into the practices of anti-colonial nationalism. Where outside groups were regarded as having benefited from colonialism to the detriment of the indigenous population, frictions between these populations complicated the racial situation. In the wake of decolonization, as Chapter 11 will discuss, such divisions often had dramatic as well as violent effects on migrant populations.

Sexual divisions were sometimes less immediately apparent than racial ones in the strategies of anti-colonial nationalisms, yet the effects of nationalist activity on the role and position of colonized women could be profound. On the one hand, the increased levels of protest that were, by the mid-twentieth century, characteristic of nationalism in colonial environments often brought women into the political arena in larger numbers. Nationalist women's organizations encouraged political participation. The first woman president of the Indian National Congress, Sarojini Naidu, was elected to that position in 1925. In the 1880s Anna Parnell's Ladies' Land League was an important element in Irish struggles over land. The United Malays national organization had a women's branch, and in India the All-India Women's Conference was highly visible and active from the late 1920s. These organizations often focused on the specific issues most pressing for women within the broader national context.

Yet it was often the case that women were asked to put their claims as women on hold, to subordinate their needs and claims to what (male) nationalists argued were the more urgent and larger issues at stake. Such arguments were often backed by claims that because of women's importance as childbearers and child-rearers, they were thus the 'mothers of the nation' whose role ought to focus on reproduction of both bodies and culture to ensure the continuance of race and culture. This fundamentally conservative view, which relegated women to a narrow and domestic role within the nationalist struggle, was a common one, and though many women accepted this as part of their commitment to nationalism, it did not always bode well for women's post-independence status. Gendered divisions were also central to how nationalisms invoked the all-important sentiment of sacrifice. Men, in effect, were called upon to be willing to sacrifice their life fighting for the cause, and women had to be willing to sacrifice husbands and sons. In that light, of course, the demand for women's rights could be made to seem deeply individualistic and somewhat selfish.

In many instances the power struggles associated with anti-colonial nationalism involved a politics of public space more readily occupied by men. Women in many colonized cultures and certainly in imperial Britain had long been expected to fulfil largely domestic roles as mothers and childcarers. Their future role was often part of the larger battlefield over what the post-colonial nation might look like. As we have seen, nationalist movements could be definitively anti-western, and they could also embrace some aspects of western culture and values. What to keep and what to reject was always a central concern for anti-colonial nationalists, and the role and position of women was invariably a key component in this determination, even as women's rights were regarded as less important than winning the fight for independence. Some sought to return women to what they saw as a proper and traditional female role, others were open to changes in women's status. In all cases, however, gender was a central concern for nationalism, even where women were asked to put nationalism before gender reform.

The position of women within the politics of anti-colonial nationalism highlights the close connections between the political and cultural aspects of imperialism. These kinds of struggles over definition and role were critical both in shaping the nature of nationalist activity and what came after. They demonstrate very clearly the common tensions between embracing and rejecting western values, for, as we have seen, it was a commonplace among colonists to represent colonials as cruel or at least indifferent to women. Did the liberation of women and a change in their social roles mean, then, that western ways had been adopted? In the controversy in the late nineteenth century over child marriage in India, this issue surfaced quite explicitly. The enforcing of an age of sexual consent upon child brides in 1891 set off a noisy protest among Hindus offended by the prospect of legitimate husbands liable to prosecution for conjugal relations, and by what they saw as a British misreading of Indian attitudes to women and to sexuality. Badly managed colonial rule in this instance led to a quickening of the pace of nationalism, another instance of Britain's seeming failure to learn from past errors, as well as a salutary reminder that nationalism could be quite conservative in its aspirations and attitudes.

The rise of anti-colonial nationalism, mostly in the twentieth century, owes its rise, then, to a complex of interrelated factors, many of which resonated beyond the colonial scene as well. The growing resentment over racial and economic inequalities in particular was exploited by other powers eager to topple Britain and its allies. Poor and often insensitive colonial governance did little to dampen this dissatisfaction. Increased contact between those who experienced colonialism helped spread nationalist ideas and tactics. Although nationalism in the colonies began life mostly in urban settings and among educated people frustrated by the limits colonial rule imposed upon them, its spread to a mass populace and to rural areas in the mid-twentieth century ensured its viability. The subsequent process of decolonization, begun in the 1940s but associated most vividly with the 1960s, owed much to the rapid spread of nationalist ideas all over imperial ground. Faced with movements that borrowed both from older local traditions and from western politics meant that the British were often facing forms of protest to which they had no obvious response. The alliances between rural and urban, between traditionalists and radicals, confounded British readings of colonial activism. British failure to understand the nature of opposition to colonial rule deepened resentment and determination among anti-colonial nationalists.

As an interesting postscript to the story of nationalism, decolonization was by no means a capstone that secured success, rendering nationalism redundant. In white settler colonies, the last half of the twentieth century witnessed considerable lobbying from indigenous groups claiming that the settlers who had arrived as a result of colonialism should recognize indigenous rights to land as well as advance cultural and social equality. Aboriginal rights organizations in Canada and Australia, for example, argued for the return of territory to indigenous peoples, a strategy based on recognition of the distinctiveness and autonomy of ethnic groups with claims to land and property. The similarities with earlier nationalist claims and demands against the colonial government suggest that the forms of nationalism peculiar to anti-colonialism are also capable of successful transformation, and that decolonization should not be considered in any way an absolute ending.

Nationalism was never a single and unified movement. Inevitably there were competing ideas as to what (or who) a nation was within the colonial arena. The ways in which imperialism had redrawn political and cultural boundaries over the years and had favoured some groups over others clouded and complicated what was already at stake: how was the nation (at whichever colonial site) to be defined, more especially after years of colonial rule had brought together hitherto separate peoples?

In India, for example, differences in that vision were by no means confined to religious sectarianism, although the communal violence that erupted so dramatically between Hindus and Muslims in the 1940s was certainly a dominant factor. But we should remember that Gandhi, so frequently depicted in popular culture as the hero of twentieth-century

Indian nationalism, had many detractors in India, and his rejection of class-based protest was not popular everywhere. As just one example, B. R. Ambedkar, who organized India's lowest caste, the *harijans*, in the 1930s, criticized Gandhi for his failure to condemn the caste system, but still identified with a broader nationalist agenda. Equally, the racial tension between Malay and Chinese residents of the Straits Settlements revealed distinctive readings of how a post-colonial state might function. These were rifts created in large measure by the vagaries of colonial rule itself, which had blurred cultural, ethnic and religious boundaries with ruthlessness and insensitivity. If decolonization, to which we now turn our attention, did not always lead to a harmonious independence, the effect of colonial rule must be seen to play some considerable role in that result.

References

1   Christopher A. Bayly, *The Birth of the Modern World, 1780–1914* (Oxford: Blackwell, 2004), p. 233.

2   Doris Lessing, *Walking in the Shade. Volume Two of my Autobiography* (New York: HarperCollins, 1997), p. 209.

3   Balfour Declaration, 1917.

CHAPTER 11

Decolonization

Anti-colonial nationalism in the twentieth century played a major role, as the previous chapter has suggested, in shaping the decolonization that dominated the politics of British imperialism after the Second World War. However, although nationalism remains a critical factor in explaining why decolonization occurred – and when it occurred – many other issues played an equally prominent role. There had never been a time when global issues – who was allied with whom, where trade routes were centred, and so forth – did not play a significant role in shaping how and where Britain colonized, and how it maintained its colonies and its status. The process of decolonization was no different in this respect. Like colonialism, decolonization too was a global phenomenon. The bulk of decolonization took place in three distinctive periods: in the late 1940s, when colonies mostly in south Asia or governed from there became independent; from the late 1950s to the early 1960s, when much of Africa gained independence; and in the late 1960s and the 1970s, when Britain decamped from its remaining colonies east of Suez and elsewhere, mostly as a result of Britain's tenaciously weak economic position.

Decolonization is a term used mostly by colonizing nations, Britain among them, to signal both the process and the period whereby former colonies gained political independence and the right to choose their own forms of rule and leadership. The process is also often referred to, not surprisingly, by those in former colonies as liberation, rather than decolonization, a preference reflecting the freedom to which anti-colonial nationalists aspired. In this chapter, unlike the last, our emphasis is on understanding from the British (and thus the colonizer's) perspective why

Caption: Queen in Barbados. Queen Elizabeth II is greeted by Errol Walton Barrow, Prime Minister of Barbados, on her arrival in Bridgetown, Barbados on 2nd February 1966. The Governor, Sir John Stow (right), also greeted the Queen and her husband, Prince Philip on their arrival from London.   Credit: ©2005 Credit:TopFoto / AP

FIGURE 25 *The 1966 royal tour of the West Indies* (Topfoto/Associated Press)

such changes occurred, and so rapidly. We are investigating principally not how former colonies won their freedom but why Britain disgorged so fully its imperial possessions in the second half of the twentieth century.

In many respects, and in many places, the world after 1945 was tremendously different from what it had been prior to six years of global conflict. The war years had speeded up technological gains, shifted political alliances and engendered radically changed economic structures. Although Britain's palpable decline in economic and political muscle was not brought about solely by the hardships and costs of war, the war escalated and intensified a trend that had long been apparent in the UK. Britain's economy and industries had felt the pressure of stiff competition throughout the twentieth century, but it was still possible between the two world wars for Britain, in large part because of its huge empire, to see itself as a major figure on the world stage, a political and diplomatic force to be reckoned with. After 1945, that image was a much harder sell, and the mantle of power, certainly in the political and economic realms, moved away from Britain and across the Atlantic Ocean to the United States.

The rise of America to world prominence was one of the most distinctive changes of the post-1945 period. The popularity of American culture and products in Britain was visible as early as the 1920s; Hollywood films, jazz and American fashion were hugely popular in interwar Britain. However, America's pivotal role in the Second World War from 1941, and its economic strength and dominance during and after the war, had a durable and powerful effect on the entire world. Put bluntly, without American money much of Europe, and Britain in particular, would have suffered severe economic hardship in the years following the war. The USA made major economic gains during the war, whereas Britain in 1945 faced a massive deficit as well as the need to rebuild many areas damaged by bombing raids.

American attitudes to colonialism, meanwhile, were complex. America had largely divested itself of its own imperial holdings, the Philippines gaining independence in 1946, although in some cases possessions were folded into statehood, as was the case for Alaska and Hawaii. American rhetoric rejected colonialism and the support of a State Department official paper, released in 1942, for national independence for colonies had angered the British. After the war, however, when the Soviets emerged as a potential rival on the world stage, American attitudes to European colonialism tended to be shaped principally by Cold War imperatives. Where colonialism was viewed as a bulwark against communism, the USA was happy to allow its retention.

Although the USA was in profoundly better economic shape at the end of the war than any of the other industrial nations, it faced nonetheless a new and powerful enemy in the Soviet Union (USSR). Despite its own imperial ambitions, the USSR found it valuable to foster and fund nationalist movements in colonies under western European rule. As mentioned in Chapter 10, the Soviets were as cynical in their exploitation of imperialism and anti-colonial nationalism as were their American rivals, funding and fostering nationalism in the colonies of the capitalist world while extending the USSR's own hold in eastern Europe with considerable brutality and little regard for national sovereignty. The spirit of capitalism so crucial to American identity and success could not but regard communist Russia – and its imperial intentions – as a threat. The so-called Cold War, which would mould so much of the world's politics until the 1990s, forged new alliances as these two 'superpowers', the USA and the USSR, worked to secure their positions. Britain, heavily reliant on infusions of American cash to save its ailing economy, and itself identified with the exploitation of colonial resources (both labour and goods), was inevitably

allied with the USA, while many of its colonies found in the USSR a generous benefactor of education, weaponry and advice in their campaigns
for independence. The Cold War's deep embroilment in the politics and
economics of imperialism had a profound effect on British decolonization.
As Britain would find out in the 1950s, moreover, the price of American
friendship could be intensely humiliating to a power that had colonized
so very much of the globe in the past. The colonial world throughout
the years of the Cold War was a theatre in which the west and the USSR
clashed, the USSR encouraging the destabilizing effects of anti-colonialism
in order to weaken the capitalist power bloc. The fear that former colonies
would turn towards communism rather than the free trade capitalism of the
western world was a critical factor affecting the process of decolonization.

Alongside Britain's unavoidable entanglement in the rivalries between
the USA and the USSR, ideas of European cooperation were strengthening, especially from the 1950s. This recognition of common European
interests was rooted to some degree in a fear that communist Russia would
turn its attention westwards. Memories of foreign occupation were fresh
in those parts of Europe where the Nazis had been temporarily successful
invaders. Alliances across western Europe, which would also foster better
trade agreements, were designed to protect these nations from the Soviet
giant on its eastern doorstep. Britain, by the late 1950s, was anxious to
play a part in this new alliance, more particularly when enhanced colonial
trade proved unable to pull Britain out of its economic slump, and unrest
in colonial arenas was growing costly to control. Britain applied for
membership of the European Economic Community (EEC) in 1961, a sign
of disengagement from its close economic ties with its colonies. France,
however, vetoed Britain's membership on the grounds that its ties to the
Commonwealth and to the USA rendered Britain insufficiently European.
Ironically, Britain's application for membership was opposed by the
very Commonwealth leaders whose ties to Britain had shaped Charles de
Gaulle's scepticism about Britain's commitment to Europe. De Gaulle
would veto Britain's next attempt in 1967 to gain membership, and it was
not until 1973 (and a change in French leadership) that Britain finally
gained entry to what is now called the European Union.

Britain's relationship to the EEC was not, however, the only way in
which Europe helped shape the course of British decolonization in the
late twentieth century. De Gaulle's decision in 1960 to abandon French
imperial claims in West and Equatorial Africa also helped accelerate
British decolonization in the region. In that same year, Belgium withdrew
quite suddenly from the Congo, which rapidly became a focal point for

political tensions that the British feared would spill over into neighbouring British colonies such as Uganda and Northern Rhodesia. Congolese
radicals founded alliances with the USSR, and Britain thus potentially
faced in this area of Africa both local turbulence and a potential Cold War
threat. Moreover, 'Africa Year' in 1960 also saw 16 newly independent
African states accepted into the United Nations (UN), an indication of
where the sympathies of the UN lay.

Anti-colonial nationalism, alongside these complex global relationships, created the conditions in which decolonization occurred. The scale
of discontent and of demands for self-direction clearly escalated after the
Second World War. In 1954 Kwame Nkrumah, who in 1949 had founded
a nationalist party in the Gold Coast in West Africa, issued his 'Declaration to the Colonial Peoples of the World'. Imperialism, he claimed, was
an exploitative system, and all peoples had the right to govern themselves.
The Gold Coast subsequently became, in 1957, Ghana, the first African
colony to gain independence from Britain. Nkrumah's defiant condemnation of the colonial system in 1954 was an important rallying call for anti-
colonial nationalism in the region for, in profound ways, the post-1945
period was truly the coming of age of western notions of democracy.
While the dispossessed in underdeveloped countries looked on, those in
the western world experienced a bountiful economic democratization in
which property and consumer goods became more affordable and available, even in economically depressed Britain. Denied in many instances
even a say in policy affecting their livelihood, their culture, their practices
and laws, colonial activists turned increasingly to demands for complete
independence. The Gold Coast's path to independence in many ways
reflects the complexities of decolonization. The colony had grown increasingly prosperous through cocoa production before the Second World
War, and colonial officials approved the moderate African politics that
seemed to dominate the colony until the late 1940s. The Gold Coast
became a far more radical environment under the growing influence
of British-educated Nkrumah, whose socialist-inspired politics alarmed
officials sufficiently for them to jail him in the 1950s. This shift from
model colony to problem child did not derail decolonization; on the contrary, it may have precipitated the change, as in India. However, the shift
illustrates the kind of assessments made by officials around questions of
suitability for independence.

In some respects, Britain's increasing economic presence in Africa in
the late 1940s and 1950s had also fuelled resentment that was easily chan-
nelled by nationalists. Britain had hoped to use the riches of its African

colonies to improve its economic situation at home. As a result, the British presence in remote rural as well as urban areas of Africa grew significantly after the war as colonial development schemes were vigorously implemented. Many Africans who had hitherto been at least directly unaware of or unaffected by a colonial presence were now irked by this intervention; it was another fertile source for nationalist organizing. Greater economic intervention in the colonies pre-dated the Second World War. Britain's weakened trading status in the interwar period had made attention to imperial markets attractive. Agencies for colonial development began to proliferate: the Empire Cotton Growing Corporation dates from 1921 and the Empire Marketing Board from 1926, yet neither these bodies nor colonial development were given the sustained funding that was needed to make the dream of a British-centred global economy a reality.

Britain's economic woes made its position an acutely difficult one. Reliant on American money and fearful of communism, saddled with the costs of running an Empire that was increasingly fractious, anxious to alleviate economic hardships and sustain welfare reforms at home, Labour and Conservative governments alike wrestled with whether the Empire was worth the money. This was no new concern; there were constant grumbles in parliament about how much the Empire cost, and indeed not all colonies were profitable, either for the state or for those investing or working in them. Things came to a head, however, after 1945 when a condition of the £3.75 billion loan Britain received from America was that sterling be made fully convertible with the US dollar. During the war, sterling earnings could be spent only in sterling-based countries, but the American loan was contingent upon opening up world markets without restriction. Britain rather cynically complied by greatly limiting the economic freedoms of its colonized peoples in order to improve the domestic situation. Africa and south-east Asia, in particular, were far more intensively exploited than they had been before the war. It would be tempting to assume that this greater attention to, and exploitation of, the valuable commodities these colonies had to offer would have enriched the local peoples. On the contrary, the stringent rules Britain imposed were designed to enhance sterling and Britain, rather than spreading the wealth more equitably. Colonial currencies were required to maintain fixed exchange rates with sterling, to sell their currency earnings to Britain in return for sterling and to permit free sterling transfers. It was a plan clearly intended to get Britain out of economic trouble at the expense of its Empire, despite the fact that many colonies suffered economic and political losses perhaps as great in some ways as those endured by Britain during the war years.

The often inflationary conditions that Britain's economic policies produced in the colonies helped to spread anti-colonial opposition.

These were economic policies that did not work, and that in every respect demonstrated British determination to use the Empire in pursuit of domestic priorities. When it became clear that the convertibility with the dollar required by the Americans was proving difficult to achieve, the Labour government devalued sterling in 1949 without bothering to consult the Commonwealth countries. It was a slap in the face for the Dominions, once more ignored on policy affecting the Empire as a whole.

Resentment of Britain by its colonies was also exacerbated by the conduct of Britain during and even before wartime. The Australians, for example, harboured a deep sense of betrayal over the Japanese invasions in the Pacific. Popular Australian sentiment blamed the British for favouring the western theatre of war, and leaving Australia vulnerable to attack. When in 1951 Australia and the USA signed a pact to protect one another from hostilities in the Pacific, the British were conspicuously excluded. The Indian soldiers who fought with the Allies played a vital role in the war and, as had been the case in the First World War, many of them hoped that their efforts would be recognized by some further degree of Indian independence. Malta and Ceylon were made wartime promises of self-government, but whereas Ceylon was granted independence in 1948, Malta had to suffice with mere internal self-government in 1947. Direct rule was reimposed there in 1959 when the British and Maltese governments failed to reach an agreement on economic questions, and it was not until 1964 that Malta enjoyed full independence. Britain's failure to reward colonies for their wartime loyalties, as we saw in Chapter 10, angered many activists. The interwar years, tellingly, had not been ones in which British governments had thought seriously about decolonization or made any preparations to embark upon such a course.

Colonialism, on the eve of decolonization, was a volatile and disparate phenomenon. The 1930s and even the war years had seen a good deal of unrest in many parts of the Empire, as we have seen. The Palestine mandate had proven to be a diplomatic minefield, and the region was further destabilized by an army rebellion against the British in 1941 in the former mandate of Iraq. British rule faced labour protests across Africa, rebellion broke out in Cyprus in 1939, and in India wave after wave of protest panicked the authorities into arresting prominent Congress Party members. Such a hugely unpopular move compounded existing and serious tensions between ruler and ruled in India. Coupled with the Japanese occupation of British colonies in south-east Asia, it was apparent even at

Westminster in the 1940s that the colonial world was under threat from many directions. The allied victory in the war in 1945 brought little relief on the colonial front. Hasty and ill-conceived decision-making and botched attempts at compromise characterized the 1947 partition of India and the declaration of the state of Israel a year later. The legacy of these earliest instances of decolonization remain among the most intractable of the world's conflicts today, as Pakistan and India continue to feud over the disputed territory of Kashmir and as people die daily in Palestine and in Israel from sectarian violence.

There is no question that in many instances, and not just in this first period of decolonization, the British had their hand forced by circumstance. Expense, political turbulence and global diplomatic considerations all affected the speed and progress of the process, although both Labour and Conservative governments throughout the period of decolonization kept up a firm rhetoric that emphasized Britain's control of events and of the overall process. Although this was frequently little more than political posturing, it nonetheless revealed a salient element of both British imperialism and its dismantling. Britain always insisted that it would be the judge, and the best judge, of when a particular colony was ready for independence. This was an attitude that grew to a large extent out of that overwhelming justification of the nineteenth-century Empire, the 'civilizing mission'. Such attitudes were not much dislodged when, after the First World War, the new League of Nations adhered to the idea of 'trusteeship' in dividing up Germany's confiscated colonies and those of the former Ottoman Empire. The hierarchy built into the classes of 'mandate' that structured post-war colonialism conceived of Africa as less capable of independence than the Ottoman states of Syria, Lebanon, Iraq and Palestine. Whereas the Middle Eastern states that made up the Class A mandates were to be advanced to independence, Classes B (German East Africa) and C (German south-west Africa and the Pacific territories) mandates were classified as territories to be governed well and humanely, but there was no timescale for granting independence. The British, clearly, were not alone in adopting hierarchies that saw some peoples as more 'advanced' than others. Thus, although the reality was often much messier, British rhetoric at any rate was that the time for decolonization was something it alone would and could determine. In practice, and though the British often put a brave face on their actions, the era of decolonization was littered with humiliating defeats. The date for Indian independence was famously accelerated by some ten months as the British faced increasing violence between Hindus and Muslims that they feared would spread to the army. Lord Mountbatten arrived in India in March 1947 to oversee the road to independence, with a date of June 1948 set for the occasion. Circumstances were such that the handover came within five months of his taking office, in August 1947.

Four years later, the British-owned oil refinery at Abadan in Iran was nationalized. Neither the UN nor the USA was prepared to sanction British military intervention to restore the refinery to British hands; two years later, however, the British and the Americans joined forces to topple the Iranian regime, fearing a growth of Soviet influence in the region, but it was clear that the senior partner in this venture was the superpower, and not Britain, and that the rationale for intervention was the Cold War rather than British oil interests. Indeed, some have argued that Britain's decision in 1956 to march into Egypt was influenced by its humiliation in Iran earlier in the decade. The record is unclear as to how far such considerations were at work, but what is not in doubt is the botched job Britain and France made in Egypt in 1956.

The Suez Crisis has often been regarded as the turning point that accelerated the pace of decolonization and ushered in its second phase, beginning just a year later in 1957 with Ghana winning its independence. Nevertheless, although Britain's showing in Egypt in 1956 vividly underscored its weaknesses and loss of world influence, the fiasco was not truly a catalyst for what would follow. Plans for Ghanaian and even Nigerian independence were already well advanced when the Suez debacle occurred; it perhaps gave many in Britain pause for thought, but Suez was not decisive for the spread of decolonization. Its principal importance in the imperial landscape is probably that it revealed so deeply that Britain was no longer a major political force and, since the possession of a large empire had been central to Britain's claims to a central world role, this diminution in status affected attitudes to Britain and in its colonies.

The Suez episode usefully highlights the tangled connections that characterized the era of decolonization, however. It was the Egyptian abandonment in 1951 of an Anglo-Egyptian treaty that set off the events leading to the 1956 invasion. The 1936 treaty had exempted the Suez Canal Zone from Britain's guarantee to withdraw its troops from Egypt, but on the outbreak of war in 1939 the British postponed their promised withdrawal. Even after the war no effort was made to withdraw and, in 1952, Gamal Abdel Nasser led a coup to unseat King Farouk, who was widely looked upon in the region as collaborating too closely with the British. Pressure for British military withdrawal from the Canal Zone intensified in the early years of Nasser's rule, and the last British troops departed the Zone in June 1956. This phased withdrawal, 20 years after the guarantees of the Anglo-Egyptian treaty, left a void that Britain was anxious to fill for this was an oil-rich region that the west was keen not to lose to the Soviet sphere of influence. To replace Egypt, Britain first sought out Iraq as its closest ally in the Middle East, having advanced that territory to independence in 1932. However, when Britain wooed Jordan to enter the 1955 Baghdad Pact it had created with Iraq and Turkey, Nasser set about organizing anti-British protests in Jordan's capital, and as a mark of his power nationalized the Suez Canal, still a hugely important thoroughfare for British shipping. Though upset by Nasser's actions, the USA was unwilling to use force in the region. Rebuffed by the Americans, the British held secret negotiations with the French and the Israelis, devising a plan that in retrospect seems little short of absurd.

The Israelis were to attack Egypt, and the British and the French would issue an ultimatum for a ceasefire knowing that Nasser would refuse. This would give them the 'excuse' required to attack Egypt. This was exactly what happened between 29 and 31 October 1956. The condemnation of the Franco-British attack was instant and unbending; the USA, the UN and the Commonwealth all decried the action, as did the Soviet Union and the Arab states, and by 7 November British forces had withdrawn under enormous pressure. The economic effects of the episode brought home to Britain just how dependent the country was on American goodwill. The Suez Crisis precipitated a run on the pound, considerably weakening sterling in the exchange market. It was only when the British agreed to leave Egypt unconditionally that the USA and the International Monetary Fund agreed to bail Britain out of this sterling crisis. If the British learned anything from Suez, it was not that decolonization was a necessity, but that new power structures meant that the meaning and muscle of its Empire had shifted radically and had been irretrievably weakened. The Suez Crisis did not usher in or even accelerate decolonization; instead, it exposed the fact that the Empire was no longer a source of political strength for Britain.

Britain would face a further major incident that vividly demonstrated its drastically reduced powers when, in 1965, white Africans opposed to black African rule in the colony of Southern Rhodesia declared their independence (UDI – unilateral declaration of independence) from the Empire under the leadership of Ian Smith. Though Britain protested and even implemented economic sanctions, apartheid South Africa, welcoming a fellow white supremacist regime close by, ignored the sanctions, ensuring supplies to Rhodesia. The imperial blow was, of course, a double one: not only had a colony rejected imperialism and claimed unilateral independence, but its closest ally was a former British colony that had withdrawn from the Commonwealth only in 1961, when new member countries objected to its racially based system of governance that denied black Africans many basic human and political rights. Britain and the white settler lands of Australia and New Zealand were willing to allow South Africa into the Commonwealth despite its apartheid rule; it was South Africa itself, faced with criticism from former colonies, that withdrew its application for membership.

Southern Rhodesia did not back down, and its declaration of independence proved a deeply embarrassing example of British weakness, both economically and politically. In some respects, the situation there was farcical. In a veritable display of the British stiff upper lip, the colonial governor – with neither salary nor telephone communication – continued to entertain guests as if nothing untoward had occurred, while the Rhodesians refused to recognize his legitimacy any more. The UN, aware of the illegality as well as the racist intent of Smith's regime, condemned the Southern Rhodesian action and called on UN member countries to refuse to recognize the new leadership. The British prime minister, Harold Wilson, was reluctant to respond with military intervention. In non-white colonies such as Kenya and Malaya and, of course, in Egypt, the use of force had been quickly deployed when nationalism erupted in violence, but Wilson was a shrewd politician and knew that military action against a white colony would be political suicide. However, these racially motivated considerations went deeper, for Wilson knew that neighbouring South Africa would be a major conduit in the event of economic sanctions, and applying pressure to as critical a trading partner as South Africa at a time of economic distress was out of the question; economics trumped any principles concerning racial equality.

In the end, Smith forced the British prime minister's hand, withdrawing from negotiations that would – in British eyes – have legitimized an illegal regime. Faced with Smith's intractable position, economic sanctions were the sole option left to the British, and they were, as expected, a miserable failure. In subsequent years the death toll from guerrilla warfare in the country rose alarmingly. It would be 1980 before the newly named Zimbabwe, with a black majority, emerged from the ruins of a bloody civil war.

The United Nations was not always as supportive of Britain as it had been in this case, and its position on Southern Rhodesia was guided critically by its disapproval of the minority white rule that Smith championed.

Five years earlier, the UN's general assembly had passed a Declaration on the Granting of Independence to Colonial Countries and People. It was, of course, by no means the first death knell sounded for European colonialism, but the UN's lending of its name and its legitimacy to post-war criticisms of colonialism was an important statement of a changed political climate.

It is worth briefly comparing the UN's 1960 Declaration with the principles enunciated at the Yalta conference in February 1945. The principle of trusteeship that had followed the First World War was extended by the Yalta agreement only to former mandate territories (some of which should have been independent by 1945 in any case) and to the colonies formerly held by Italy. For French and British colonialism the status quo remained unchanged, though only fifteen years later the UN found colonialism a sufficiently odious mechanism of governance to condemn it. Clearly, the post-war period fostered a new climate less amenable to the political, if not necessarily the economic, inequities of European colonialism.

In the reshaping and reorganization of the Commonwealth, the British hoped to foster goodwill and continued relations with former colonies in a world that clearly no longer found full-scale colonialism acceptable. The Commonwealth was often little more than a public relations exercise; Britain had seen no reason to consult Commonwealth countries over Suez or over its bids for EEC membership. Yet money and effort went into making this body seem an important and mutually respectful and beneficial one. The term 'Commonwealth' had been chosen by the newly federated Australia in 1900 as one that did not imply colonial domination. The Balfour Report of 1926 defined Commonwealth countries as characterized by a common allegiance to the British Crown, and in 1931, as we have seen, the Statute of Westminster legally embodied their status as equal partners, confirming the full independence of member states whose acts could not be invalidated by the Westminster parliament. At this juncture, of course, Commonwealth membership was limited to those settler colonies where self-governance was already a fact. In the 1940s, the British envisaged a two-tier Commonwealth in which the non-white colonies of Asia and Africa would occupy a lesser form of membership.

Commonwealth eligibility required reconsideration when the newly independent republics of south Asia were born. Constitutional experts regarded allegiance to the monarch as incompatible with the republican nature of these new nations. Republics – as far back in British imperial terms as 1776 when the American colonies broke away – specifically rejected monarchical loyalty, and it was republican refusal in Ireland to pledge such loyalty that had wrecked the 1920 Home Rule plans there (see Chapter 10). However, Britain wanted to foster continued ties with India and Pakistan, if principally to ensure that they would not be brought within the Soviet sphere of influence. As a result, in 1949 the Commonwealth was redefined to allay republican doubts and to make full membership of the new south Asian nations possible. But though the make-up of the Commonwealth changed considerably after the war, it was never a body with any real power, and its representativeness of the Empire was, at best, spotty. None of Britain's former Arab or Middle East colonies ever joined the Commonwealth and, as we have seen, South Africa withdrew its application for membership in 1961.

The Commonwealth, then, was an idea more than a functioning reality, but its rhetoric – however unreflective of the actual situation – is a useful guide to the complex mechanisms at work in the disbandment of the Empire. In particular, the palpable fact that, for all the talk of equality, there was no way in which to ensure that Britain consulted Commonwealth nations suggests that the gap between principle and reality was always important. Britain wanted to hold on an at least to idea of its continued global importance in the face of shrinking influence and economic decline. The Empire was, to all intents and purposes, the only place where such a posture was at all possible, and even there, as we have seen, compromise was frequently forced upon Britain. Still, British politicians maintained a rhetoric of power and self-determination. The Labour foreign secretary, Ernest Bevin, dreamed in the post-war 1940s of the Empire providing precious economic resources that would be the envy of the superpowers, an extraordinary vision for a country so wholly dependent on foreign aid. At the start of the 1960s, and in the wake of serious nationalist violence in many parts of the Empire, Bevin's colleague and former prime minister Clement Attlee seriously proposed that Britain stood out among imperial powers in history as the only empire that 'voluntarily surrendered its hegemony over subject peoples'.[1] The events of the 1950s belie his statement: Britain fought nationalist uprisings in Malaya, Kenya, Cyprus, Iraq, the Gold Coast and Egypt, and often with considerable violence.

Yet, as we have seen in the case of Southern Rhodesia, the use of force was sometimes not an option, and the key determination of this was clearly race. Britain was reluctant to take up arms against white societies, reserving military intervention and police action in the main for its dealings with peoples of colour. Cyprus may be the exception here, but the rising level of terrorism on the island in the 1950s coupled with its 'easterly' associations with the former Ottoman Empire singled the colony out. Elsewhere it was almost always against Asian, African and Middle

Eastern peoples that force was employed. This racial consideration influenced the decolonization process in many ways, and was a legacy that affected not only Britain but the Dominion nations for whom white settler identity was a key identification. Australia from its birth as a nation had prevented non-white immigration (and would do so until 1966), and during the First World War it was the white settler colonies who protested against Britain's insistence on making India a member of the Imperial War Conference to which the self-governing colonies had been invited. The idea of trusteeship, as we have seen, was applied only to predominantly non-white colonies regarded as not yet ready for independence. Such thinking shaped the timetable of decolonization as well.

In the late 1940s Britain saw India and the Middle East as far more suitable candidates for independence than supposedly 'backward' Africa. It was a view that conveniently ignored Britain's own unwillingness over the years to fund and to promote economic development and better health and education practices in its African colonies. As other chapters have suggested, Britain's colonial reckoning was always a hierarchical one in which some races were endowed with superior power and control. It was the Aryan racial characteristics of Indians that elevated them in imperial eyes above the Africans. In African settler contexts, Britain not only avoided the use of force wherever feasible, but until quite late in the decolonization process worked hard to avoid black African majority rule, so tenacious was the belief that such peoples were unready for political responsibility. Alan Lennox-Boyd, colonial secretary from 1954 to 1959, publicly decried Africans as too backward for independence. More bizarrely, proponents of what had become known as ethnopsychiatry (the study of the psychology and behaviour of non-western peoples) argued that many of those who sought independence in Africa were motivated not by politics but by psychopathology – in short, that their demand for freedom from colonial rule was evidence of mental illness.[2]

Yet there was little real surprise for Britain when the demands for independence grew in the 1950s. In 1939 Lord Hailey, an experienced colonial administrator, was commissioned to examine British governance in Africa with a view to ultimate self-government there. Hailey's views were pessimistic; he saw little prospect of goodwill towards British rule among Africans. His report became buried as economic development issues took precedence at the Colonial Office, prompted by Britain's economic anxieties. Nonetheless, its commissioning, as well as its conclusions, suggests that some far-sighted officials saw the prospect of decolonization looming even as war broke out in 1939.

Africa was on the agenda once again, however, after the war ended, this time in connection with ensuring that the Middle East did not fall under Soviet influence, and that the USSR did not claim territory in Africa. Ernest Bevin supported a consolidation of defence forces to protect the Middle East, the Mediterranean and Africa. His idea for a 'Lagos–Mombasa line' became part of a broader strategy in the late 1940s to develop Africa as a bulwark against communism and as an economic boon for Britain. These plans show a great deal more concern with British than with African prosperity and security.

The Middle East, where the economic importance of oil and a very different colonial history lent the region some political purchase, became increasingly important to Britain's imperial goals. It was only late in the nineteenth century, and mostly after the First World War, that Britain had much of a foothold (other than in Egypt) in the Middle East. Prior to the insatiable thirst for oil so characteristic of the twentieth century, Britain's principal interest in the region had been as a route through to India and other colonies, both overland and by sea. However, the mandates created by the League of Nations after the First World War made the region increasingly important. Britain acquired an interest and a stake in the Arab world at a time of growing Arab nationalism and increased Zionist migration to Palestine. In the era of decolonization, the area would be a critical one.

As we have seen, the Suez Crisis was not truly a catalyst for decolonization, but it certainly served as an illustration of the growing force of Arab nationalism, and Britain's handling of the situation there had not made it any friends in the Arab world. Even earlier, in 1947, Anglo-Arab relations were strained when Britain turned the future of Palestine over to the UN for resolution. As we have noted, Britain found itself in an impossible situation, bound by Balfour's 1917 promise to protect a Jewish homeland but faced with vigorous Arab opposition. The pro-Zionist stand of America was not unimportant, given Britain's need for American aid, yet imperial concerns, as well as British oil interests, relied on Arab goodwill, for Britain was the largest western presence in the area. Complicating matters was that in 1945 many European Jews were clamouring to move to Palestine after experiencing the brutal anti-Semitism of the 1930s and 1940s. Britain was assailed on all sides: Palestinians made it clear they wanted the country to retain an Arab majority; Jews in the region took up increasingly violent tactics to force their desire for a Jewish state. Even in Britain there was no unanimity on the issue. The Colonial and the Foreign Offices, who shared the administration of the territory, favoured different solutions. Britain resigned the mandate in September 1947 when the UN recommended separate Arab and Jewish states; Israel subsequently declared its independence in May 1948, an action that precipitated the immediate outbreak of a conflict still burningly alive today.

The crisis over Palestine was one of the two major colonial problems Britain faced in the immediate post-war years, the other being the partition of India. The 1950s brought little relief. Cyprus, Malaya and Kenya all erupted in violent opposition to colonialism. The defeat of the French in Indochina in 1954 and the Algerian war of independence the French also fought until 1962 were reminders to the British that anti-colonial nationalism had roots both deep and broad.

Less than two years after its debacle in Egypt, Britain's power in the Middle East was further eroded by the Iraqi revolution of 1958, in which a Soviet-backed regime toppled the ruling pro-British party, jeopardizing Britain's capacity to maintain military bases in Iraq. There can be no doubt that one factor in the Iraqi coup was the pro-British stand of the ousted monarch, just as had been the case in Egypt in the 1952 coup.

With the loss of Iraqi cooperation, the mess surrounding Suez and Britain's earlier expulsion from Iran, it was to the colonial port and Protectorate of Aden, now part of Yemen, that the British turned. A huge new oil plant under construction there was intended to make up for the nationalization of the British refineries in Iran. Aden became the British military headquarters in the Middle East from the late 1950s; it was from here that the British despatched troops to shore up the Jordanian regime in 1958, to Kuwait to stem Iraqi hostilities in 1961, and to Yemen in 1962 against nationalists there. Setbacks in the region from nationalist activism did not deter the British from staking colonial claims there by whatever means.

Aden would see its own share of instability in the 1960s, when the civil war in southern Yemen (Britain's last colonial acquisition, by the 1934 treaty of Sana'a, though it had been ceded to Britain by Turkey as early as 1839) spilled over into the territory, fanned by an active Arab nationalism. Aden's constitution was suspended and direct rule reimposed in 1965, but the violence did not stop. Britain ultimately withdrew from the colony in November 1967, a decision that would have a considerable effect on the final major phase of decolonization; it was in the wake of that decision that the larger policy of withdrawing from the Empire 'east of Suez' was made by a Labour government weighed down by economic disintegration. In 1967, following another currency devaluation, the British government announced its intention to withdraw from the Persian

Gulf and the Malay archipelago by 1971, the so-called 'east of Suez' arena. Simultaneously, large tracts of the British West Indies and of British island colonies in the Pacific secured independence, including Fiji, Dominica, the Bahamas and the Turks and Caicos Islands. The pace of decolonization in the late 1960s and 1970s was rapid and, since virtually all of British Africa had gained independence by the time this new policy of withdrawal was announced, the Empire as a formal entity was, certainly symbolically, becoming a relic, with only a few small colonies and dependencies remaining.

Yet the end of the Empire was not by any means the close of a chapter, for the long-term impact and consequences of British imperialism are with us still. Many of the most intractable and violent of contemporary political trouble spots share a colonial British legacy. Whether we seek to understand the stand-off between Palestinians and Israelis, the rise of the Ba'ath party in Iraq, the violence in Kashmir or in Northern Ireland, in all these instances British influence has been central. Much of the interethnic violence that has followed and still follows decolonization – in Iraq, in Uganda, in Nigeria, in Zimbabwe and elsewhere – is also part of the legacy of colonialism. Not only was the uneven, rapid and often panicked withdrawal of British rule in many places a necessarily destabilizing factor in itself, with new nations economically ill placed for success and survival, but in many instances the British grouped together for administrative convenience peoples with very little in common beyond geographical proximity. The massive upheaval that followed the clumsy partition of India in 1947 should have alerted the colonists to such problems, but the lesson remained unlearned. In south Asia, millions of people found themselves virtually without warning in potentially hostile territory – Muslims in Hindu territory and vice versa. The bloodbath of communal violence that overtook newly independent Pakistan and India forced many to cross the border and begin anew in what was, religion aside, now a foreign country. The turmoil and damage was both broad and deep, and has left a lasting scar on the region.

Yet when Nigeria was created as an independent nation just over a decade later in 1960, the authorities did not look back and take stock as they might have done. This was not an easily or obviously definable country or, indeed, one in which an obvious group of leaders had emerged. Critical cultural and linguistic as well as political and religious divides were well known to the British authorities, and were in place at the very birth of the Nigerian nation. Civil war – almost inevitably – ensued within a decade. It was a story that would be repeated over and over again. In

Fiji, violence has divided the immigrant Indian community brought over by the British as indentured plantation labour from indigenous Fijians. In Kenya and Uganda in the 1960s, south Asians were forcibly expelled in a wave of 'Africanization'. In Malaysia, there has been chronic tension between Chinese encouraged by the British to migrate there in the nineteenth century and indigenous Malays. In the Sudan, there has been little peace between rival factions since independence in 1955. The list goes on.

However, if this rather grim list suggests that decolonization *produced* violence that the British had formerly kept in check, it is worth bearing in mind the violence with which the British often met anti-colonial nationalisms in their Empire. Violence was not the exclusive characteristic of colonial peoples. In Cyprus, in Malaya, in Kenya and in India, the British fought bloody campaigns to stem the rising tide of nationalism. For most of the 1950s, troops were stationed in Malaya to combat a strong and disciplined communist–nationalist guerrilla force. In Kenya the British spent the 1950s attempting to quell the Kikuyu-led Mau Mau, detaining thousands of suspects in internment camps and enclosed villages. It was not lost on angry locals that by the end of the Mau Mau emergency, the white death toll was around 70 and the black death toll around 10,000. Whether in Africa, India or even Cyprus, the British never hesitated to incarcerate nationalist leaders, often on flimsy charges. In Malaya, compulsory resettlement of village Chinese thought to be potential supporters of the guerrillas was a heavy-handed piece of coercion, part of a vast clampdown on civil rights designed to isolate and oust the guerrillas. Britain, it might be said, was fighting for its imperial life, and was more than willing to employ violence in selected contexts to secure that end.

The last such fight that Britain would undertake was also perhaps its oddest, for it occurred after almost the entire empire had broken up, and when few people in Britain really saw the nation as defined by empire. In 1982, just months after the naval presence at the Falkland Islands was withdrawn, as part of a cost-cutting exercise by the government, this obscure surviving outpost of the British Empire was invaded by neighbouring Argentina, which had long clamoured for sovereignty over the territory. Margaret Thatcher, the British prime minister, countered by sending troops to regain the islands in a hugely popular military battle. The whole affair was over in three months and the naval presence restored along with British rule, and while some of the popularity of this adventure can be explained by the fact that the Argentinian leader was a widely reviled and brutal dictator, there was a very substantial element of revealingly imperial sentiment in the affair. Popular opinion saw the British success as a reminder of past glories and strengths, of a time when Britain ruled the seas and a hefty portion of the globe. In practical terms, the British in the years after the Second World War may have deemed their colonial possessions not 'worth' the expense or too burdensome to maintain, but the image of empire as epitomizing British power and glory nonetheless remained a strong undercurrent in national self-reckoning. Whether it was reliance on America in the late 1940s, humiliation in the Middle East in the 1950s, or continued and long-term economic decline – and really a potent brew of all these and more – that led to Britain's abandonment of its idea of itself as politically prominent, the idea of empire remains palpable.

Some argue that imperialism has successfully survived the mechanics and process of decolonization, and continues to operate today. Inequities in wealth, in the ability to use resources, in education and in literacy, in health care and any number of other critical factors keep previously colonized nations in thrall to the wealth of developed countries, many of them former colonizing powers. If Britain's Empire is but a shadow of its earlier and massive presence, its legacy indubitably lives on.

References

1   Clement Attlee, *Empire into Commonwealth* (London: Oxford University Press, 1961), p. 1.

2   See, for example, J. C. Carothers, *The Psychology of Mau Mau* (Nairobi: Government Printer, 1954).

Further reading

Chapter 1: Uniting the kingdom

The literature on internal colonialism is surprisingly small. Michael Hechter's study *Internal Colonialism: The Celtic Fringe in British National Development* (2nd edn, New Brunswick, NJ: Transaction Publishers, 1999), remains the major work in the field. R. R. Davies's *Domination and Conquest: The Experience of Ireland, Scotland and Wales, 1100–1300* (Cambridge: Cambridge University Press, 1990) is a helpful introduction to the earliest relations between England and the countries it colonized over time to create the United Kingdom. Laurence Brockliss and David Eastwood (eds), *A Union of Multiple Identities: The British Isles, c. 1750– c. 1850* (Manchester: Manchester University Press, 1997) takes as its premise a colonialism already in place.

Works on the individual states affected by British internal colonialism abound. For good overviews of the history of Scotland, see Christopher T. Harvie, *Scotland and Nationalism: Scottish Society and Politics, 1707 to the Present* (4th edn, London: Routledge, 2004) and Rosalind Mitchison's *A History of Scotland* (3rd edn, London: Routledge, 2002).

For Wales, John Davies's *A History of Wales* (London: Penguin Books, 1994) is a good general history, and would be well supplemented by the questions around nationalism posed in the collection edited by Ralph Fevre and Andrew Thompson, *Nation, Identity and Social Theory: Perspectives from Wales* (Cardiff: University of Wales Press, 1999). For a lengthier sweep of chronology, readers might also profit from *Modern Wales: A Concise History, c. 1485–1979* by Gareth Elwyn Jones (Cambridge: Cambridge University Press, 1984).

For Ireland, Terrence McDonough's edited collection *Was Ireland a Colony? Economics, Politics, and Culture in Nineteenth-century Ireland* (Dublin: Irish Academic Press, 2005) speaks directly to the topic of this chapter. In *Colonialism, Religion, and Nationalism in Ireland*, Liam Kennedy (Belfast: Institute of Irish Studies, Queen's University of Belfast,

1996) draws out the connections that link religious difference and colonial rule there. R. F. Foster's *Modern Ireland, 1600–1972* (London: Allen Lane, 1988) is a standard text. *Victoria's Ireland? Irishness and Britishness, 1837–1901*, edited by Peter Gray (Dublin: Four Courts Press, 2004) examines the relationship between Irish and British identity in the years after the Union of 1800. Two edited collections – Kevin Kenny's *Ireland and the British Empire* (Oxford: Oxford University Press, 2004) and Keith Jeffery's *An Irish Empire? Aspects of Ireland and the British Empire* (Manchester: Manchester University Press, 1996) – explicitly connect Ireland to the rest of the Empire. Nicholas Canny's *Making Ireland British, 1580–1650* (Oxford: Oxford University Press, 2001) treats of an earlier period of Irish colonial experience, and *Britain and Ireland in the Eighteenth-century Crisis of Empire* by Martyn J. Powell (New York: Palgrave Macmillan, 2003) contextualizes the Irish question during the period of the so-called First British Empire.

Chapter 2: Slaves, merchants and trade

Brendan Bradshaw and John Morrill's collections of essays on *The British Problem, c. 1534–1707: State Formation in the Atlantic Archipelago* (New York: St Martin's Press, 1996) is a helpful introduction to the larger questions posed in this chapter. David Brion Davis has been among the most prominent scholars to write about slavery. His *The Problem of Slavery in Western Culture* (Ithaca, NY: Cornell University Press, 1966) remains a valuable contribution some 40 years after its first publication. In an edited collection, *Discourses of Slavery and Abolition: Britain and its Colonies, 1760–1838* (New York: Palgrave Macmillan, 2004), Brycchan Carey, Markman Ellis and Sara Salih specifically pair colonialism with slavery. Colin A. Palmer's collection of essays entitled *The Worlds of Unfree Labour: From Indentured Servitude to Slavery* (Aldershot and Brookfield, Conn.: Variorum, 1998) discusses the most characteristic forms of labour that enriched the early Caribbean and Atlantic colonies. Among James Walvin's extensive writings on slavery, see especially *Slaves and Slavery: The British Colonial Experience* (Manchester: Manchester University Press 1992). For moving reminiscences of slave life, see the stories told in Philip D. Curtin (ed.), *Africa Remembered: Narratives by West Africans from the Era of the Slave Trade*, (Madison: University of Wisconsin Press, 1967).

Kenneth Morgan's *Slavery, Atlantic Trade and the British Economy, 1660–1800* (Cambridge: Cambridge University Press, 2000) focuses on the clear economic relationship between slavery and eighteenth-century commerce and trade, and *The Many-headed Hydra: The Hidden History of the Revolutionary Atlantic* by Peter Linebaugh and Marcus Rediker (Boston: Beacon Press, 2000) looks at the role of what the authors call 'sailors, slaves, commoners' in the profitable Atlantic trade. *Soldiers, Sugar, and Seapower: The British Expeditions to the West Indies and the War against Revolutionary France* by Michael Duffy (Oxford: Clarendon Press, 1987) puts that trade into the perspective of European warmongering, as does Bruce Lenman in *Britain's Colonial Wars, 1688–1783* (Harlow: Longman, 2001).

For the experiences of women slaves, see *Slave Women in Caribbean Society, 1650–1838* by Barbara Bush (Kingston: Heinemann Caribbean and Bloomington: Indiana University Press, 1990). In *The Caribbean Slave: A Biological History*, Kenneth F. Kiple (Cambridge: Cambridge University Press, 1984) looks at the medical and biological issues slaves faced as a result of their situation. For slavery outside the Atlantic but within the British Empire, see *Gender, Slavery and Law in Colonial India* by Indrani Chatterjee (New Delhi: Oxford University Press, 1999).

The British anti-slavery movement boasts a large literature. Among the major works in this area are Roger Anstey, *The Atlantic Slave Trade and British Abolition, 1760–1810* (Atlantic Highlands, NJ: Humanities Press, 1975), Clare Midgley, *Women Against Slavery: The British Campaigns, 1780–1870* (London: Routledge, 1992) and David Turley, *The Culture of English Antislavery, 1780–1860* (London: Routledge, 1991). In *The Mighty Experiment: Free Labor Versus Slavery in British Emancipation* (Oxford: Oxford University Press, 2002) Seymour Drescher looks at the consequences and impact of the abolition of slavery in the British Empire.

Chapter 3: Settling the 'New World'

Bernard Bailyn's *The Ideological Origins of the American Revolution* (Cambridge: Belknap Press of Harvard University Press, 1992) offers a perspective on the political philosophies that informed American discontent in the eighteenth century, while his co-edited collection, *Strangers Within the Realm: Cultural Margins of the First British Empire* (edited with Philip D. Morgan; Chapel Hill, NC: Published for the Institute of Early American History and Culture, Williamsburg, Virginia, by the University of North Carolina Press, 1991) looks at the diverse groups that made up this colonial arena. In *British America, 1500–1800: Creating Colonies, Imagining an Empire* (London: Hodder Arnold, 2005), Steven

Sarson provides a long view of the expansion of British American colonialism, as do the essays in the collection edited by David Armitage and Michael J. Braddick, *The British Atlantic World, 1500–1800* (New York: Palgrave Macmillan, 2002).

Crucible of War: The Seven Years War and the Fate of Empire in British North America, 1754–1766 (New York: Knopf, 2000) by Fred Anderson gives a detailed account of the impact on the American colonies of what was perhaps the key colonial war of the eighteenth century for this region. P. J. Marshall's *The Making and Unmaking of Empires: Britain, India, and America c. 1750–1783* (Oxford: Oxford University Press, 2005) offers a valuable perspective on the relations between the different colonial possessions of the period.

Two books that do a lot to flesh out a picture of life in colonial America are *Down and Out in Early America* (ed. Billy G. Smith; University Park, Pa: Pennsylvania State University Press, 2004) and *The Creation of the British Atlantic World* (eds, Elizabeth Mancke and Carole Shammas; Baltimore: Johns Hopkins University Press, 2005). *Born to Die: Disease and New World Conquest, 1492–1650* by Noble David Cook (Cambridge: Cambridge University Press, 1998) vividly describes the toll disease took on the indigenous peoples as they encountered microbes new to the region.

In *Epic Journeys of Freedom: Runaway Slaves of the American Revolution and their Global Quest for Liberty* (Boston: Beacon Press, 2006), Cassandra Pybus tells of what happened to slaves who took the opportunity offered by the revolutionary war to escape enslavement.

Chapter 4: After America

For an overview of the expansion of this period, Philip Lawson's *A Taste for Empire and Glory: Studies in British Overseas Expansion, 1660–1800* (Brookfield, Conn.: Variorum, 1997) is helpful and comprehensive. '*A free though conquering people': Eighteenth-century Britain and its Empire* by P. J. Marshall (Aldershot and Burlington, Vt.: Ashgate, 2003) covers some of the same territory. *The Global Reach of Empire: Britain's Maritime Expansion in the Indian and Pacific Oceans, 1764–1815* by Alan Frost (Carlton, Vic: Miegunyah Press, 2003) reminds us of the critical importance for colonial expansion of Britain's naval power in this period. C. A. Bayly's *Imperial Meridian: The British Empire and the World, 1780–1830* (London: Longman, 1989) offers a broad and important perspective on the global reach of Britain's imperial interests.

Stuart Macintyre's *Concise History of Australia* (2nd edn, Cambridge: Cambridge University Press, 2004) and Philippa Mein Smith's *Concise History of New Zealand* (Cambridge: Cambridge University Press, 2005) are excellent introductions to the histories of these respective colonies. *Making Peoples: A History of the New Zealanders, from Polynesian Settlement to the End of the Nineteenth Century* (Honolulu: University of Hawaii Press, 2001) by James Belich is another excellent national history.

In *Invisible Invaders: Smallpox and Other Diseases in Aboriginal Australia, 1780–1880* (Carlton South: Melbourne University Press, 2002), Judy Campbell explores the impact of European diseases on Aboriginal populations, and James Belich reads New Zealand through the lens of racial inequality in *The New Zealand Wars and the Victorian Interpretation of Racial Conflict* (Auckland: Auckland University Press, 1986). *Encounters in Place: Outsiders and Aboriginal Australians, 1606–1985* by D. J. Mulvaney (St Lucia: University of Queensland Press, 1989) discusses some of these same questions in the Australian context.

Aboriginal history, and the effect of settler colonialism on the earlier inhabitants of Australia, are discussed in Richard Broome's *Aboriginal Australians: Black Responses to White Dominance, 1788–2001* (3rd edn, Crows Nest, Australia: Allen & Unwin, 2002), Henry Reynolds's *Frontier: Aborigines, Settlers, and Land* (St Leonards, NSW: Allen & Unwin, 1987) and Ann McGrath (ed.), *Contested Ground: Australian Aborigines under the British Crown* (St Leonards, NSW: Allen & Unwin, 1995).

In *Dancing with Strangers: Europeans and Australians at First Contact* (Cambridge: Cambridge University Press, 2005), Inga Clendinnen looks at the earliest relations between settlers and indigenes.

Depraved and Disorderly: Female Convicts, Sexuality and Gender in Colonial Australia by Joy Damousi (Cambridge: Cambridge University Press, 1997) offers an excellent account of the life and status of women convicts in early Australian history.

Chapter 5: Britain in India

C. A. Bayly's *Indian Society and the Making of the British Empire* (Cambridge: Cambridge University Press, 1988) is a comprehensive view of relations between Britain and India. P. J. Marshall has written extensively on the early British Empire in India. Among his many works, see in particular *East Indian Fortunes: The British in Bengal in the Eighteenth Century* (Oxford: Clarendon Press, 1976) and *Problems of Empire: Britain and India 1757–1813* (London: Allen & Unwin, 1968).

On the East India Company, a good general history is provided by Philip Lawson in his *The East India Company: A History* (London: Longman, 1993). In *Reading the East India Company, 1720–1840: Colonial Currencies of Gender* (Chicago: University of Chicago Press, 2004) Betty Joseph provides a cultural studies perspective on the company. Like Joseph, Lata Mani is interested in exploring gendered issues within colonial Indian history. Her study of suttee, *Contentious Traditions: The Debate on Sati in Colonial India* (Berkeley: University of California Press, 1998) offers a broad reading of gender relations under colonialism in early nineteenth-century India. In a series of imaginative essays, the late Bernard S. Cohn discusses language, clothing, textiles and much more in his innovative *Colonialism and its Forms of Knowledge: The British in India* (Princeton, NJ: Princeton University Press, 1996).

Useful general texts include *Modern South Asia: History, Culture, Political Economy* by Sugata Bose and Ayesha Jalal (2nd edn, New York: Routledge, 2004) and *Ideologies of the Raj* by Thomas R. Metcalf (Cambridge: Cambridge University Press, 1994).

In *The Indian Princes and their States* (Cambridge: Cambridge University Press, 2004), Barbara N. Ramusack gives a helpful history of those princely states formally beyond British control but often a critical component of colonial rule.

The economics of colonial India are the topic of Neil Charlesworth's *British Rule and the Indian Economy, 1800–1914* (London: Macmillan, 1982).

Chapter 6: Global Growth

A good number of general histories of the Empire in this period have been published in the last few years. Among them are Willie Thompson, *Global Expansion: Britain and its Empire, 1870–1914* (London: Pluto Press, 1999), Andrew S. Thompson, *Imperial Britain: The Empire in British Politics, c. 1880–1932* (Harlow: Longman, 2000), *Britain's Imperial Century, 1815–1914: A Study of Empire and Expansion* by Ronald Hyam (3rd edn, New York: Palgrave Macmillan, 2002), *The British Empire and Commonwealth: A Short History* by Martin Kitchen (New York: St Martin's Press, 1996) and Timothy Parsons, *The British Imperial Century, 1815–1914: A World History Perspective* (Lanham, Md.: Rowman & Littlefield, 1999).

There is also, of course, a huge literature on the individual history of particular colonies. *India and the World Economy 1850–1950*, edited by

G. Balachandran (New Delhi: Oxford University Press, 2003) is a helpful overview of India's place in the increasingly global economy crafted by colonialism in the nineteenth and twentieth centuries.

The growing colonial interest in Africa is discussed in Roland Oliver and Anthony Atmore, *Africa Since 1800* (5th edn, Cambridge: Cambridge University Press, 2005), in *The Scramble for Africa, 1876–1912* by Thomas Pakenham (New York: Random House, 1991) and in *Africa and the Victorians: The Official Mind of Imperialism* by Ronald Robinson, John Gallagher and Alice Denny, first published in 1961 and much reprinted and revised thereafter (London: Macmillan).

For east and south-east Asia, John M. Carroll's *Edge of Empires: Chinese Elites and British Colonials in Hong Kong* (Cambridge, Mass.: Harvard University Press, 2005) does an excellent job in revealing the collaboration necessary to successful colonization. Nicholas Tarling's *The Cambridge History of Southeast Asia, Volume II, The Nineteenth and Twentieth Centuries* (Cambridge: Cambridge University Press, 1992) offers an extensive overview of British interests in the region.

Chapter 7: Ruling an empire

In *Colonizing Nature: The Tropics in British Arts and Letters, 1760–1820* (Philadelphia: University of Pennsylvania Press, 2005) Beth Fowkes Tobin demonstrates not just the interest generated by colonial expansion but the kinds of celebratory superiorities that accompanied the growing expansion of the Empire. V. G. Kiernan's classic study *The Lords of Human Kind. European Attitudes to the Outside World in the Imperial Age* (Harmondsworth: Penguin Books, 1972) details the attitudes of colonizers towards those they colonized, and in *Racism and Empire: White Settlers and Colored Immigrants in the British Self-governing Colonies, 1830–1910* (Ithaca, NY: Cornell University Press, 1976), Robert A. Huttenback reveals the racist attitudes that shaped the forms of settler colonialism in its most expansive era.

There is much good work on missionaries and the Empire. *Missionary Writing and Empire, 1800–1860* by Anna Johnston (Cambridge: Cambridge University Press, 2003), Jeffrey Cox, *Imperial Fault Lines: Christianity and Colonial Power in India, 1818–1940* (Stanford, Calif.: Stanford University Press, 2002) and Andrew Porter's *Religion Versus Empire? British Protestant Missionaries and Overseas Expansion, 1700–1914* (Manchester: Manchester University Press, 2004) all offer fresh perspectives on the missionary mind. A useful collection of original essays on missionaries is *Missions and Empire*, edited by Norman Etherington (Oxford: Oxford University Press, 2005)

Chapter 8: Being ruled

In *Black Experience and the Empire* (Oxford: Oxford University Press, 2004), editors Philip D. Morgan and Sean Hawkins have collected a series of interesting essays on the meaning of race and skin colour within the imperial framework.

The experience of indentured workers under colonialism in the Caribbean is the subject of Madhavi Kale's study *Fragments of Empire: Capital, Slavery, and Indian Indentured Labor Migration in the British Caribbean* (Philadelphia: University of Pennsylvania Press, 1998).

Equal Subjects, Unequal Rights: Indigenous Peoples in British Settler Colonies, 1830–1910, edited by Julie Evans (Manchester: Manchester University Press, 2003), looks specifically at the experience of indigenous peoples affected by settler colonialism, and the essays in Martin Daunton and Rick Halpern's collection *Empire and Others: British Encounters with Indigenous Peoples, 1600–1850* (Philadelphia: University of Pennsylvania Press, 1999), although also investigating the experience of the colonized, looks at a broader range of colonial experiences. Read together, they are an excellent introduction to the topic, and over a lengthy period.

Chapter 9: Gender and sexuality

A number of edited collections engage the relations between gender history and the history of the Empire. Clare Midgley's *Gender and Imperialism* (Manchester: Manchester University Press, 1998) and Philippa Levine's *Gender and Empire* (Oxford: Oxford University Press, 2004) deal specifically with the British Empire.

For the experience of African women under colonialism, *Women in African Colonial Histories* (Bloomington: Indiana University Press, 2002), edited by Jean Allman, Susan Geiger and Nakanyike Musisi, is an invaluable collection.

For discussions of the relationship of British women to the Empire, see *Married to the Empire: Gender, Politics and Imperialism in India, 1883–1947* (Manchester: Manchester University Press, 2002) by Mary A. Procida, which looks at British women living in the Empire. Antoinette Burton's *Burdens of History: British Feminists, Indian Women, and Imperial Culture, 1865–1915* (Chapel Hill: University of North Carolina Press,

1994) looks critically at the attitudes espoused by British feminists towards colonized women in the high colonial era.

For a discussion of colonial masculinity, see Mrinalini Sinha, *Colonial Masculinity: the 'manly Englishman' and the 'effeminate Bengali' in the Late Nineteenth Century* (Manchester: Manchester University Press, 1995). In *Martial Races: The Military, Race and Masculinity in British Imperial Culture, 1857–1914* (Manchester: Manchester University Press, 2004), Heather Streets compares Scottish and Indian military regiments in a study of military masculinity. *May the Best Man Win: Sport, Masculinity, and Nationalism in Great Britain and the Empire, 1880–1935* (New York: Palgrave Macmillan, 2004) by Patrick F. McDevitt looks at questions of gender and masculinity through the growth of sporting events and new sports in the Empire.

Sexuality, and especially male sexuality, is the theme of Anne McClintock's *Imperial Leather: Race, Gender, and Sexuality in the Colonial Context* (New York: Routledge, 1995), and in *Prostitution, Race and Politics: Policing Venereal Disease in the British Empire* (New York: Routledge, 2003) Philippa Levine explores questions of colonial sexuality through an investigation of venereal disease policy throughout the Empire.

Chapter 10: Contesting empire

The classic study of colonialism and nationalism is Benedict Anderson's *Imagined Communities: Reflections on the Origin and Spread of Nationalism* (London: New Left Books, 1991), although British colonialism is not his major focus. Nonetheless, the book remains a key work in the area. Also of considerable importance is Partha Chatterjee's *Nationalist Thought and the Colonial World: A Derivative Discourse?* (Minneapolis: University of Minnesota Press, 1998).

The Idea of Freedom in Asia and Africa, ed. Robert H. Taylor (Stanford: Stanford University Press, 2002) is a useful collection detailing the ideas that spread through colonial territories as nationalism gathered steam. D. A. Low's *Britain and Indian Nationalism, 1929–1942: Imprint of Ambiguity* (Cambridge: Cambridge University Press, 1997) details the intense fight for self-determination in interwar India, and in *The Turning Point in Africa: British Colonial Policy, 1938–48* (London: Cass, 1982), R. D. Pearce discusses African nationalism and protest.

Bernard Porter investigates how British radicals understood African colonialism in his *Critics of Empire: British Radical Attitudes to Colonialism in Africa 1895–1914* (New York: St Martin's Press, 1968).

In *American Intellectuals and African Nationalists, 1955–1970* (New Haven, Conn.: Yale University Press, 1991), Martin Staniland explores the growing connections between African-American activists and African nationalists.

In *Gender and Nation* (Thousand Oaks, Calif.: Sage, 1997), Nira Yuval-Davis explores the links between gender and nationalism, as do the essays in *Gendered Nations: Nationalisms and Gender Order in the Long Nineteenth Century* (eds Ida Blom, Karen Hagemann and Catherine Hall; New York: Berg, 1996). One valuable case study of gender and nationalism is Cora Ann Presley, *Kikuyu Women, the Mau Mau Rebellion and Social Change in Kenya* (Boulder, Col.: Westview Press, 1992). Kumari Jayawardena's *Feminism and Nationalism in the Third World* (London: Zed Books, 1986) was one of the first studies to explore this critical link.

Chapter 11: Decolonization

M. E. Chamberlain, *Decolonization: The Fall of the European Empires* (2nd edn, Oxford: Blackwell, 1999) is a helpful overview, as are Raymond F. Betts, *Decolonization* (2nd edn, New York: Routledge, 2004) and Nicholas J. White, *Decolonisation: The British Experience since 1945* (Harlow: Longman, 1999).

In *The End of the British Empire: The Historical Debate* (Oxford: Blackwell, 1991) John Darwin surveys the different rationales that historians have offered for why decolonization occurred when and how it did.

A much longer perspective colours D. George Boyce's views on decolonization in his *Decolonisation and the British Empire, 1775–1997* (New York: St Martin's Press, 1999), where he analyses eighteenth-century dissatisfactions with imperial rule alongside the more typical concentration on the twentieth century. A. N. Porter and A. J. Stockwell straddle the divide of the Second World War in *British Imperial Policy and Decolonization, 1938–64* (Basingstoke: Macmillan, 1987), and John Springhall sees the post-war years as more critical in his *Decolonization Since 1945: The Collapse of European Overseas Empires* (Basingstoke and New York: Palgrave, 2001).

Chronology

1562   Sir John Hawkins's first English Atlantic slave voyage

1564   Hawkins's second expedition establishes slaving as a commercial operation

1578   Humphrey Gilbert secures patent from Elizabeth I to found colonies in lands 'not actually possessed of any Christian prince or people'

1600   Establishment of English East India Company under royal charter

1607   First permanent English settlement at Jamestown, Virginia

1612   Development of tobacco in Virginia; first importation of slaves

1613   First British factory established at Surat, India

1615   Moguls grant Britain permission to trade in India

1619   First sale of blacks in Jamestown, Virginia

1620   *Mayflower*, headed for Virginia, blown off course, landing at Cape Cod and founding Plymouth

1664   Settlement at Jamaica begins

1672   Royal African Company incorporated to control British slave trade

1673   First major slave revolt, Jamaica

1698   Attempted settlement at Darien by Company of Scotland

         Slave trade opened to private traders

1701   Founding of the Society for the Propagation of the Gospel in Foreign Parts (Church of England)

1704   British occupy Gibraltar

1707   Act of Union between England and Scotland

1708   British occupy Menorca

1713   Right to supply slaves to Spanish colonies (*asiento*) shifted from the French to the British

1718   Penal transportation introduced

1756   Siraj-ud-Daula (nawab of Bengal) captures Calcutta

1757   Defeat of Siraj-ud-Daula at Plassey (India)

1758   British drive French out of West Africa

1763   Defeat of France in Seven Years War; Treaty of Paris cedes all French territory east of Mississippi River to Britain (Grenada, Dominica, St Vincent and Tobago)

       Creation of East and West Florida, and of Quebec (all by royal proclamation)

       Annexation of Senegal

       Annexation of Prince Edward Island as part of Nova Scotia

       Proclamation Line sets limits of British colonization in America at the Alleghenies

1764   Falkland Islands (off the coast of Argentina) declared British

1765   Stamp Act rejected by American colonists

       Treaty of Allahabad guarantees East India Company the *diwani* (revenue control) in Bengal

1766   First British garrison at West Falkland

       Stamp Act repealed after rioting in America

       Declaratory Act asserts British rights to govern in colonies

1768   Establishment of Colonial Department (abolished after American Revolution)

       Captain Cook's first voyage

1770   Cook claims South Island of New Zealand

1772   Mansfield judgment ends slavery in Britain by ruling that enslaved persons landing on English soil were free

1773   Tea Act in the American colonies prompts the 'Boston Tea Party'

Regulating Act establishes governor generalship and supreme court for British India

1774   Quebec Act gave Catholics in Canada political and religious equality

First Continental Congress of the American colonies

Coercive Acts, America

Britain withdrew from Falkland Islands

Initial battles of American–British War at Lexington, Bunker Hill and Quebec City

1776   Second Continental Congress of the American colonies

American Declaration of Independence

1781   Cornwallis surrenders to Washington at Yorktown, ending Revolutionary War

1782   Colonial affairs moved to the domain of the Home Office

1783   Peace of Versailles marks American independence and Britain's loss of the American colonies

Rights of the British over the Gambia River estuary (Africa) recognized

1784   India Act (authored by Pitt) passed, giving the Crown greater control of British India

1786   Purchase of Penang by the East India Company marks the first British settlement on the Malay coast

Decision to establish penal colony at Botany Bay

1787   Establishment of Sierra Leone as a settlement for freed slaves

Society for the Abolition of the Slave Trade founded

1788   First fleet arrives at Botany Bay, and establishes the first Australian penal colony at Port Jackson

Penal colony established in the Andaman Islands

1791   Canada Act creates Upper (Ontario) and Lower (Quebec) Canada, each with a governor and an elected assembly

1792   Bill to abolish slave trade within four years passes in the House of Commons, defeated in the House of Lords

Baptist Missionary Society founded

1793   Lord Cornwallis's permanent settlement of the Bengal revenues

Upper Canada passes an anti-slavery law

1794   First Christian church built in New South Wales

1795   London Missionary Society founded

Trincomalee and Cape Colony captured from the Dutch

Mungo Park's first expedition to trace the course of the Niger

1796   Scottish Missionary Society founded

East India Company takes parts of Ceylon from the Dutch

Andaman Islands penal colony abandoned

1797   St Lucia, Martinique, Tobago taken from the French

Malacca and Dutch Guiana captured from the Dutch

Merino sheep introduced in New South Wales

1798   Rebellion in Ireland

British establish control of Belize

1799   Defeat of Tipu Sultan at Seringapatam, India

Church Missionary Society founded as the Society for Missions in Africa and the East

1800   Province Wellesley (Malay peninsula) acquired

British drive French out of Malta

1801   Annexation of the Carnatic and Oudh, India

Act of Union joins Ireland to the UK

Creation of Colonial Department within Department of War and Colonies

1803   St Lucia, Demerara and Surinam captured

Dominica formally recognized as British

First European settlement of Van Diemen's Land, Australia

Tobago and Trinidad ceded to Britain

Denmark becomes the first country to halt the slave trade

East India Company leases St Helena to the Crown for the internment of Napoleon

1804   British and Foreign Bible Society founded

1806   Foreign Slave Trade Act

British reoccupy Cape of Good Hope

British occupy Buenos Aires

British settlers in the Cape forbidden to own slaves

1807   Abolition of slave trade in British Empire

Heligoland and Malacca seized from Dutch

1808   Sierra Leone becomes a Crown Colony

1809   British drive French out of Ionian Islands

1810   British capture Mauritius, Martinique, Guadeloupe, Seychelles and Réunion

1811   Java seized from the Dutch; Raffles appointed governor

Import of slaves to Bengal prohibited

1812   War with USA over border with Canada (until 1814)

1813   Wesleyan Methodist Missionary Society founded

East India Company Charter Act opens Indian trade and allows missionaries into India

Import of slaves to Bombay and Madras prohibited

1814   Formal British annexation of Cape of Good Hope

Annexation of Dutch colonies of Berbice, Demerara and Essequibo

Ionian Islands and Malta annexed

First English missionaries arrive in New Zealand

British persuade European powers to declare the slave trade repugnant at Congress of Vienna

Dutch abolish the slave trade in their colonies

1815   Treaty of Vienna guarantees Britain's possession of St Lucia, Trinidad, Tobago, British Guiana, Berbice, Demerara and Essequibo

European powers agree to outlaw slave trade

British occupy Ascension Island, administered by the Admiralty Office until 1922

All of Ceylon brought under British control

Ionian Islands become a British Protectorate

1816   Maratha War, India (until 1818)

Bathurst (Banjul Island, The Gambia) established as a base (garrison) for Anti-Slavery (West Africa) Squadron

British resident appointed to Nepal

Annexation of Tristan da Cunha (South Atlantic)

1817   Creation of post of Secretary of State for Colonies

War against Xhosa, South Africa (until 1819)

1819   Trading station established at Singapore

British laid claim to British Antarctic Territory

1821   Bathurst and Gold Coast placed under Crown rule, administered from Sierra Leone

1822   First Britons cross the Sahara

Source of Niger River established by A. G. Laing

Liberia established for freed slaves by American Colonization Society

1824   Anglo-Dutch Treaty divides Malay archipelago into two spheres of influence

First Anglo-Burmese War (to 1826)

Britain recognizes independent republics in Latin America

First bishoprics in Barbados and Jamaica established

First British settlement of Natal

1825   Tasmania (Van Diemen's Land) becomes a separate colony

1826   Establishment of Straits Settlements consisting of Penang, Province Wellesley, Malacca and Singapore, administered until 1867 by the government of Bengal

British win trading concessions in Siam

New Zealand Company founded

Rejection by British government of a request to make Tahiti a Protectorate

1828   Cape Khoikhoi confirmed as a free people by ordinance, South Africa

1829   Entire continent of Australia declared British

Swan River Colony established in western Australia

Edward Gibbon Wakefield's *Letter from Sydney* published, laying out his vision for free settlement

1830   Wakefield founds Colonization Society

Mysore added to British holdings in India

Royal Geographical Society founded

1831   Baptist War (slave revolt) in Jamaica, Barbados and other Caribbean islands

1832   First resident appointed for New Zealand

Falkland Islands declared a Crown Colony

1833   Emancipation Act abolishes slavery in British Empire from 1 August 1834

East India Company loses its China trade monopoly

Import of Nepalese slaves to India prohibited

1834   Introduction of large-scale indentured labour to the Caribbean

War against Xhosa in Cape Colony (until 1835) ends slavery

St Helena becomes a Crown Colony

South Australia established by Act of Parliament

1835   Boers at Cape Colony begin the 'Great Trek' to settle further north on the Orange River

1836   First colonial railway in the British Empire opens east of Montreal

1837   Rebellions in Upper and Lower Canada over subjugation of legislative assembly to governor and council

1838   Abolition of slave apprenticeships

Establishment of Boer republic in South Africa

1839   Aden seized by East India Company, administered by government of Bombay

Indentured labour from India prohibited

Lord Durham's *Report on the Affairs of North America*

First Opium War prompted by the confiscation by the Chinese government of colonial-grown opium

Grand Trunk Road linking Calcutta and Delhi, Calcutta and Bombay, Bombay and Agra begun: completed 1840

British invade Afghanistan to prevent Russian advance towards India's north-west frontier

African Civilization Society founded to establish model settlements in Africa

1840   Transportation to New South Wales ended

Treaty of Waitangi in which Maori chiefs acknowledge Queen Victoria's sovereignty in return for guaranteed ownership of lands

1841   British consul established at Zanzibar (administered until 1873 by government of Bombay)

Sultan of Brunei appoints James Brooke Rajah of Sarawak

Union of Upper and Lower Canada

1842   Treaty of Nanking ends the Opium War, cedes Hong Kong to Britain, and opens five treaty ports in China to foreign trade

British troops attacked, and retreat from Afghanistan

New South Wales granted representative government

1843   Hong Kong becomes a Crown Colony

Annexation of Natal, South Africa

Annexation of Sind, India

Legal support for slavery in India withdrawn

The Gambia becomes a Crown Colony

1844   Indentured labour from India re-authorized

Gold Coast comes under direct British rule

1845   Natal declared a dependency of the Cape

1846   Western USA/British North America set at 49th parallel

Responsible government granted to Nova Scotia

Irish famine begins

Labuan acquired from the Sultan of Brunei

1847   Establishment of the colony of British Kaffraria

Sweden abolished slave trade in its Caribbean colonies

1848   Annexation of Orange River Sovereignty, South Africa

Labuan becomes a Crown Colony

France and Denmark abolish slavery

1849   Indentured labour from India again suspended

Annexation of the Punjab

Repeal of Navigation Acts

Vancouver Island becomes a Crown Colony

1850   Australian Colonies Government Act extends charter for responsible self-government to Victoria, South Australia and Van Diemen's Land

1851   Indentured labour from India resumed

Prince Edward Island attains responsible government

1852   New Zealand Constitution Act gives self-government to New Zealand

Sand River convention recognizes Boer independence in Transvaal

1853   Transportation to eastern Australia ends

David Livingstone traverses Africa

1854   Creation of the Colonial Office as a stand-alone department

Bloemfontein Convention grants Orange Free State full sovereignty

Representative government established in Cape Colony

New Brunswick and Newfoundland granted responsible self-government

First telegraph line, from Calcutta to Agra, in India

1855   New South Wales, Van Diemen's Land, South Australia and Victoria acquire elected legislatures

Windward Islands Crown Colony established (St Lucia, St Vincent, Grenadines, Grenada and French Martinique)

Britain and Afghanistan declare war on Persia (until 1857)

1856 Responsible, which replaced representative, self-government granted to New Zealand

Annexation of Oudh, India

Second Opium War, after the Chinese seize a British-colonial ship

Responsible replaces representative government in New South Wales

Separation of Natal and Cape; Natal becomes a Crown Colony

1857 Indian Mutiny (until 1858)

Cocos (Keeling) Islands in the Indian Ocean annexed

1858 East India Company abolished

Act for the Better Government of India establishes the India Office as a formal branch of British government

Foundation of colony of British Columbia

Second Opium War ends but China refuses to ratify terms of peace treaty

Penal colony established at Port Blair, Andaman Islands

1859 Queensland separated from New South Wales

Cayman Islands become a Crown Colony

1860 Maori Wars (until 1863)

Acquisition of Kowloon and Stonecutters Island extends territory of Hong Kong

Convention of Peking gives Europeans greater rights in China

Slave ownership prohibited in India

1861 Annexation of Lagos, administered from Sierra Leone

First English cricket teams visit Australia

Bahrain (Persian Gulf) becomes a Protectorate

1862 British representative established at Mandalay

British Honduras (Belize) formally colonized, administered from Jamaica until 1884

1864 First black Anglican bishop appointed to Sierra Leone: Samuel Adjayi Crowther (c. 1805–1891)

Ionian Islands ceded to Greece

1865   Colonial Laws Validity Act gave Westminster the right to invalidate colonial laws that ran counter to British statute law

Morant Bay uprising, Jamaica

Trade treaties open Japan to merchants

1866   British Kaffraria incorporated into Cape Colony

Jamaica becomes a Crown Colony

1867   Straits Settlements become a Crown Colony

British North America Act federates the Dominion of Canada; Newfoundland chooses not to join

Maoris given four seats in New Zealand's general assembly

Fenian agitation in Britain for Irish independence

1868   Aboriginal cricket team toured England

Basutoland becomes a Protectorate

End of transportation to Western Australia

1869   Opening of the Suez Canal

Hudson's Bay Company lands pass to Crown

Britain acquires Nicobar Islands from the Danes

1870   Western Australia acquires representative government

1871   Annexation of Griqualand West

Basutoland transferred to Cape Colony

Leeward Islands Federation established (Dominica, Antigua, St Christopher, Nevis, Montserrat, British Virgin Islands)

1872   Responsible self-government granted to Cape Colony

First Maoris appointed to New Zealand's upper house

1873   Aden Protectorate formed

Spain abolishes slavery in Puerto Rico

1874   Treaty of Pangkor: sultans of protected Malay States accept British residents

Fiji becomes a Crown Colony

Gold Coast becomes a Crown Colony

1876   Empress of India Act

Canadian Trans-Pacific Railway completed

Perim and Socotra (offshore islands close to Aden) become a British Protectorate as part of Aden

Last full-blooded Tasmanian Aboriginal dies

1877   British re-annex the Transvaal

North Borneo ceded to the British by the Sultan of Brunei

1878   British Protectorate, Walvis Bay, South West Africa

Cyprus placed under British administration, leased from Sultan of Turkey

Cocoa production introduced to Gold Coast

Congress of Berlin to avert a European war over the disintegration of the Ottoman Empire

1879   Irish Land War (until 1882)

Zululand becomes a Protectorate

Second Anglo-Afghan War after British resident in Kabul murdered

New Zealand introduces manhood suffrage

1880   First Anglo-Boer War (until 1881)

First refrigerated meat from Australia lands in Britain

1881   Battle of Majuba Hill – British defeated by Boers, retaking Transvaal

Pretoria Convention recognizes self-government for Transvaal, Britain retaining nominal control over foreign relations

Royal charter granted to British North Borneo Company

Urabi revolt, Egypt

1882   Occupation of Egypt

Emirs of Bahrain enter into treaties of protection with British

1884   Britain expelled from the Sudan

Establishment of British Somaliland Protectorate (on the Red Sea, across from the Gulf of Aden), administered from India until 1898

Papua New Guinea becomes a British Protectorate

Bechuanaland returned to British protection

Berlin Conference establishes rules for African partition – imperial power had to substantiate territorial claims by demonstrating 'effective administration'.

1885   Formation of Indian National Congress

General Gordon killed at Khartoum

Anglo-Egyptian forces withdraw from the Sudan

Niger Districts Protectorate established

Upper Burma annexed

Crown Colony of Bechuanaland created in Southern Africa

1886   Colonial and Indian Exhibition staged in London

Spain abolishes slavery in Cuba

Gilbert and Ellice Islands become British

1887   Informal Anglo-Russian division of Persia into spheres of interest

Anglo-French Pacific condominium over New Hebrides

Maldive Islands (Indian Ocean) become a Protectorate, administered from Ceylon

Treaties of protection with Arab Trucial States

Annexation of Zululand

Cecil Rhodes founds British South Africa Company

1888   British residency established at Pahang

Protectorates established in North Borneo, Sarawak and Brunei, Cook Islands

Charter granted to Imperial British East Africa Company

The Gambia re-established as a Crown Colony

Trinidad and Tobago governments united as a Crown Colony

Slavery abolished in Brazil

British New Guinea becomes a Crown Colony

Christmas Island (Indian Ocean) annexed by the British; administered by Singapore until 1958

1889   Second Berlin Conference agrees spheres of influence in the Pacific

1890   Zanzibar declared a Protectorate

Heligoland ceded to Germany

Labuan incorporated into North Borneo

Joint Protectorate between British and Transvaal over Swaziland

Western Australia granted responsible self-government

1891   British Central African Protectorate created

Niger Districts Protectorate becomes Oil River Protectorate

1892   Protectorate established in Gilbert and Ellice Islands

Dadabhai Naoroji elected Liberal MP for Central Finsbury constituency, London

1893   Natal granted responsible government

British Protectorate established over southern Solomon Islands

New Zealand women win the right to vote

Oil River Protectorate becomes Niger Coast Protectorate; Yoruba added to the territory

1894   Buganda (East Africa) declared a British Protectorate

First English cricket teams visit South Africa

Women granted vote in South Australia

1895   Jameson Raid, Transvaal

Anglo-Ashanti War (until 1896) – British overrun Ashanti and annex as far as the Gold Coast

Rhodesia established as a Protectorate

1896   Federated Malay States (Perak, Selangor, Negri Sembilan, Pahang) established as a Protectorate

1897   First English cricket teams visit West Indies

Zululand annexed to Natal

1898   Sierra Leone Hut Tax rebellion (until 1901)

Anglo-Egyptian administration (condominium) established in the Sudan after its reconquest at Battle of Omdurman

Leasing of New Territories as part of Hong Kong

Wei-hai-wei in north China leased to the British

Fashoda Crisis (Sudan) – confrontation with French on Upper Nile

1899   Bloemfontein Conference failure leads to Boer War (until 1902)

Samoa divided between Britain, Germany and USA

Acquisition of Solomon Islands and Tonga

New Zealand restricts non-white immigration

1900   Annexation of Orange Free State and Transvaal

Ruler of Tonga places himself under British protection

Britain acquires Ghana

Buganda Agreement guaranteeing African land rights

Niue (South Pacific) becomes a British Protectorate

1901   Australia acquires a national constitution and becomes the Commonwealth of Australia

Australia restricts non-white immigration

Annexation of Asante (West Africa) as a Crown Colony

Ugandan railway completed

Southern Rhodesia separated

1902   Boer War ends; Treaty of Vereeniging (forced Transvaal and Orange Free State into Empire)

Seychelles become a Crown Colony

1904   Anglo-French entente (Entente Cordiale), recognizing respective interests in Egypt and Morocco

Gandhi founds his first newspaper, *Indian Opinion*

1905   Partition of Bengal against Indian desires

1906   Formation of Muslim League in India

Zulu rebellion in Natal (until 1908)

North Borneo becomes a Crown Colony

Anglo-French condominium of the New Hebrides (Vanuatu) formed

1907   Dominion Division established at Colonial Office when New Zealand, Canada, Newfoundland and Australia declared Dominions

Responsible government granted to Orange Free State and Transvaal

1908   British control of South Georgia and South Sandwich Islands as the Falkland Island Dependencies

1909   Anglo-Siamese Treaty: Unfederated Malay States (Kelantan, Trengganu, Kedah, Perlis) placed under British protection

1910   Creation of the Union of South Africa (Cape Colony, Orange Free State, Natal, Transvaal)

1911   Treaty with ruler of Bhutan guaranteed internal autonomy in exchange for British control of foreign policy

Delhi Durbar marks coronation of George V

Northern Rhodesia separated

1912   Home Rule Bill for Ireland passes

Foundation of South African Native National Congress

Establishment of Afrikaaner National Party by James Hertzog

Reunification of Presidency of Bengal

1913   South African Natives Land Act creates rural reserves for Africans

Women's campaign against pass laws, South Africa

South Africa restricts non-white immigration

1914   Irish Home Rule implementation delayed by outbreak of First World War

Egypt becomes a Protectorate

Cyprus becomes a colony when Turkey declares war on Britain

1915   Gilbert and Ellice Islands become a Crown Colony

1916   Easter Rising, Dublin

British occupation of Palestine and Syria

Qatar enters treaties of protection with British

Empire Day established in Britain (24 May)

Kamaran Islands become part of British Protectorate of Aden

1917   Indentured labour from India to Caribbean halted

Imperial War Conference and cabinet established

Balfour Declaration commits Britain to a national Jewish homeland

Britain acquires Palestine from Turkey

Rioting in Quebec in response to conscription

Montagu Declaration promises eventual Indian self-governance

Claim to British Antarctic Territory defined

1918   Montagu–Chelmsford Report on Indian self-governance

Foundation of National Congress of British West Africa by J. E. Casely Hayford

1919   Amritsar massacre, India

Rowlatt Acts, India, extended wartime restrictions on civil liberties into peace years

Anglo-Irish War (until 1921)

Government of India (Montagu–Chelmsford) Act permits partial self-government

Britain acquires part of German Cameroon (incorporated into Niger Protectorate) and some of Togoland

German colony around Walvis Bay becomes part of South Africa mandate

Tanganyika (German East Africa) becomes a British mandate

British invasion in Afghanistan to quell unrest

Jamaican women win the vote

1920   East Africa Protectorate renamed Kenya and becomes a Crown Colony

British mandate in Iraq, Transjordan and Palestine

Kikuyu Association founded in Kenya

1921   Malta granted a legislature

Control of Palestine passes from Foreign Office to Colonial Office

Chamber of Princes established in India as a consultative body

1922   Founding of Irish Free State

Declaration of Egyptian independence (Britain retains control of Suez Canal)

Violence at Chauri Chaura leads Gandhi to suspend his non-cooperation campaign

Chanak Crisis when Britain, on the verge of war with Turkey, was refused aid by the Dominion countries

Ascension Island brought under the Colonial Office

Iraq establishes treaty of alliance with Britain

1923   Britain recognizes rights of Dominions to freedom in treaty-making

Southern Rhodesia granted responsible self-government

Devonshire White Paper declares Kenya 'primarily an African territory'

Creation of Arab kingdom of Transjordan

Antarctic (Ross Dependency) placed under New Zealand jurisdiction

Canada's Immigration Act excludes Chinese settlers from Canada

1924   Crown rule replaces company rule in Northern Zambesia

Northern Rhodesia becomes a Crown Colony

St Lucia granted representative government

1925   Dominions Office separated from Colonial Office

Cyprus becomes a Crown Colony

South African Native National Congress changes its name to African National Congress

1926   Dominions now known as Commonwealth

Balfour Report defines dominion status as autonomous communities within the Empire

African National Congress adopts tactics of passive resistance

1929   Arab revolts against Jewish immigration to Palestine

Colonial Development Act

1930   Anglo-Iraqi Treaty

Gandhi's Salt March to Dandi

Wei-hai-wei returned to China

1931   Statute of Westminster granted Dominions full independence, dissolving the Colonial Laws Validity Act (1865)

Ceylon granted partial self-government

1932   Gandhi imprisoned and Indian National Congress banned

Formal independence of Iraq

1934   Treaty of Sana'a: Yemen became last territorial acquisition of the British Empire

Establishment of Australian Antarctic Territory

1935   Government of India Act gave responsible self-government to Indian provinces and promised eventual self-government for India

1936   Anglo-Egyptian Treaty recognized Egyptian sovereignty

Arab rebellion in Palestine

1937   Irgun (Jewish Activist group) begins terrorist campaigns against Arabs in Palestine

Separate government for Burma created

Irish Free State becomes Eire

Aden becomes a British Crown Colony

1938   Moyne Commission proposes social, economic and governance reforms for the Caribbean

Tristan da Cunha Islands becomes a dependency of St Helena

1940   Colonial Development and Welfare Act

Jinnah's Lahore Resolution calling for the creation of a separate Muslim state of Pakistan

Change in definition of Commonwealth to permit republics to remain members

Italians occupy British Somaliland

1941   Atlantic Charter between USA and UK

Britain occupies Iraq until 1947

Restriction of Jewish immigration into Palestine

1942   Quit India movement

Japanese occupy Singapore, Hong Kong, Burma, Malaya, Sarawak, North Borneo, Andaman and Nicobar Islands, Solomon Islands and Gilbert and Ellice Islands

1943   Colonial secretary's pledge that Britain would 'guide colonial people along the road to self-government within the British Empire'

1944   Universal suffrage introduced in Jamaica; formation of semi-responsible government headed by Alexander Bustamente

New constitutions in Trinidad and British Guiana

1945   Ceylon acquires responsible self-government

Colonial Development and Welfare Act

Singapore, Burma, Malaya and Hong Kong recovered from Japanese

1946   Crown rule replaces Brooke dynasty in Sarawak

North Borneo becomes a Crown Colony

Transjordan gains independence

1947   Partition of India and Pakistan

Dominions Office renamed Commonwealth Relations Office

Palestine question referred by British to UN

Malta granted self-government

Nicobar and Andaman Islands passed to newly independent India

1948   Declaration of the State of Israel; Britain withdraws from Palestine

Irish Republic leaves the Commonwealth

Burma and Ceylon gain independence; Burma opts not to join the Commonwealth

Creation of Federation of Malaya; state of emergency declared in Malaya

Gold Coast riots (starting in Accra and spreading)

British Nationality Act – first time UK citizenship defined

Maldives granted self-government

1949   Kwame Nkrumah founds Convention People's Party in the Gold Coast

1951   ANZUS Pact, Britain excluded

1952   King Farouk of Egypt deposed in a military coup by Gamal Abdel Nasser

State of emergency declared in Kenya as Mau Mau rebellion grows

1954   Anglo-Egyptian agreement to withdraw British forces from Canal Zone

1955   Britain's last annexation: island of Rockall, North Atlantic

1956   Suez Crisis; establishment of Egypt as a republic

1957   The Gold Coast becomes independent as Ghana, the first African colony to win independence

Malaya becomes independent

1958   Coup in Iraq and establishment of an Islamic Republic

Empire Day becomes Commonwealth Day

1959   Declaration of a state of emergency in Nyasaland

Cayman Islands become a separate colony

Northern Nigeria given internal self-government

1960   Nigeria becomes independent

Cyprus gains independence

British Somaliland gains independence

Sudan gains independence

UN General Assembly passes Declaration on the Granting of Independence to Colonial Countries and People

Lancaster House conference recommends majority rule for Kenya

State of emergency in Kenya lifted

Montserrat acquires partially elected executive and legislative councils

Tanganyika acquires responsible self-government

1961   Sierra Leone and Tanzania (Tanganyika until 1964) gain independence

South Africa withdraws from Commonwealth over objections about apartheid from new member nations

Kuwait gains independence

Cameroons gain independence

Barbados and British Guiana granted internal self-government

Bechuanaland acquires an elected legislature and an executive council

1962 Western Samoa gains independence

Uganda gains independence

Trinidad and Tobago and Jamaica gain independence

First barriers to Commonwealth citizens' entry to UK established

Britain declares a British Antarctic Territory

1963 Kenya granted internal self-government in June and independence in December

Zanzibar granted internal self-government, and then full independence

Federation of Malaysia (Malaya, Sarawak, North Borneo (now called Sabah)) formed

Nigeria becomes a republic

1964 Nyasaland (Malawi) and Northern Rhodesia (Zambia) become independent

Malta gains independence

Tanganyika unites with Zanzibar and becomes Tanzania

Bahamas and British Honduras granted internal self-government

Self-government introduced in Gibraltar

1965 Southern Rhodesia's Unilateral Declaration of Independence

The Gambia gains independence

Cook Islands become independent

Islands that were dependencies of Mauritius and Seychelles placed under direct British administration as British Indian Ocean Territory

Anglo-French Pacific condominium over New Hebrides

Maldive Islands gain independence

Aden emergency: British troops attacked by Egypt-backed Front for the Liberation of Occupied South Yemen

1966   Guyana (British Guiana) and Barbados become independent

Lesotho (formerly Basutoland) and Botswana (formerly Bechuanaland) gain independence

1967   British withdraw from Aden; collapse of South Arabian Federation; establishment of Republic of South Yemen

Leeward Islands and Windward Islands gain internal self-government

Virgin Islands confirmed as a British colonial dependency

Gibraltar referendum overwhelmingly votes to stay British

Swaziland granted internal self-government

1968   Mauritius, Swaziland and Nauru gain independence

British troops begin withdrawing from Persian Gulf and Singapore

Bermuda gains internal self-government

1969   Anguilla brought back under direct British administration as a dependency

St Vincent acquires internal self-government

1970   Fiji and Tonga become independent

1971   Bahrain and Qatar gain full independence

Arab Trucial States gain independence as United Arab Emirates

1972   Ceylon becomes Sri Lanka

Cayman Islands become a British Dependent Territory

1973   Bahamas gain independence

Turks and Caicos Islands become a separate colony

Papua New Guinea granted self-government

1974   Grenada gains independence

Niue gains internal self-government

1975   Papua New Guinea gains full independence

Ellice Islands become independent as Tuvalu

Seychelles granted internal self-government

1976   British Indian Ocean Territory islands (except Chagos, retained by British) returned to Seychelles

Solomon Islands granted internal self-government

1978   Dominica gains independence

Solomon Islands gain full independence

Sierra Leone becomes a one-party state

Northern Territory (Australia) becomes self-governing

Seychelles gain full independence

1979   Kiribati (Gilbert Islands) gains independence

St Lucia gains independence

St Vincent and the Grenadines gain full independence

1980   Vanuatu (New Hebrides) and Zimbabwe (Rhodesia) become independent

Anguilla Act formalized Anguilla as a British Dependency

1981   Antigua and Barbuda, and Belize win independence

British Nationality Act denied right to live in Britain to British overseas citizens and citizens of British Dependent Territories

1982   Argentinian invasion of Falkland Islands leads to Falklands War

1983   Brunei becomes an independent state

St Kitts and Nevis gain independence

1984   Anglo-Chinese agreement to restore Hong Kong to China in 1997

1990   South West Africa Protectorate and Mandate become independent as Namibia

1994   South Africa rejoins Commonwealth; abolition of apartheid

1995   Bermudans reject independence in a referendum

1997   Hong Kong returned to China

Index

slave revolts, 18, 20–1, 108
slave ships, 17, 27
slave women, 19, 20
slavery, 13–26, 27, 31, 34, 91, 92,
    128, 132, 133
  abolition of, 15, 23–4, 25, 41, 58,
    70, 125, 126
  anti-slavery, 21–3, 29
  anti-slavery squadrons, 91
  characteristics of Atlantic, 15
  conditions under, 17–18
  Consolidated Slave Acts, 18
  in Britain, 22
  profit from, 24–35
  sexual exploitation in, 20
Smith, Adam, 21, 29
Smith, Ian, 200–1
Smuts, Jan, 171
Society for the Abolition of the Slave
    Trade, 22
Society for the Preservation of the Irish
    Language, 10
Socorro, 88
Somaliland, 94, 182
Somersett, James, 22
South African Industrial and
    Commercial Workers' Union, 181
South African Native National
    Congress, 181
South Australia, 47, 51, 53, 54, 129
South Sea Company, 26
Spain, 2, 7, 8, 26, 28, 40, 59, 60
  rivalry with, 18, 28, 43, 44, 60
Speke, John H., 93
Stamp Act, 38
Stanley, Henry Morton, 121
Statute of Westminster, 172, 202
Steckel, Richard, 20
Strachey, John, 107
Straits Settlements, 57, 95, 128, 138,
    190
Sudan, 94, 208
Suez Canal, 90, 96, 98, 180, 199, 200
Suez crisis, 199–200, 205
sugar, 15, 18, 19, 20, 25, 34, 36, 37,
    41, 55, 62, 97, 116, 130, 133, 135
Sumatra, 56, 57, 64
superiority, British sense of, 103–4,
    107

suttee, 71–2, 146
Swan River Colony, see Western
    Australia
swaraj, 173
Switzerland, 34
Syria, 89, 90, 198

Tahiti, 44
Tanganyika, 94
Tasmania, 46, 47, 48, 49, 50, 51, 53
taxation, 35, 37, 66–7, 76, 130, 136,
    174
tea, 38, 64, 97, 155
  Boston Tea Party, 38
  Tea Act, 38
technology, 96, 98–9, 116–17, 192
terra nullius, 50, 131
Thailand, 57, 89
Thakombau, 87
Thatcher, Margaret, 208
Thuku, Harry, 179
Tientsin, Treaty of, 76
timber, 34, 36, 45
tobacco, 16, 19, 34
Tobago, 21, 28
Tone, Wolf, 2, 7
trade
  Atlantic, 13
  colonial, 4–5, 13, 26–7, 32, 36, 63,
    87, 88–9, 91–2
  with indigenous peoples, 107, 132
  see also free trade
transportation, 16, 48, 53, 63, 132
Transvaal, 93, 133, 134, 135
treaty ports, 85, 119
Trincomalee, 57
Trinidad, 21, 117, 134
Turkey, 74, 90, 97, 170, 180, 200, 206
Turks and Caicos Islands, 207

Uganda, 93, 135, 195, 207, 208
Unilateral Declaration of Independence
    (UDI), 200–1
United Company of Merchants
    Trading in the East Indies, see
    East India Company
United Malays, 187
United Nations, 195, 199, 200, 201–2,
    205